Working in hotels and catering

The hotel and catering industry is one of the most heterogeneous of industries, consisting as it does of businesses ranging from the most humble café to the largest luxury hotel. Strong images of the glamorous nature of the work are often conjured up by the popular media, and sit alongside the lures of an industry in which it is theoretically possible to rise to the top from the very lowest levels.

This book provides an insight into the circumstances under which hotel and catering services are provided in reality. It is the first text to provide an overview of existing research in the industry, and Wood's account is both wide-ranging and accessible. He highlights many previously overlooked aspects of the industry, including such characteristics as low wages, high labour turnover, lack of unionisation, and heavy-handed management, which are identified and explored in such a way as to illuminate current practice.

The depth and range of themes covered, together with the author's underlying sociological approach to the material, will ensure that this work is of value to students and professionals in hospitality management, who find that existing material bears increasingly less relevance to the world in which they work. Wood draws on the experiences of the full range of employees, from the hardest pressed operative worker to top hotel managers, to inform his text throughout, and in particular his final conclusions about future developments in the nature of hotel and catering employment.

Roy C. Wood is currently a lecturer at The Scottish Hotel School of the University of Strathclyde. He has published articles on a range of topics, including social aspects of food and eating, and has acted as a Chief Examiner for the HCIMA in Gastronomy.

Working in hotels and catering

Roy C. Wood

London and New York

First published in 1992
by Routledge
11 New Fetter Lane, London EC4P 4EE

Simultaneously published in the USA and Canada
by Routledge
a division of Routledge, Chapman and Hall Inc.
29 West 35th Street, New York, NY 10001

© 1992 Roy C. Wood

Typeset by LaserScript, Mitcham, Surrey.
Printed and bound in Great Britain by Biddles Ltd, Guildford and King's Lynn.

British Library Cataloguing in Publication Data
Wood, Roy C. (Roy Christopher) 1959-
Working in hotels and catering.
1. Great Britain. Catering establishments
I. Title
646.9402341

Library of Congress Cataloging in Publication Data
Wood, Roy C., 1959-
Working in hotels and catering/
Roy C. Wood.
p. cm.
Includes bibliographical references and index.
1. Hotel management. 2. Caterers and catering – Management.
I. Title.
TX911.3.M27W67   1992
647.94'068–dc20

91-12880
CIP

ISBN 0–415–04782–X (hbk)
ISBN 0–415–04783–8 (pbk)

For Malcolm, Margaret and Keith Wood

Contents

Acknowledgements

A number of people have provided practical and moral support during the writing of this book. I owe a great debt to Chris Rojek for his initial interest in the development of the text and to Elisabeth Tribe, my editor at Routledge who provided unobtrusive but effective encouragement throughout its preparation. My colleagues Philip Houghton, John Lennon and Dr James Steel gave their advice freely and willingly but I have chosen not to hold this against them. Professor Kit Jenkins offered quieter but no less valuable support. On more than one occasion, Elizabeth Steel provided much needed hospitality and respite for which I am indeed grateful. The ideas developed in this book owe a great deal to the comments, criticisms and encouragement of students past and present. I am particularly indebted to Sophie Heiser, Kevin Gardner, Arséne Aslan, Shona Fraser, Arnaud Frapin-Beaugé, Philip Backhouse, Donald Sloan, Alan Archbold and Lore Grigg for their interest and support. Gareth Currie's constant solicitousness about the progress of the manuscript prevented any serious slacking on my part. Ian Macaulay provided many useful comments on the completed text for which I am grateful. Patricia Kelly prepared the manuscript for publication: her good humour, expert skill and human insight was invaluable. I should also like to extend my gratitude to Professor John O'Connor for giving me a chance, and to Walker Graham for giving me another.

Finally here, it is true to say that this book would never have been written without the support and encouragement of Linda McKie, who talked me into submitting the original proposal after years of vacillation on my part, and subsequently provided unqualified encouragement and sound advice. None of what follows necessarily represents the views of the aforementioned persons. All errors are those of the author alone.

Roy C. Wood
Glasgow
January 1991

1 Sociology, work and the hotel and catering industry

The hotel and catering industry is one of the largest employers in the United Kingdom and many other developed (and, increasingly, less developed) countries. Some 10 per cent of the British workforce are engaged in hotel and catering employment, representing somewhere between two and two and a half million persons. The hospitality industry, as it is now commonly referred to, is the most important element in the wider tourism sector. Economists frequently point to its heterogeneous nature: the industry comprises units ranging from the most humble café to the largest luxury hotel owned by a multinational corporation. Hospitality industry employers stress the caring people-oriented nature of hotels and catering, generating a glamorous mystique that is all too easily reinforced by images in popular media (Wood, 1990a). Further, the industry is often presented as a paragon of conservative virtues. Low barriers to entry mean that, in theory at least, the hotel and catering sector is fertile ground for the small-time entrepreneur. Similarly, a view is promulgated of career development in the industry as open and meritocratic: even the kitchen pan washer can rise to become general manager of the hotel with hard work and dedication. Supporting these powerful images is an educational system that for post-school students separates out courses in hotel and catering management from those in general business studies, encouraging an insularity that is characteristic of the industry as a whole.

This insularity manifests itself in a variety of ways, most commonly in pleas from those connected with it for the industry to be regarded as unique and 'special', requiring specialist skills and training, a special attitude of mind and body, specialist professional associations and, above all, special academic understanding. Those engaged in the hotel and catering industry at all levels have elevated special pleading to a fine art but the mythologies that surround the industry cannot disguise the true nature of much hospitality industry employment, of low wages and poor working conditions, of exploitation and minimal job security, of monotonous yet demanding work, of degrading and low status occupations.

Evidence for all of these is to be found in a substantial body of published research concerned with the nature of hotel and catering employment. Broadly speaking, this literature can be divided into five categories:

1 a number of sociological studies of work and employment in hotels and catering the majority of which are concerned with workplace relations;
2 a body of quasi-sociological research addressed to one or other of the hospitality industry's labour 'problems', for example labour turnover and the adoption of flexible working strategies in hotel and catering organisations;
3 a literature combining sociological, economic and social policy concerns and centring on the nature of hotel and catering labour markets (Henderson, 1965; Witz and Wilson, 1982; Alpert, 1986; Crompton and Sanderson, 1990);
4 a variety of mainly official reports by government and other organisations on the condition of labour in the industry and the nature of labour problems in hotels and catering; and
5 similar reports published by campaign and pressure groups, most notably in Britain, the Low Pay Unit network.

The casual researcher would be hard pushed to find mention of this material in the many textbooks devoted to personnel management in hotels and catering. These manuals, purporting to apply 'human resource management' techniques to the hospitality industry are for the most part 'how to do it' manuals which often verge on the anodyne. Their content bears little relevance to either the realities of work experience in the industry or actual labour management practices. Most are written without reference to hard research data, exhibiting instead a tendency to offer prescriptive and generalised solutions to personnel issues (Mars, Bryant and Mitchell, 1979: 128).

This book draws across the range of studies of hotel and catering work though the main objective is to construct, in the broadest sense, a sociological account of employment in the hospitality industry. This presents an immediate problem for, despite the existence of a small literature, within the mainstream of sociological studies of work and industry more generally, hotels and catering along with other service industries have attracted little research attention compared to manufacturing. This reflects wider societal attitudes towards service industries which vary from the indifferent to the outrightly hostile. A commentator in the *Guardian* newspaper (2 July 1987) observed of economic trends that 'we are left with the distinctive feeling that the country is being seduced by the short-term palliatives of the candy-floss tourist economy'. Attitudes like these undoubtedly have some grounding in hard economic and social analysis but they are also the product of a deeply ingrained snobbery that characterises British social institutions. The academic establishment is not immune to such prejudices and amongst industrial sociologists it is difficult to find a satisfactory explanation for the general neglect of service employment. As Crompton (1989: 129) in a review of Gabriel's *Working Lives in Catering* (1988) puts it: 'Much of the empirical research and theorising current in the Sociology of Work is derived from what are now outdated studies of predominantly male, predominantly white production workers'.

Crompton's strictures identify only one of the problems attendant on any discussion of the sociology of work. Internal debates about the scope and methods of industrial sociology and the use of a range of terms to describe what appear to be roughly similar areas of concern are two further barriers to clarity. Salaman (1986) summarises the problems well:

> by talking of the sociology of work we are avoiding an issue: there is no sociology of work. There is sociology, and there is work but the former is not homogeneous in its treatment of the latter, and sociologically, the latter is not homogeneous either. Sociologically, there are a number of discrete but overlapping sub-disciplines which define their subject-matter in terms of work activities and institutions, e.g. the sociology of organization, of occupations, of professions, of industry, of industrial relations. All this need not matter but simply be another indication of the strange, arcane, hopelessly 'academic' nature of the discipline. But for our purposes there is an implication: the different sub-disciplines treat the object of our analysis in significantly different ways, thus providing the diversity mentioned above.
>
> (Salaman, 1986: 74–75)

Detailed examination of both the historical development of industrial sociology as a field of study and the preoccupations of its major sub-disciplines fall outside the scope of this discussion (see Rose, 1988 for an outstanding historical account and Watson, 1988 for an excellent overview of many of the specialisms). However, some brief sketch is necessary in order to demonstrate those connections that do exist between the mainstream of industrial sociology and existing sociological analyses of hotel and catering work.

THE SOCIOLOGY OF WORK AND INDUSTRY

The origins of industrial sociology lie in the attempts of the classical sociologists Marx, Weber and Durkheim to assess the impact of industrialisation on society within more general theories of social development. It is the work of F. W. Taylor however that is generally accepted as marking the beginnings of a specialist sociology of work (see Figure 1.1). His development of 'scientific management' (Taylorism) entailed the application of supposedly scientific techniques to the analysis of employment for the purposes of controlling and quantifying labour and resources in order to eliminate industrial inefficiency, inefficiency perceived as deriving both from workers' attempts to control and limit output in order to maximise rewards and the ignorance of managements as to the nature of the productive process. If not quite the original 'time and motion' man, Taylor proposed strategies based on the acquisition of workers' knowledge and its vesting in separate and specialist managerial functions combined with systems of reward that would appeal to employees' self-interest. In short, with sufficient encouragement, money could buy anything including the acquiescence of the greedy worker.

Much of Taylor's theory of scientific management was derived from close observation of work at plant level and the tradition of 'plant sociology' with its emphasis on workplace behaviour was continued under the auspices of those researchers committed to a human relations perspective. Rose (1975) has remarked that Taylor and other early industrial sociologists were not, in point of fact, sociologists at all, and early social scientific interest in industry was more to do with improving management and productivity than with intellectual inquiry. To some degree, the human relations perspective was perhaps the first 'movement' in the study of industrial sociology to strive for credibility in both respects. In many ways a reaction against Taylorism, the human relations movement emphasised a vastly different view of human nature based on the idea of people's need for sociability, a need regarded as being constrained by then prevailing modes of factory work organisation. The best known studies of the human relations movement are the 'Hawthorn experiments' conducted for the Western Electric Company. After the Second World War, human relations, like Taylorism, fell into disrepute, criticised for favouring managerial problematics and priorities and neglecting conflict and the wider socio-economic and political context in which work was performed. It was around this time that the sociological study of work began to become more obviously fragmented into specialisms. Plant studies continued to dominate, though now the focus shifted to the role of technology in determining work experiences, workplace behaviour and organisational form to the extent that the British Tavistock Institute 'developed' the concept of socio-technical systems, most clearly associated with the work of Joan Woodward (1958, 1965) who claimed to have found that management style and formal work organisation were determined for the most part by technology. This post-

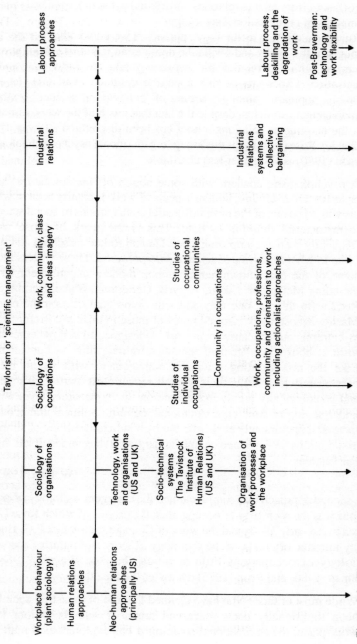

Figure 1.1 Theoretical strands in the sociology of work and industry

war offshoot from human relations constituted in the most general sense the beginnings of organisational sociology.

Running alongside technology approaches were two other perspectives. Throughout the 1950s and 1960s the neo-human relations school was also concerned with the relationship between work, the individual and the organisation. Exponents of this approach continue even now to enjoy enormous popularity amongst writers of 'behavioural science' textbooks for management students, despite the fact that much of the work associated with the neo-human relations school has been discredited (if ever it were creditable). Rose (1975) calls this group 'organisational psycho-technologists'. Watson (1980) is altogether less charitable:

> A psychologistic concern with some notion of 'human nature' as the basis for understanding human aspects of work is clearly seen in what is proving to be one of the most influential contributions of social scientists to managerial thinking to date. This is the work of those writers frequently seen as composing a neo-Human Relations school and whom I like to label *behavioural science entrepreneurs*. These writers include some of the best known names among modern management writers, including McGregor, Likert, Argyris, Gellerman, Blake, Herzberg and Reddin [to this list one may add with some qualification the name of Maslow whose work inspired many of those in this list]. I refer to them as entrepreneurs because their work is designed to sell, whether in the form of books, management seminars, training films or consultancies. Like the task-splitting scientific management with whom they so passionately take issue, their work is reductionist, partial, evangelistic and sociologically highly inadequate on the explanatory level with its underplaying of structural, situational, cultural, political and economic factors. It is ultimately simplistic but by a judicious mixing of simplistic assumptions and pseudo-scientific jargon it has made itself highly marketable.
>
> (Watson, 1980: 38)

The second approach that complemented the emergent sociology of organisations was the sociology of occupations, the origins of which Rose (1975) traces to the early 1940s and the work of Chicago sociologist E.C. Hughes. Many introductory texts on the sociology of work and industry accord the sociology of occupations little attention (but see Watson, 1988 and Salaman, 1986) and Rose (1975) dismisses the area thus:

> While most of those who have claimed the title of industrial sociologist have traditionally been concerned primarily with behaviour in the work-place, the occupational sociologist has explored such matters as

the subjective consequences of work for the individual, its meaning to him, its effect on his attitudes and relationships in other social contexts, and the tactics which members of an occupation adopt to increase their rewards, security and prestige. . . . Generally speaking, however, occupational sociology can be regarded as complementary to traditional industrial sociology.

(Rose, 1975: 18)

This dismissiveness presents something of a difficulty here since many sociological studies of work in hotels and catering are within the broad tradition of occupational sociology, a point that will be elaborated upon later in the chapter.

Diversification of sociological interest in work in the post-war period makes it possible to speak of distinct sub-disciplines or thematic orientations, but it is necessary to appreciate that such distinctions disguise overlapping concerns and are thus necessarily artificial. Having said this, the two final 'strands' depicted in Figure 1.1 – industrial relations and labour process approaches – represent slight deviations from this norm. The industrial relations approach is exceptionally difficult to define in terms of scope and interest, maintaining at one level an extremely formal interest in the mechanisms of the relationships between capital and organised labour – most notably collective bargaining, trade union organisation and behaviour, and the relationship between trade unions and employer organisations in terms of the maintenance of stability and control in industry. At another level, more radical perspectives have eschewed this institutional approach in favour of the analysis of industrial conflict in terms of irreconcilable class interests and class conflict and the dislocation of trade unions' behaviour and activity from the (supposed) real interests of their members (Hyman, 1975). Whilst there are clear overlaps of interest between industrial relations and other branches of the sociology of work and industry, the links are, in some areas at least, arguably weaker than those that exist between other sub-disciplines. The same cannot be said of labour process approaches. In 1974, Harry Braverman's *Labor and Monopoly Capital* offered a trenchant reassertion of the Marxist analysis of work that sought to eliminate what the author viewed as the artificial complexities erected by sociologists in an effort to understand the nature of work, and reassert a view of work as degraded as a result of the application of Taylorist techniques to labour processes. The extent to which the labour process approach has dominated recent sociology of work cannot be underestimated. Despite accusations of 'Bravermania' (Salaman, 1986: 24), as debates have developed, a much richer vein of analysis that draws on many of the other traditions in industrial sociology has been tapped – on organisational and occupational control and resistance to work degradation and deskilling – whilst at the same time extending the scope of sociological analysis to take into consideration, in a more explicit way, economic factors influencing labour and work.

HOTEL AND CATERING WORK

The foregoing discussion is necessarily skeletal and professional industrial sociologists will readily note its inadequacies and omissions. The important point is that the preoccupations of mainstream industrial sociology have left the analysis of hotel and catering work relatively untouched. The earliest systematic study of hotel and catering labour was W.F. Whyte's *Human Relations in the Restaurant Industry* (1948) which was firmly rooted in the human relations tradition. It was followed a year later by an article on similar themes in the *American Journal of Sociology* (Whyte, 1949). From the general perspective of organisational sociology, Bowey (1976) attempted to apply a form of action theory to the analysis of restaurants and Shamir (1978) examined the implication of contingency theories of organisation for an understanding of hotel work. (See Thompson and McHugh, 1990, for an excellent discussion of the basic elements of these theories.) Industrial relations approaches have generated a small number of case studies of trade union activity in hotels and catering (Horowitz, 1960; Chopping, 1977; Wood and Pedlar, 1978) and the labour process debate has also made its mark, though only on a limited scale (Bagguley, 1987; Gabriel, 1988; McKenna, 1990).

As would be expected, despite being undertaken from different theoretical and methodological standpoints, many of these studies are loosely bound together in terms of certain shared concepts, ideas and assumptions. There is little theoretical synergy however. Indeed, if the sociological study of hotel and catering work to date has any defining feature it is the triumph of empiricism over theory, of data collection and description over systematic attempts to relate data to wider theoretical issues in the sociology of work and to the experiences of labour in other industries. The empirical base is a very narrow one at that but has come to form the bedrock of an orthodox perspective on hospitality employment, a 'dominant research paradigm' (Lennon and Wood, 1989).

This orthodoxy tends to depict hotel and catering employment as a special analytic case and is accepting of the industry's own self-perception of itself as 'unique', as a closed industrial and social system sustained and influenced by its own structures and procedures to the near exclusion of the effects of exogenous factors. Many operational and labour problems are seen as deriving from the singular service nature of hotel and catering operations. Whyte (1948) recognised and to some extent attempted correction of this view by drawing attention to both the production and service elements of restaurant operations, an observation subsequently reiterated more famously and in more general terms by Levitt (1972):

> Purveyors of service think that they and their problems are fundamentally different from other businesses and their problems. They feel that service is people-intensive, while the rest of the economy is capital intensive. But these distinctions are largely spurious. There are no such things as service industries. There are only industries where service components are greater or less than those of other industries.
>
> (Levitt, quoted in Mullins, 1981: 33)

To many, the observations of Whyte (1948) and Levitt (1972) may appear blindingly obvious but the assumptions described by the latter continue to enjoy substantial currency. One consequence of approaching the hospitality industry as a 'special case' has been a tendency to adopt a 'problem-solving' approach to hotel and catering work that treats the principal features of industry employment as immutable. From this position, many of the industry's labour problems are seen as emanating from, what are usually presented as, antediluvian management practices amenable to improvement through alterations to organisational design and management style. As might be anticipated, there are elements of this approach in the human relations work of Whyte (1948). In a somewhat exaggerated response to *Human Relations in the Restaurant Industry*, Rose (1988: 162), with dismissive clinical disapprobation, remarks that the book is 'a popularly written work with much advice to restaurant managers on keeping employees happy, containing little systematic theorizing'. Rose has a point. Whyte suggested, *inter alia*, that conflict between food production and service staff might be reduced if management introduced communication devices that eliminated face-to-face contact. For Whyte, face-to-face contact allowed the pressure under which food service staff were placed to be articulated in hostility to food preparers and others, a hostility compounded by the possibilities for wider conflict based on status differences. Both themes are returned to later in the text. Whyte's 'problem solving' orientation is evident in several other pieces of advice to managers as Rose suggests, and other writers have been similarly eager to present their theoretical predilections as possessing the potential for problem solving. For example, Bowey (1976) in her study of restaurants sets out to:

> test the validity of William Foot Whyte's interpretations and analyses of the behaviour of the employees in restaurants (Whyte, 1948). During this investigation it became clear that the inadequacies of Foot Whyte's

work were due to the shortcomings of the 'Human Relations' theory which he used. It did not afford a sufficiently accurate model of behaviour in organisations for adequate interpretations to be made of that behaviour. The aim of this book is to present a model of behaviour in organisations, which can be used by research sociologists (organisation theorists) and by practising managers for diagnostic organisational analysis.

(Bowey, 1976: 15)

In describing certain sociological perspectives on hotel and catering work as constituting an orthodoxy, it is not the intention to suggest that these perspectives are in any way invalid. Piecemeal and limited development of research in the field has made it to some degree inevitable that certain key studies have assumed special importance as a basis for informing other commentaries on hotel and catering employment. The orthodox view does, however, present an incomplete and occasionally distorted perspective on hospitality industry employment, placing undue stress on internal workplace processes and neglecting the wider social and economic context in which work is performed (cf. Gabriel, 1988). Indeed, there is a noticeable tendency in much research to present hotel and catering employment as an atypical intellectual curiosity, obscuring the very real drudgery faced every day by many of the industry's employees.

For the most part, the orthodox view has grown out of a very narrow occupation-based approach to the study of hospitality industry employment. Even writers like Whyte (1948) and Bowey (1976) who have ostensibly been concerned with broader theoretical issues have ultimately directed their attention towards the relationship between occupational groups in the industry. At the wider theoretical and empirical level, sociologists of occupations have been concerned with six inter-related issues (see Dunkerley, 1975; Salaman, 1974, 1986; Watson, 1988). The first of these is *occupational recruitment and socialisation* by which, through the interaction of both formal and informal procedures (including education, certification and modes of recruitment), an occupational set creates and recreates itself. Studies of *occupational careers* have elaborated the scope for progress and development within particular occupational sets, including analyses of hierarchical career structures and the nature of work careers in occupations where the scope for upward movement is limited by the social and technical components of the occupational set – class, economic position, skill, gender and so forth. Thirdly, studies of *occupational strategies and professionalisation* have examined, *inter alia*, the processes whereby occupational solidarity is encouraged via some form of professionalisation. These processes need not be confined to occupations conventionally understood as professions: attempts to emulate the procedures and practices of the professions have filtered through to other occupational groups involving, in varying degrees, attempts to exercise some form of control over occupational recruitment and career structure. Clearly, there are many occupational sets who can proceed only so far down the road towards professionalisation by arguing that they possess particular competencies. This points towards the fourth area of interest of occupational sociologists, and that is the extent to which occupations are *socially constructed and reproduced*. To a large degree, the distinctiveness of any occupational set relies on the extent to which the claims of members of that set for such distinctiveness can be justified to the wider society and other occupational groups with whom they engage in the workplace. Occupations are therefore dynamic, subject to pressures of both internal and external change. This can be seen, fifthly, in the nature of occupational cultures and ideologies, which provide a system of values that bind occupation members together and serve to legitimate their collective and individual interests. Shared ideologies provide a source of strength for bargaining over power, privileges and rewards particularly if they are linked to concepts of professionalism predicated on the possession of scarce skills and knowledge. Finally in this catalogue is the study of *occupational communities* (see Salaman, 1974, 1986) that embraces two areas of enquiry – communities at work and work within communities. The former is concerned with growth of community in particular occupations. People share a social and cultural network of values but do not usually live together though they may share similar work and leisure interests. The study of work within communities is represented by a much more distinctive sociological literature usually focused on a discrete geographical area where a particular form of work or occupation is the dominant form of labour. The most famous example of this kind of study is *Coal is Our Life* by Dennis, Henriques and Slaughter (1956) but there are others such as Tunstall's (1969) study of fishermen.

Rarely in the study of hotel and catering work are these areas of interest explored in any systematic way. Notable exceptions would include Chivers' study of chefs and cooks (Chivers, 1971, 1973), Saunders study of the social stigma of occupations, with particular emphasis on the role of kitchen porters in the catering industry (Saunders, 1981a), and Shamir's analysis of hotels as workplace communities (Shamir, 1981). The vast majority of what may be termed 'mainstream' *sociological* studies of hospitality industry occupations have been of food (and drink) service staff. Put crudely, many elements in what has been described here as the orthodox approach to the study of hotel and catering employment derive from studies of waiting-on-table, and the experience of food service staff and their relationships with other workers (notably chefs and cooks), have been generalised to the workforce as a whole (e.g. Mars, 1973; Bowey, 1976; Butler and Snizek, 1976; Howe, 1977; Mars, Bryant and Mitchell, 1979; Butler and Skipper, 1981; Mars and Nicod, 1981, 1984). The majority of these studies differ from the work of writers like Chivers, Saunders and Shamir and others in an important methodological sense. The bulk of studies on non-food service staff have utilised what may be termed in the broadest sense a survey/questionnaire/interview style of methodology. Research on food service staff in contrast has almost invariably entailed some (usually extensive) element of ethnographic research involving participant observation. In some cases this reflects the social anthropological training of the researchers concerned, as in the case of Mars and Nicod who, in their examination of waiting-on-table, claim that 'the methods anthropologists use to study, say, the New Guinea Highlanders are also ideally suited to a study of the "tribe" of waiters at work in Western hotels' (1984: 2).

The extravagant confidence of this claim is highly suspect. The principal tool of the social anthropologist is ethnography. Participant observation usually involves living or working alongside the group under study either openly or, more commonly, covertly so that the subjects under scrutiny are unaware of the researcher's status. The latter is generally justified in terms of the naturalistic data that may be collected. In contrast, in making evident to a community under scrutiny that they are being studied by the ethnographer, the activities of subjects may be affected and altered thereby reducing the reliability of experiential evidence. A problem with ethnographic technique in general and participant observation in particular concerns the possibility of the researcher 'going native', becoming so much a part of the fabric of the research situation as to be unable to adequately discriminate 'relevant' from less relevant data. Some researchers have in fact suggested that 'going native' is to some extent a necessary and integral part of competent ethnography. Collins (1984) argues that for sociologists of science researching scientific controversies in which the emergence of a new piece of knowledge is at stake, technical and cultural immersion – what he calls participant comprehension – is a vital aspect of adequate understanding without which the researcher is unlikely to penetrate fully to the social processes entailed in scientific debate. This may well be fair comment but it obscures the danger that in 'going native' researchers' analyses will tend toward the insular. Ethnography, almost by definition, is concerned with the behaviour of discrete groups of people in a given social setting or settings.

The charge of insularity could no doubt be levelled against many sociological studies of occupations but it is one that has especial salience for the analysis of hotel and catering work. Ethnographic studies of food service personnel have tended to focus attention upon the 'soft underbelly' of work processes in that occupational group, particularly in respect of concentrating upon the efforts of waiting staff to secure tips, and the extent to which they engage in acts of petty (and not so petty) theft. The study of workplace relations and conflict in hotels and catering is almost entirely based on evidence of the conflict between food service personnel. This leads conflict to be regarded as a pathological expression of industry 'culture' rather than a response, at least in part, to the more general social and economic disadvantage faced by many employees. To cap it all, the culture of the industry is seen as encouraging large numbers of 'marginal workers' to enter the ranks of the workforce – not primarily marginal in their relationship to labour markets, that is in the context in which they sell their labour, but in the sense of being socially-psychologically disposed to 'enjoying' the kinds of work experience offered by the hospitality industry. An appreciation of these three concepts – the marginality of the workforce, the nature of remuneration in the industry, and the nature of conflict – is fundamental to a wider understanding of employment in hotels and catering and forms the subject matter of the next chapter.

To end this discussion it is necessary to reiterate that the core of sociological literature that represents the orthodoxy described above is small. Its influence is much wider and echoes of the 'dominant paradigm' will be found throughout the text. This is unavoidable: it is only possible to work with that material which is available. However, with all the major topics examined below, an attempt has been made to 'explode' discussion, to relate what is known about hotel and catering work to wider issues in industrial sociology. This effort to broaden discussion is on a small scale, confined, for example, to examining trends in industrial conflict and the role of trade unions in the hospitality industry (Chapter 4) and trends towards deskilling and 'flexible working' (Chapter 5). Indeed, the structure of the text is deliberately programmatic in order that it may fulfil its primary purpose as a reference point/sourcebook.

CONSIDERATIONS AND CAVEATS

Any attempt at synthesising an account of hotel and catering work is necessarily schematic, if only because the available source material is limited and patchy in its coverage of the industry. Many studies of hotel employment are of chain-owned hotels and/or those operating in the middle and luxury markets. In contrast, many studies of restaurants are of relatively small, often independent owned units. In both cases, individual research reports have tended to focus on a small number of units and, in many cases, single establishments. In short, there is a problem of representativeness not only in the findings of individual studies but in the relationship the types of establishment bear to other establishments and sectors in the industry. For example, there are few studies of work in non-commercial catering services. Further, any survey of the literature reveals there have been few investigative incursions by sociologists into the world of high-technology, high-capital food provision – the world of fast food and advanced process catering. Indeed, most research has focused on 'traditional' forms of hospitality operating, detracting from the extent to which the growth of the hotel and catering industry in recent years has been predicated on high levels of capital investment in fabric and technology. Hotels are certainly not immune to these processes. Many hotel customers would be surprised and probably irked to find that their *haute cuisine* meal began life in a food processing factory, was committed to a foil dish or plastic bag and then transported to the hotel where, with a suitable delay after being ordered (to give the appearance of meticulous preparation), it was regenerated in one or other kind of oven along with half a dozen identical packages before being presented for consumption. Customers would be further surprised to see that the hotel kitchen was not that much bigger than a large school classroom and possibly shocked, if their attention was drawn to these things, to be given a bill at the end of their meal reflecting prices based on the cost of preparation of fresh ingredients.

A further problem of representativeness arises from the fact that much data on hotel and catering work derives from occupational studies. The experience of individuals and occupational groups cannot be viewed independently of organisational structures. Yet, one of the biggest weaknesses in current understandings of the hospitality industry is the absence of comparative studies of how organisational and occupational structures are mediated at unit level as a result of the particular market circumstances of individual establishments. It is common to assume that occupational structure in the hotel and catering industry corresponds to organisational structure, each department in the organisation corresponding to an occupation, for example housekeeping (cleaners), front of house (receptionists), kitchen (chefs and cooks) and so on. To a very large degree this is an accurate view but account needs to be taken of the ways in which departmental organisation differs from or coincides with organisation according to functional and cost-centre criteria. For example, department activities tend to be aggregated and subsumed under higher-order organisational categories such as food and beverage (food and wet in some operations) and accommodation. A corollary of this is that the existence of a particular organisational structure does not necessarily imply that that structure is the basis for systems of organisational control.

Shamir (1978) demonstrates this in his use of the distinction between mechanistic and organic organisations originated by Burns and Stalker (1961). Mechanistic organisations are characterised by high levels of bureaucracy, extensive specialisation and division of labour and hierarchical structures of control. Organic organisations are characterised by less pronounced bureaucracy, more flexible task performance, lateral communication and less rigid rules and systems of control. The essence of contingency theories is that the success of a particular organisation is contingent upon it choosing a structure most suited to its environment. Shamir shows that hotels tend to exhibit a formal mechanistic structure behind which lies an organic informal structure characterised by informal and lateral communication, an ability to transfer labour resources across departments, and the maintenance of a reserve of labour in the form of live-in staff. Further, the relative autonomy of hotel departments appears to vary greatly and hotels appear to be centralised and devolved at one and the same time, some departments coming under central control, others being allowed a degree of autonomy. Shamir additionally argues that most large hotels appear to lack any formal integrating mechanisms for the control of organisational elements short of co-ordinating managers with responsibility for several departments. He concludes that traditional hotels resolve the conflict between the demands of bureaucracy and of hospitality by preserving a mechanistic façade whilst practising organic styles of organisational control. The general point here is that organisational structure can have a profound effect on the experience of work, whether this be individual or collective experience. Whilst the literature on hotel and catering work provides many instances of how organisation impinges upon this experience, there is little in the way of systematic analysis and thus there are limitations in what may be regarded as 'typical' organisational influences on the performance of work.

Whilst representativeness is a problem, it is to some degree counteracted by a relatively high measure of agreement as to the principal features of hotel and catering work though, as indicated in the previous section, the interpretive scope of many studies is somewhat limited. Having said this Lowe (1988), on the basis of detailed examination of the independent small-hotel sector in Scotland, has cast both implicit and explicit doubts upon the extent to which research findings from studies of large hotels can be generalised. Lowe found relatively reasonable working conditions and a moderately content workforce, experiences arising in part from the role of the hotel and catering industry within the surrounding community and the economy of the local area. Lowe and many others have drawn attention to the ever more complex diversity of the industry and every effort has been made in what follows to specify what type of operation is being discussed.

Cross-sectoral and intra-sectoral variations serve as a reminder of the dangers in drawing far-reaching conclusions from limited data. This should not, however, serve to detract from general trends and repeated observations of the conditions and experiences of hotel and catering labour. For many employees – probably the majority – labouring in hotels and catering is a last ditch option characterised by exploitative and conflictual relationships. The wider social emphasis on service work as servitude, as inferior to manufacturing work, does little for the morale of the industry's employees and, indeed, permits employers to maintain terms and conditions of employment that in many respects are still medieval in character. The frequently patronising approach of academic analysts to services in general and hotels and catering in particular plays its part in obscuring the extent to which work in hotels and catering differs little in kind and quality from similar work in manufacturing. Intellectual treatments of service industries often contain a strong undertone of moral disapproval that might perhaps be best expressed in·a paraphrasing of Orwell's creatures in *Animal Farm* – 'producing things good, serving things bad'. Any study of hotel and catering employment is essentially a study of neglect. Put another way, it is concerned with people's responses to the knowledge of others' employment in hotels and catering which all too frequently takes the form of 'Oh, couldn't you get anything better?'

2 Organising themes in the study of hotel and catering work

Although sociological knowledge about work in hotels and catering derives from a disparate body of literature, certain common themes can be discerned. Three of these in particular are important to a wider understanding of the issues covered in this book. They are: the nature and composition of the hotel and catering workforce; the forms of remuneration prevalent in the industry; and the influence of organisational and status factors on employee's experiences of work. The following discussion deals with each in turn and seeks to link long-standing preoccupations in research on hotel and catering work to wider concerns in industrial sociology. For example, in the case of the nature and composition of the workforce, some effort has been made to highlight the relevance of certain concepts in labour market analysis, hitherto largely neglected in industry-specific studies. In the discussion of remuneration, some weight has been given to the statutory context of payment in hotels and catering which until recently (Lucas, 1989, 1990) has also been largely ignored. It needs to be emphasised that in sociological terms this is not the stuff that interpretive miracles are made of, but rather the beginnings of a necessary correction to the insularity of many existing perspectives on employment in the hospitality industry.

GETTING THERE: WORKERS IN HOTELS AND CATERING

It is generally accepted that the historical origins of the hotel and catering workforce lie in the class of domestic servants who maintained the homes of the ruling classes in the latter half of the nineteenth century and first half of the twentieth (Saunders, 1981a; Riley, 1985). According to Saunders (1981a) the decline in the number of domestic servants in the first part of the twentieth century coincided with the first significant growth in hotel employment. Many domestic workers were leaving their employment as a result of 'push factors' such as lack of employment protection (which made domestic labour less attractive) and the improvements being made in domestic technology (that reduced the need for servants). Riley (1985) argues that the location of much domestic servant employment geographically mapped the growth areas for hotel and catering, most notably in seaside resorts, country spas and large urban conurbations. Saunders argues that this process of labour transfer meant that by the end of the Second World War, conditions 'made it seem logical that substantial numbers of male and female domestic staff drift into the expanding hotel and catering industry' (Saunders, 1981a: 83).

Clearly, the persistence of hotels and catering as major employers cannot be explained in the terms proposed by Riley and Saunders. Other contemporaneous discussions of hospitality industry employment tend to be couched in terms of the attractiveness of such work to persons who are in some way socially and/or psychologically marginal (Mars, Bryant and Mitchell, 1979). Thus, in explaining the attractiveness of hotel and catering work in the face of poor formal rewards, Mars and Mitchell (1976) argue that hotel workers obtain satisfaction from their employment that is not easily obtained in other occupations, satisfaction which can offset low earnings. This view can be traced back to Whyte (1948) who commented that: 'Apparently, there are many people who require a high rate of social activity and changes in physical activity in order to be happy in their work. The restaurant fills this need for them' (Whyte, 1948: 13).

In a later work, Mars, Bryant and Mitchell (1979: 79) report a hotel manager as describing hotel workers as 'misfits' who enjoy 'dealing with basic human elements that people have to have – the necessities of life'. This respondent went on to argue that 'other jobs are more remote from people's needs – hotel workers are people who cannot cope with remoteness'. Echoing Whyte's remarks, Mars, Bryant and Mitchell write:

> The industry seems to attract those for whom the making of more permanent relationships, either in personal or professional life, is difficult and who derive satisfaction in situations in which a large number of ephemeral but jovial relationships can be made.
>
> (Mars, Bryant and Mitchell, 1979: 89)

Similar statements concerning the social psychological marginality of the hotel and catering workforce abound in the literature. Despite lack of detailed empirical support there has been an invidious tendency to depict many hotel workers as 'deviants', and the hospitality industry as attracting a large number of people with 'personal problems'. Mars, Bryant and Mitchell (1979) and others have argued with some justification that employees themselves share these views. In their interviews with operative staff, Mars and his colleagues found a perception of the workforce as being comprised of 'nomadic' and 'non-conforming' members of society, and affected by a disproportionate amount of dishonesty, delinquency and psychological perversion. One executive is quoted as stating that the industry tends to attract 'all kinds of crooks, queers, men on the run, alcoholics' and those who for whatever reasons find mobility agreeable (Mars, Bryant and Mitchell, 1979: 79). Certainly the folklore of the industry supports the view that there are many employees with alcohol problems but any cause–effect relationship is unclear. The problem lies in visibility: are those with alcohol problems simply more visible within the food and accommodation industries? Or are alcoholics attracted to the industry? Or does the industry make alcoholics of many employees because the ready availability of alcohol is useful in coping with, for example, stress? Clearly, put this way there is a danger of descent into the absurd, though such arguments may merit serious investigation. Whyte, Hamilton and Whiley (1964) report that workers at the 'Hotel Tremont' drank a great deal, not for relaxation but for 'total blackout'. Visibility is also the key to understanding the other oft vaunted proposition that the hospitality industry has within its ranks a greater proportion than would be expected of male homosexuals. Folklore is here supported by coy references to homosexuality in the academic literature. Again, causality is impossible to establish, even if such an exercise were worthwhile. The disturbing thing about both examples is the ready tendency of some academic commentators to resort to simplistic psychologisms in explaining complex phenomena.

Shamir offers a similar account that exhibits minor tendencies in this direction but which is otherwise useful in demonstrating the extent to which hotel organisations embrace a culture that is potentially causal in stimulating petty criminal behaviour and other 'deviations' from conventional social mores. Shamir studied eight English hotels at a time when the hotel industry faced an acute labour shortage and was exceptionally willing to offer accommodation as a means of tempting workers to join their organisations. Many of the hotel workers he interviewed felt that those employed in the industry were 'running away from something', for example failing or failed marriages and difficulties with parents. These are hardly exceptional experiences unique to hotel industry employees but Shamir argues that many people are attracted to hotel and catering work precisely because the living-in facility helps them escape their background. He found that the core of live-in workers provided a focus for a workplace community that also embraced those employees who lived away from the hotel. The latter spent a good deal of non-work time in the hotel because their breaks, engendered by a split-shift system, were too short for them to go elsewhere. These workplace communities constituted, according to Shamir, a near-family-like surrogate that substituted for the absence of alternatively satisfying social relationships.

Shamir's point is that the workplace community, founded on the live-in arrangement, encourages and/or attracts those who are, in normative terms, socially marginal or deviant. Thus, many of the youngsters in the hotels studied could not, for a variety of reasons, live with their parents. At the same time, Shamir considers two aspects of hotel life which, if not actually causal of 'deviant' behaviour, certainly reinforce it. The first of these is the opportunity structure of the workplace. Because customer–worker contacts in certain areas are difficult to control, as are physical commodities and the amount of money changing hands, the poor pay and conditions of employees can create a high level of instrumentalism amongst the workforce that takes form in acts of petty pilferage and other kinds of fraudulent behaviour. A further aspect of this opportunity structure is the tendency of some clients to take a 'moral holiday' when staying in a hotel, thus providing workers with the chances to facilitate sexual and other non-legitimate services to clients. Indeed, it appears that some employers capitalise on this tendency for clients to take moral holidays. The trade journal *Caterer and Hotelkeeper* (25 June, 1987) reported that a company called Rainbow Mini Holidays was offering 'discreet weekends' where hotel staff asked no questions. The company is reported as saying that 'it's a fact of life that hotel affairs do take place' and that it hoped to make the secret or clandestine weekend easier to book. Further support for Shamir's claim comes from an American study. Prus and Vasilakopoulos (1979) studied male desk-clerks in two 'shady' (i.e. disreputable) inner-city American hotels. A significant contribution to the hotels' income came from prostitution, a trade supported by both a diverse bar clientele of businessmen and blue-collar workers and a staff comprised in part of ex-convicts and criminals, many of whom were engaged in other covert activities involving acts of fraud against their employers, fencing stolen property, dealing drugs and bookmaking. In both hotels, the relationship between prostitutes and clients and the hotel desk clerks was one of mutual, though not necessarily equal, benefit. The presence of prostitutes ensured the development of a sub-clientele desirous of their services; this generated takings at the bars since it was a rule that all women touting for business must have a drink. Further, a successful approach by a client led to further purchases including, at one of the hotels, the sale of a room, usually taking the form of a short-let. Typically therefore, a number of successful contracts between prostitute and client could generate a substantial income in any one night, and the desk-clerk acted as an intermediary between the two. The clerks maintained order, organised room lets and 'watched the backs' of the prostitutes, for example by calling rooms at specific times in order to check that the women were unhurt and not in difficulty. In return for these services, desk clerks expected and received tips from prostitutes, usually paid when the latter left the hotel. This payment of gratuities built up goodwill for the prostitute and compensated the clerk for the inconvenience caused.

The second aspect of hotel life which, in Shamir's view, encourages deviance, is the fact that hotel workers labour in the leisure time of other people. They often find themselves temporarily out of phase with the rest of society, unable to easily form social relationships outside of the industry. This can lead to the formation of community and occupational sub-cultures characterised by insularity and an exaggerated reaction against the norms of 'outsiders' such that engaging in deviant acts serves as a way of reinforcing the identity of workers whilst shocking 'normal' people. Shamir is clearly aware of the essential relativism attendant on concepts of 'normality' and 'deviance' but persists in ascribing activities such as pilfering, procuring prostitutes for guests and indulging in other acts of theft as part of a unique hotel culture, an assumption that permeates the work of many other writers who seek to advance essentially individualistic and psychologistic explanations of hotel and catering workplace behaviour. Hotel and catering workers are seen as victims not of an economic and social system that marginalises and exploits their labour but of their personal psychologies and the deficiencies of their private lives. The danger of this approach is that it depicts hotel workers as passive dupes, and frequently verges on the patronising as when Shamir writes:

> Hotel employees thus find themselves facing temptations to join customers or to assist them in non-legitimate or deviant activities. While in most cases the hotel workers who co-operate with customers in illegal activities stand to profit from their co-operation, it must be noted that customers' involvement in such activities may 'legitimise' some of them in the eyes of the workers, both because many of the customers have a higher social status than the co-operating employees and because it is the official aim of the hotel to serve the customer.
>
> (Shamir, 1981: 48)

There are clearly severe problems with explanations of the composition and motivations of the workforce in terms of 'deviant' psychological characteristics. Acts of theft may be seen, for example, as a perfectly rational response to low wages and poor conditions of employment. The claim that hotel workers derive satisfaction from their labour not easily accessible to those in other occupations is hardly commensurate with the suggestion that the hotel industry attracts social misfits. Some people may indeed derive psychological benefits from hotel *life* but this is not the same as obtaining satisfaction from hotel work. Indeed, attempts by researchers to assess the image of the industry held by the workforce and potential workforce reveals an almost uniformly negative response to hotel and catering employment. Despite the usually optimistic conclusions of many such studies that, if only hospitality work could be made to appear more attractive then difficulties attendant on recruitment and workforce stability would disappear, it is clear that antipathy to hotel and catering work is less to do with a lack of appreciation of the industry's image than an all too knowing suspicion of what hotel and catering employment is really like.

Underlying most of this research is the idea that people have a choice in deciding whether to work in hotels and catering. This in itself is an ideological gloss because to depict choice as an absolute value renders attitudes a matter of individual preference alone. As Snow (1981) points out, it is necessary to differentiate between degrees of freedom in choice. He postulates a somewhat simple dichotomous positive-negative model of motivation to explain the (un)attractiveness of hotel and catering occupations. In his study, positive choice (a conscious decision to enter hotel and catering employment because of its perceived attractiveness) was most common amongst chefs. In contrast, many other employees chose hotel and catering work for largely negative reasons – mainly because of a lack of positive alternatives.

Corcoran and Johnson (1974) explored career teachers' images of cooks, waiters, porters and room maids and asked respondents to compare each occupation with jobs of a similar level in other industries in terms of wages, hours of work, welfare facilities, career structure, pleasant working environment and scope for discretion. Cooks and chefs emerged from this exercise with reasonably favourable images whilst waiters, porters and room maids were regarded unfavourably, with few respondents actually differentiating between them on the criteria measured. One respondent cited by the authors summarised the central finding of the study:

> The main problem appears to be status. Compared with the Continent, a waiter's job here is normally regarded with contempt – as are most 'service' jobs in this country. Change the attitude and you will revolutionise the catering industry.
>
> (Corcoran and Johnson, 1974: 16)

Corcoran and Johnson conclude that in the main, there is no career structure for most waiters, porters and room-maids (and by extension many other jobs) and that hotel and catering posts are perceived as 'dead end', thus making them less likely to attract long-stay recruits.

Ellis (1981) also found that the occupations of chef/cook and waiter/waitress were the two jobs most associated with the industry and that chefs were viewed as sound and relatively attractive career options whereas waiters and other occupations elicited a more neutral response, a finding later confirmed by the Hotel and Catering Training Board (1989). Ellis

(1981) sampled 1,926 members of the general public, 361 job seekers interviewed whilst using Job Centre facilities and 3,042 school pupils in the final year of compulsory schooling with a view to eliciting images of work and occupations in the hotel industry. Two-thirds of the general public associated the industry with good jobs and three-quarters felt catering work offered valuable opportunities for young people, though men were less likely to find hotel and catering jobs attractive and a predictable class difference emerged in so far as those in higher social groups were less likely to nominate a suitable hotel and catering job, implying that there still exists a distinction between the service class and the serviced class. Ninety-six per cent of the job seekers said they would be willing to consider a job in the industry. Within this sample a clear hierarchy of suitable preferred occupations emerged with cashiers, barpersons and receptionists felt most desirable and room-maid, porter and housekeeper least so. The centre ground preferences included manager, kitchen/counter assistant, cook/chef and waiter/waitress. Amongst school pupils, the two least acceptable jobs to emerge were room-maid and porter; key deterrent factors in evaluating such work being the perceived low status, repetitive and unskilled nature of the job. At best, the school pupil results show a gentle indifference to hotel and catering jobs and at worst their assessments are potentially negative. What is most interesting about this part of the survey is the extent to which the author regards data drawn from these responses as intrinsically unreliable because of pupils' generic ignorance about the 'real' nature of hotel and catering jobs!

It is difficult to do justice to a complex report such as that by Ellis (1981) yet the author exhibits a peculiar unwillingness to accept the obvious (negative) interpretation of his findings, an unwillingness that makes traditional academic caution look like reckless abandon. Other studies of industry image exhibit similar caution and fail to grasp anomalies arising from their own data. For example, the County of Avon Careers Service (1988) found that employers regarded a willingness to work unsocial hours as a prerequisite for a career in the hospitality industry and yet at the same time expressed the view that the lack of young people interested in a hotel and catering job was due to a *misinformed* image of the industry as offering poor pay, ill-defined career structures and – surprise – unsocial hours of work. The extent to which employer attitudes can alert prospective employees to the down side of hotel and catering work also emerged from the report with many employers reaffirming the industry's hostility towards qualifications. Most were interested in taking on college trained and YTS (Youth Training Scheme) workers (one wonders, somewhat less than innocently, if this is because of the lower cost and fewer employment rights of such workers) but in general saw qualifications as not being overly important, except in the case of chefs where relevant craft certificates were required. The Avon report confirms a trend that is manifest throughout the industry – it is a trend of thoughtlessness combined with a hint of the 'we had to suffer why shouldn't you' attitude. The UK trade journal *Caterer and Hotelkeeper*, hardly a source of radical agitprop, frequently reports the views of employers on a variety of issues, including the image of the industry. On 11 February 1988, they covered a careers convention: 'When the careers Convention panel was asked by one student about salary levels in the industry, the reply from John Herdman, general manager of the Imperial Hotel, Blackpool, came back swiftly: ' "If you want to work a 39-hour week in this industry, you'll stay in the potwash. Rewards are there for the taking but they have to be worked for" ' (1988: 9). Even the *Caterer and Hotelkeeper* correspondent was, in winding up the piece, moved to spell out rather drily that 'The implication was that to earn good salaries in the catering industry, they must be prepared to worker harder and longer than in other occupations' (1988: 9).

However employers present themselves in their public statements, it is difficult to overcome the fundamental objection that the image of the industry as being low paid, offering poor conditions of employment and low status jobs reflects to a very large extent the reality of work in hotels and catering. What has perhaps changed is that many more potential employees are now recognising this and voting with their feet. The Hotel and Catering Training Board (HCTB) (1989) study of employment in London found that amongst job seekers interviewed at Job Centres the most important attributes of employment were salary, good training, pleasant working environment and interesting work. Only one-third of respondents felt that pay levels in the industry were attractive. Desperate to explain away the image and reality of low pay, the HCTB comment:

> A substantial contributory factor to this appeared to be the way in which hotel and catering jobs are advertised inside Job Centres . . . very few mentioned or quantified tips as part of the total remuneration on offer.
>
> (Hotel and Catering Training Board, 1989: 7)

The indifference or hostility of *potential* employees is disturbing enough for employers but the HCTB also explored the views of other adults on the image of the industry and found that the 80 per cent of men and 58 per cent of women cited poor salaries and long working hours as a source of discouragement to working in hotels and catering. More worrying still was the response of those already employed in the industry – more than half of those questioned stated that they had considered looking for a job outside the industry, for preference the most frequently mentioned alternatives were selling, retailing, office work and manufacturing. The irony of this situation is that whereas movement of hotel and catering workers has traditionally been *within* the industry, the gradual progression towards a low-wage economy in areas that may be seen as a close substitute for hotel and catering work – areas such as retailing – means that moves outside are no longer improbable, especially since 92 per cent of the employees interviewed said they would leave their jobs because of low pay.

Research on the image of employment in hotels and catering goes beyond explanations of the composition of the hotel and catering workforce in terms of social-psychological marginality. A harsher reality can be discerned, one that becomes clearer through close analysis of structural aspects of the labour market. Picking up on the theme of workforce marginality, the American writer Henderson (1965) laid the foundations for such analysis in the hotel and catering context. He referred with no seeming intention to be pejorative to hospitality industry workers as 'substandard':

> The term, 'substandard', merely refers to labor groups who are weak in bargaining power and who, for one reason or another, are easily discriminated against. . .they enter the labor market with certain handicaps in their dealings with employers. . .the substandard labor groups most prominent in the lodging industry are women, children, immigrants. . .Puerto Ricans, Mexicans, Negroes, unskilled laborers, and persons with prison records.
>
> (Henderson, 1965: 51)

The remainder of this discussion focusses on two groups of workers in the labour market who are 'marginal' both because of their limited bargaining power and other factors that allow employers to discriminate against them in a variety of ways. These are women and ethnic minority and migrant workers. The issue of young workers will be briefly examined in the later discussion on remuneration in the industry.

Women workers in hotels and catering

Robinson and Wallace (1983) found that between 1971 and 1981 employment in hotels and catering rose at more than twice the rate of employment in service industries as a whole with the share of hotels and catering in total service industry employment rising from 4.4 per cent to 5.1 per cent for men and 7.6 per cent to 8.2 per cent for women. The creation of additional part-time jobs was wholly responsible for the increase in women's employment and for 69 per cent of the increase in male employment. By 1981, the industry accounted for about 12 per cent of part-time employment in all industries and 13.5 per cent of part-time employment in service industries with 36 per cent of all part-timers being men and 67 per cent women.

Robinson and Wallace (1983) argue that over the decade, the growth in part-time employment has occurred at the expense of full-time jobs, particularly those of women. In short therefore, the position of women workers in the hotel and catering industry is inextricably linked with part-time employment.

The most comprehensive recent report on the position of women in the hotel and catering industry in Britain was published by the Hotel and Catering Training Board (HCTB) (1987). This report uses the categories of Main and Subsidiary Activity Centres to describe the industry and thus adopts as its baseline for calculations the workforce total of 2.3 million persons. The Main Activity Centres include hotels, guesthouses, other tourist accommodation, restaurants, cafés, snackbars, public houses, bars, night clubs and licensed clubs, canteens and messes operated by contract caterers and the category 'other' made up of the self-employed. These areas between them accounted at the time for some 1,332,000 workers of whom 375,000 were employed in hotels, guesthouses and other tourist accommodation, 304,000 in restaurants, cafés and snackbars and some 373,000 in pubs and bars. The Subsidiary Activity Sectors accounted for 998,000 employees working in tourism and travel catering, public services catering (education, public administration and the National Health Service), retail distribution, personal and domestic services and industry and office catering. Crudely speaking, the HCTB's Main Activity Centres probably account for the bulk of commercial catering whereas the Subsidiary Activity Centres account for the majority of public sector catering. This interpretation is supported by Robinson and Wallace (1983) who note that an earlier HCITB survey in 1977:

> reported a workforce total of 2,137,000 compared with 853,000 in the DE's [Department of Employment] Census of Employment. Over half the difference arose from the inclusion in the HCITB results of 670,000 workers in the National Health Service, local authority and industrial catering employment.
>
> (Robinson and Wallace, 1983: 268)

The main findings of the 1987 HCTB report can be summarised as follows:

1 17 per cent of all women in paid employment are in hotel and catering jobs: of the 2.3 million workers in the hotel and catering industry some 74 per cent or 1.7 million are women of which between 50 and 60 per cent are employed in subsidiary sectors of the industry;
2 of the 1.3 million jobs in the Main Activity Centres of the industry some 830,000 are held by women: there are thus 1.6 women for every man, the corresponding figures for the Subsidiary Sectors being ten women for every one man;

3 by any estimate around 70 per cent of all women workers in the hotel and
  catering industry are employed in operative grades: some 47 per cent of
  all managers are women and, whilst this is the highest proportion of
  women managers in any industry, it does not reflect the overall percentage – 74 per cent – of women workers in the industry nor the number
  of females studying on hotel management courses (75 per cent all levels;
  75 per cent on full-time university undergraduate courses in hotel and
  catering management and 67 per cent on CNAA degree courses in hotel
  and catering management); and
4 of the 2.3 million jobs in the hotel and catering industry some 1.3 million
  or about 56 per cent are part-time: the majority are held by women with
  three-quarters of part-time jobs in the Main Commercial Sectors being
  held by women.

Several reasons have been advanced in order to account for the predominance of part-time employment in the hotel and catering industry. First, the
erratic nature of the demand for hotel and catering services with many peaks
and troughs throughout the day means that it is difficult to utilise full-time
labour effectively or economically. Secondly the industry has faced periodic
labour shortages such that sources of labour other than full-time workers
have become attractive to employers. Airey and Chopping (1980) speculate
that the growth in female employment in general may have been attributable
to the recruitment of women at lower cost during periods when unemployment was low and the cost of male labour more expensive. Equal pay
legislation has theoretically eliminated such discrimination. However, the
simple fact is that part-time workers earn less than their full-time counterparts because they work less. Advantages also accrue to employers in the
hospitality industry in utilising part-time workers when needed – at peak
business hours – thus eliminating 'idle time'. This gives rise to significant
cost advantages. As Robinson and Wallace (1983) note:

> Most managers reported an ample supply of workers seeking full-time
> employment but the ability to engage staff able to work only for the
> hours during which labour was needed yielded direct savings in wage
> costs. Although at macro-level there is evidence that higher hourly rates
> of earnings are paid to full-time than to part-time catering workers in the
> same occupation, the main cost advantage within a particular organisa-
> tion stemmed from the reduced hours of work associated with part-time
> employment.
>
> (Robinson and Wallace, 1983: 276)

Finally here, many sectors of the hotel and catering industry, particularly in
such areas as education and public and industrial catering, operate only at

certain times of day and thus find employment of part-time workers more attractive.

Of course, the demand for part-time workers does not simultaneously explain why women tend to fill such jobs. Conventional explanations of women's participation in the workforce tend to emphasise what Howe (1977) calls the 'pink blanket' theory of socialisation, where women are viewed as being socialised into particular norms and values which predispose them to seeking work in occupations which reflect and extend these values. Much evidence exists to support this view. For example, Witz and Wilson (1982) note that in the service industries, women predominate in occupations that mirror their unpaid functions in the home. Employers are able to utilise their skills at low cost since women acquire them outside of the labour market and employers do not have to bear the cost of training. Such explanations have been common in accounting for the presence of women in the hotel and catering industry. A 1967 Hotel and Catering Economic Development Committee (HCEDC) report argued that because hotel and catering work was domestic in nature, it was 'particularly suitable' to women who employers could recruit without having to undertake extensive training. The HCEDC further argued that the scope for part-time work in the industry might be viewed as attractive by married women who required jobs that could be fitted around domestic and childcare responsibilities. This is a familiar argument that resurfaced in a study by the Hotel and Catering Industry Training Board (HCITB) (1983) who observed that housewives constituted a large source of labour for all sectors of the industry, some 21 per cent of industry employees having been housewives prior to entering the industry. This is not to ignore the fact that many women in family units find it necessary to work in order to sustain an adequate 'family wage'. Similar explanations of women's participation in the workforce couched in terms of their lack of commitment are also suspect. The HCEDC (1967) argued that much part-time work is seasonal and therefore suits women workers who do not want to make a longer-term employment commitment, stating at the same time that the nature and lack of stability of hotel and catering employment makes it less attractive to men. However, Robinson and Wallace (1983) have demonstrated that seasonal changes in employment in the hotel and catering industry are seemingly met by wider fluctuations in the number of full-time than part-time jobs. The idea that women in general lack commitment to full-time employment must therefore be viewed with caution.

This is particularly so in the light of evidence showing that however dismal hotel and catering employment is overall, the terms and conditions of employment for men are often superior to those enjoyed by women. Men fair better on a range of criteria that demonstrates the depth of the structures of discrimination against women irrespective of whether the latter are of part- or full-time status. For example, Knight (1971) notes that whilst overall, some 64 per cent of experienced staff had never progressed beyond operative level, when broken down according to gender this showed that only 45 per cent of men had never progressed compared to 74 per cent of women. A breakdown by full- and part-time working is not given. Similarly, in an HCITB (1983) report, it was found that 15 per cent of industry employees claimed some formal qualification but men were more than twice as likely to possess qualifications as women. The HCTB (1987) survey of women in the industry found that after three years of employment, women straight out of college did less well than men, with the number of men in supervisory/management positions having increased threefold but women only twofold. At management level, this may be as much due to that ever discreet form of discrimination, 'channelling', as to women taking career breaks (see Chapter 3's discussion of women managers). The crucial period at management level seems to be for women in their mid-twenties. Prior to this women and men managers are roughly equal in number (though not proportions) but men then begin to overtake women. The gap reduces after age 45 but never returns to the earlier balance. Sectorally there are also clear imbalances. An HCITB (1985) study calculated that in 1981 only 36 per cent of hotel managers, 55 per cent of restaurant managers and 43 per cent of public house managers were women. The highest proportion of women managers was to be found in the subsidiary sectors of education (67 per cent). The HCTB (1987) later found that women craft students in a two-tier study conducted in the periods 1975–1978 and 1980–1984 were more highly qualified than men in so far as 71 per cent of female students had at least one GCE O level examination pass compared to 58 per cent of men. In the 1975 study it was found however that only some 16 per cent of women had been promoted compared to 40 per cent for men. Channelling may be an important barrier to development in those areas of the industry that have a career or promotional structure (e.g. management posts). The vast majority of women do not work in such areas however, but in part-time operative jobs where even the full-time equivalent posts have little career structure or prospects. Part-time employment in the industry is closely associated with certain occupational groups: waiting-on-table, chambermaids, washers-up and cleaners (Airey and Chopping, 1980). The HCTB (1987) noted that women's concentration in the lower occupational groups combined with their part-time status meant that their earnings were approximately 75 per cent of men's.

Sociological perspectives on the nature of labour markets are of value here in illuminating the position of women workers, though only the most cursory discussion is possible within the constraints of the text. The first area of importance is the nature of occupational segregation whereby the structuring of male and female participation in the labour market entails a distinctive separation between the types of jobs performed by men and women. This segregation occurs at two levels. *Horizontal segregation* entails the separation of men and women into different industrial spheres – different industries. *Vertical segregation* involves men and women working in different areas of the same industry – mainly different occupational levels. For 1982, Witz and Wilson report that three-quarters of the female labour force worked in service industries with 57.9 per cent concentrated in just three areas: distributive trades, professional and scientific, and miscellaneous services. As was demonstrated earlier, women comprise in excess of two-thirds of the hotel and catering workforce yet are concentrated for the most part in operative roles whilst men dominate in management.

Occupational segregation is best understood in the context of dual labour market theories of job allocation (Barron and Norris, 1976; Doeringer and Piore, 1971) underlying which is the assumption that the labour market is not unified but structured into distinct segments, usually a primary and secondary sector. In primary labour markets, jobs are supplied by large firms that are highly profitable; characterised by a high capital to labour ratio and high productivity resulting from large scale production predicated on capital investment in technology; and stable demand for the products arising from international as well as national markets. In primary labour markets, wages and skill levels are relatively high; there are opportunities for training and advancement; employment is stable and there are high levels of unionisation (Witz and Wilson, 1982). The characteristics of primary labour market employment arise for the most part from employers' interest in maintaining stable workforces in order to ensure minimum disruption to production. In contrast, secondary labour markets are characterised by the provision of jobs by small firms where there is a low capital-to-labour ratio; production is small scale and intensive; and local and regional markets with irregular and/or seasonal patterns of demand predominate. Whereas primary labour markets tend to correspond with firms located in highly concentrated industries, secondary labour markets are more likely to be associated with unconcentrated industries where there are large numbers of small firms. Secondary labour market jobs are characterised by low wages, unstable employment, few training and advancement prospects, low skill levels and low levels of unionisation. A further crucial difference between primary and secondary labour markets is the role in the former of *internal* labour markets. Opportunities for advancement in primary labour markets are related to the hierarchical structure of markets where progress upwards is clearly demarcated in terms of skill level and rewards and where recruitment to higher positions is from lower positions in the same hierarchy rather than external labour markets. Recruits to jobs in the secondary labour markets by way of contrast are almost exclusively from the open labour market to which employees return when they leave a job. At the level of individual firms and units, most of the evidence for the hotel and catering industry suggests that employers tend to rely on recruitment from external labour markets and internal labour markets are relatively poorly developed (Simms, Hales and Riley, 1988).

Dual labour market theorists argue that secondary labour markets are characterised for the most part by high female participation rates in the labour force. According to writers like Barron and Norris (1976) secondary labour markets exhibit a number of characteristics that 'match' those of certain social groups, such as women – they are easily dispensable; can be sharply demarcated from other groups of workers on the grounds of a conventional social attribute (i.e. gender); they have a relatively low motivation to acquire training; they do not rate economic rewards particularly highly; and are unlikely to develop solidarity with other employees. However, these claims rely for the most part on stereotypical assumptions about women rather than concrete evidence (Beechey, 1987). Further, specific to the hotel and catering industry, whilst men may do better than women on a whole range of criteria concerned with terms and conditions of employment, it is still the case that the operative workforce as a whole fares rather badly. In other words, dual labour market theories are of rather limited value in making comparisons *within* industries. As Beechey (1987: 38) notes, the horizontal and vertical segmentation of women in the labour market means that the treatment of women in terms of a heterogeneous category of secondary sector workers obscures differences between the types of work women do. A further problem with dual labour market theory – at least as proposed by Barron and Norris (1976) – is, according to Beechey (1987), its tendency to treat the dynamics of the labour market as the determining factor in explaining the position of female labour. In so doing, dual labour market theorists ignore the position of female labour in domestic and family contexts and the wider complex of patriarchal relationships that influence the supply of labour. A similar point is made by Witz and Wilson (1982) who argue that segmentation theories do not explain *why* women should be drawn into service industry employment in preference to men. They argue that 'This reveals one of the major weaknesses of labour market segmentation theories which is their apparent inability to explain why it is that women are confined to secondary labour markets' (Witz and Wilson, 1982: 52).

Dual labour market theory provides explanations of women's labour market position that transcend simplistic theories of socialisation and explanations couched in terms of discrimination against women. Of equal value are theories of the feminisation of labour. Dual labour market theories tend to treat employers' strategies for the recruitment and retention of labour as at least partly given. Explanations of differences in employer strategy in primary and secondary sectors are also couched in suspiciously asymmetrical terms. Thus, in primary sectors, employers pursue a rational strategy to retain a stable workforce but in secondary sectors they do not. The reasons as to why the latter should be the case are not clear. Theories of the feminisation of labour view the position of female labour as at least partly arising from managements' attempts to degrade and deskill work in order to secure control over labour processes and improve access to easily disposable and cheap pools of labour (see Chapter 4).

In essence, the feminisation of labour is a process whereby the low status and rewards of jobs become associated with the performance of such jobs by women. This comes about as capital attempts to lower the value of labour power, often by deskilling a job and offering it to women workers. A frequently cited example of this process is clerical work, once the domain of middle-class males but through the introduction of clerical technologies now a predominantly low-paid 'typical' female occupation. The central problem with the feminisation thesis is the dispute that exists over whether deskilling takes place prior or subsequent to an occupation coming to be dominated by women. As Thompson (1989) observes, it is quite possible that both types of feminisation have occurred and continue to occur. Jobs which are seen as a natural extension of women's role such as nursing and primary school teaching are those in which devaluation takes place subsequent to such jobs being defined as women's work. In contrast, there is some evidence to suggest that feminisation takes place after an occupation or work task has already been deskilled. Indeed, Thompson (1989) argues that clerical work falls into this category. New technology helped women into offices by creating new categories of work not in direct competition with those of men: women were originally employed in offices because they were cheaper than men. Office technology already had a grip on clerical work, though the transformation of clerical work from a virtually all-male to all-female area of employment was relatively rapid. Thompson (1989) also makes an important point when he says that not only may the two variants of the feminisation thesis take place at different times in the same occupations but they may operate co-jointly within a single sector at any one time.

The importance of sociological attempts to explain the labour market position of women lies in the extent to which they transcend the normally simplistic accounts of women's position proffered by employers and many of the less imaginative texts on personnel management practice. Clearly, the marginality of female workers reflects deep-rooted structures of inequality characteristic of women's social position more generally. A recent study of hotel and catering employment in the English seaside resort of Brighton offers one final thought on part-time female work in the industry (Brighton Council Economic Development Committee, 1988). The authors of this report found that in pay terms women appear to have consistently lower aspirations than men whilst having more exacting demands in respect of childcare facilities, maternity/paternity leave, time off for family sickness, late night transport and flexibility in hours of work. The authors of the study conclude that women's desire for temporary and part-time employment derives from the lack of permanent jobs (not only in the hotel and catering industry) with hours that suit childcare and other family responsibilities that normally fall to women. The absence of full-time jobs with adequate supporting facilities and conditions of employment means that women are obliged to consider part-time, casual and temporary work. In other words, women's seeming predilection for part-time work is little more than an expression of the constraints that govern women's lives more generally.

Migrant and ethnic workers

Discussions of ethnic and migrant workers in the literature on hotel and catering work are complicated by a failure to define terms such as migrant and ethnic. The terms are often used interchangeably. Rarely are indige-nous ethnic populations distinguished from visiting workers. Knight (1971) is typical in simply referring to foreign workers. His study revealed that one-seventh of industry employees began their working lives outside Great Britain and that one-twentieth of the workforce was Irish (again, it is unclear as to whether the term is being used generically or to refer to the Republic) and the majority of other non-British workers came from Western Europe or Asia. Of all foreign staff in catering, some three quarters entered the industry as their first job in Britain and more than a quarter had held catering occupations (mostly as cooks and waiters) before coming to Britain. Further: 'it appears that foreign staff are more likely, as opposed to more willing, to work long hours than the rest of the catering workers and more likely to work shifts and week-ends.' (Knight, 1971: 170).

Knight's comments obscure a complex of racial discrimination and exploitation of ethnic minorities. There are many reasons as to why over-seas workers (as opposed to indigenous members of the ethnic minority population) come to work in UK catering jobs. Catering work in Britain can pay better and provide overseas workers with career opportunities often absent in their home countries. Others come for reasons of learning English and the desire to travel (Bowey, 1976). At the same time, the willingness of firms to employ overseas workers is because of difficulties in finding members of the indigenous population prepared to work for the kind of wages on offer. The clear implication here is that whatever the relative position of overseas workers in the British catering industry *vis-à-vis* their countries of origin, the majority come to occupy positions in the industry that are amongst the worst paid. Placing the role of overseas catering workers in the British hospitality industry into historical perspective, Dronfield and Soto note that in the late 1960s not only were hotel employers failing to attract the indigenous unemployed into jobs in the industry but in many cases 'must have actually chosen migrant workers in the belief that they would be more docile and hard working' (Dronfield and Soto, 1980: 16), a view loosely supported by Bowey (1976). During this period, hotel employers, particularly those with large units in London, actively recruited overseas workers. Many ended up in the poorer jobs (Byrne, 1986).

In the past, migrant workers to Britain had to live in constant fear that employers would revoke their work permits. The potential threat of having permission to work withdrawn often led migrant workers to acquiesce to employers' demands with little legal protection from the unreasonable or unscrupulous. However, the role of work permits in the employment of overseas workers has changed considerably in recent years. Byrne (1986: 13) points out that whereas over 15,000 permits a year were issued for the industry in the mid-1960s, subsequent tightening-up on the part of governments means that in 1983 only 267 were issued for hotel and catering. Whilst changes in the work permit system have largely put an end to the use of cheap, unskilled, overseas labour Byrne argues, exploitation continues in other ways. Methods of recruitment have changed but foreign nationals continue to be employed in significant numbers by the use of migrant students and visitors: the numbers of student visas issued has risen from 91,000 in 1974 to 124,000 in 1984, though no statistics exist to show the numbers of students and visitors who drift into hotel and catering work.

All in all, Byrne (1986) estimates that around 115,000 workers in the hotel and catering industry are migrants and that many more are members of ethnic minorities indigenous to the population. The contribution of ethnic minorities to the industry is considerable, particularly in certain geographic areas. Byrne cites a study of London hotels where 45 per cent of workers were from ethnic minorities. In contrast, the Commission for Racial Equality (1991) found that in Bradford, where a high proportion of the population are members of ethnic minorities, a number of hotels had all-white staffs. As with women and migrant workers, members of ethnic minorities are often regarded as a source of cheap labour. They also have to contend with both explicit and implicit racism. Byrne (1986) reports that in

1985 the National Federation for Self-Employed and Small Businesses argued that Wages Council protection should be abolished in order that black workers could then undercut the wages of the majority. This was presented as a means of countering employers' discrimination! Similarly, in the same year the Institute of Directors argued that Wages Councils' minimum rates discouraged employers from taking on blacks who 'for a number of socio-economic reasons have a lower marginal productivity than whites' (quoted in Byrne, 1986: 9). As the evidence on Wages Council regulation discussed later in the chapter will show, minimum rates cannot be reasonably cited as relevant to recruitment in this context, since they are often the 'going rate' for jobs in hotel and catering. Further, productivity in hotels and catering is in any case low and primarily a function of markets and the state of technology rather than the quality of labour or its deployment. Indeed, as Potter (1988) notes, 'the reluctance of employers to take on black workers is nothing to do with "lower marginal productivity" and everything to do with deeply embedded racist views' (1988: 19).

Much of what Byrne (1986) alleges about the employment of ethnic minorities in the hotel and catering industry is confirmed by the Commission for Racial Equality (CRE) (1991) who found that their Code of Practice in Employment, issued in 1984 and offering practical advice on implementing effective equal opportunity policies, had met with little response from hospitality industry employers compared to other service sector employers:

> The hotel industry has a reputation for giving a low priority to personnel issues, but the almost universal disregard of the Code's recommendations which we found cannot be justified, either on the grounds of inadequate personnel resources or the inappropriateness of the Code for use in the industry. Many large industries, (including some household names in retailing) with similarly decentralised recruitment and a high turnover of unskilled staff have found it possible, and indeed useful, to follow the recommendations of the Code of Practice.
>
> (Commission for Racial Equality, 1991: 34)

The CRE argues that the diverse recruitment methods employed by hotel and catering organisations for different grades of jobs, when combined with a general lack of systematic personnel and recruitment procedures, is detrimental to the recruitment of ethnic minority employees. Where recruitment techniques were supported by specialist personnel staff as opposed to being the sole responsibility of a member of the unit management team, better procedures appeared to exist.

The CRE also examined the recruitment policies and techniques of colleges offering hospitality management courses. Members of the ethnic minorities tended to be concentrated on courses in technical rather than managerial skills and were not well represented in course literature and recruitment documentation. Further, three London colleges reported that they had encountered problems securing industrial placements for ethnic minority students and felt this was due to racial discrimination. Three colleges reported similar difficulties in ethnic minority students' attempts to find permanent employment. This is supported by earlier evidence from Dronfield and Soto (1980: 17) who state that nearly all the black people they talked to were working in jobs that did not involve contact with the public. They also cite college lecturers as indicating that securing industrial placements in public-contact jobs for black students was difficult. It is unsurprising in the light of this evidence that the CRE found that ethnic minority employees were under-represented in management, supervisory and clerical grades throughout the country.

Much of what was said earlier with respect to women in the labour market is not without relevance for an understanding of the position of ethnic minorities (Hill, 1981; Thompson, 1989). There seems to be some consensus that whilst ethnicity is not unimportant in the allocation of jobs, skill levels and factors like gender and class remain more important differentiators. According to Hill (1981) there is evidence to suggest that on occasions, race may lead to forms of segregation in which whites and members of the ethnic minorities do not compete for the same types of work. It is important not to become complacent on the question of ethnicity in employment however. The CRE report and other evidence discussed above suggests that discrimination in one form or another remains an important element in explaining the position of women and members of the ethnic minorities in the workforce. Within the hotel and catering industry, as with other industries, gender and ethnicity also have important implications for occupational status and remuneration as later discussion will show.

BEING THERE: REMUNERATION AND 'INCENTIVE'

The previous section identified evidence supportive of the idea that both potential and actual hotel and catering industry employees have a negative view of work in the industry. What are the foundations for such a view? One complex of reasons relating to labour markets was highlighted earlier, namely the extent to which for many, hotel and catering work is a last resort, mundane and degrading employment with few opportunities for even limited advancement. Another reason centres on the nature of remuneration in the industry. Most commentators (but few employers) are agreed that the hotel and catering industry is characterised by low pay.

However, it has been argued that for some hospitality industry occupations at least, income is greater than may be reflected in formal remuneration. This point of view has been most forcefully advanced by Gerald Mars and his various colleagues (e.g. Mars and Mitchell, 1976; Mars and Nicod, 1981, 1984) and has been widely accepted, only recently attracting limited critical review (Johnson, 1982, 1983a; Lennon and Wood, 1989). The idea of total and informal rewards is crucial here. Mars and Mitchell (1976: 27) argue that in addition to basic pay, hotel and catering workers have access, in varying degrees, to a variety of other rewards. They define the total rewards system as comprising BASIC PAY + SUBSIDISED LODGING + SUBSIDISED FOOD + TIPS OR SERVICE CHARGE + 'FIDDLES' AND 'KNOCK-OFFS'.

In this formula, basic pay constitutes formal reward as, to some extent, do subsidised food and lodging. The term 'informal', generally refers to tips or service charge, fiddles and knock-offs. Crucial to the analysis of the total rewards system are three related concepts. The first centres on the generally accepted view that because levels of demand for hotel and restaurant services are largely unpredictable, management are unable to develop tightly controlled and systematic responses to the requirements of the market and thus respond in an *ad hoc* or flexible manner that gives rise to a culture of authoritarianism. Secondly, in order to attempt some response to an uncertain environment, managements form *individual contracts* with key staff. Individual contracts govern not only basic pay but the access workers may have to other elements in the total rewards system. The basis of the individual contract is secrecy. Some workers are rewarded better than others but the allocation of such rewards is almost always conditional on a private agreement between managers and individual workers. This leads, thirdly, to the concepts of *core and peripheral workers*. Core workers are those who benefit substantially from individual contracts. They are key workers whose labour is perceived by management as vital to the smooth operation of the enterprise because of some special skill(s), technical knowledge, loyalty and so on. Peripheral workers are those who benefit less from individual contracts. The relationship between core and peripheral workers in this context is seen as progressive: most hotel and catering workers beginning as peripherals and many moving eventually into the core. Not all peripheral workers move into the core however, as the earlier review of the nature of the workforce would suggest, and there are a large group of stigmatised workers in the lowest grades who never leave the periphery. The concepts of *ad hoc* management, individual contracts, and core and peripheral workers figure prominently not only in discussions of pay in the industry but in the study of the hotel and catering workplace more generally as will subsequently be demonstrated.

Basic pay

The majority of academic evidence concurs in suggesting both that basic rates of pay in hotels and catering are inadequate and employers are frequently ruthless in pursuing low-pay strategies. For comparative purposes and in order to establish the historical facticity of low pay in hotels and catering it is worth offering a short summary of key studies in recent years. The Hotel and Catering Economic Development Committee (1975) calculated that on the basis of a low pay criteria of 60p an hour for men and 55p per hour for women, 49 per cent of full-time adult men and 88 per cent of full-time adult women in hotels and catering were low paid compared with 11 per cent and 53 per cent respectively in 'all industries'. Thomas and Erlam (1978) in a Low Pay Unit report found that 'Male catering workers are the lowest paid men in any industry listed in the Government's New Earnings Survey' (1978: 1). Taylor, Airey and Kotas (1983: 157) noted that the balance of evidence supported the view that pay in the industry consistently falls behind that of other industries. Byrne (1986) estimated that for 1985 average earnings in hotels and catering fell more than £60 behind the average in the rest of the economy and that anywhere between 57 and 64 per cent of full-time workers were low paid, defined as earning less than two-thirds of the male median earnings. Croney (1988: 15) estimated that for 1987 the average gross weekly earnings for manual men in the industry was 60.4 per cent of the average earnings for all industries and services whilst for manual women this figure was 83.4 per cent. The British trade journal *Caterer and Hotelkeeper* (1990: 12–13) reported that the 1989 British Hotels, Restaurants and Caterers' Association wages survey revealed catering managers as earning 27 per cent less than the average non-manual worker whilst non-management employees earned 28 per cent less than the average manual worker (in both surveys, overtime was excluded). Earlier in the chapter the specific issue of women's earnings was considered, and it is worth pointing out that, in both 1972 and 1982, full-time men in manual catering employment earned the lowest wages of any considered in 125 industries, whereas for women, catering earnings exceeded only hairdressing for fifty-one industries studied, whilst part-time women workers in catering were the lowest in both 1972 and 1982 (Robinson and Wallace, 1984: 144).

Low pay persists despite the existence of minimum-wage fixing legislation for certain industries administered under the Wages Council system. Wages Councils originated as part of a strategy by governments to provide safety net protection for the low paid in (principally manufacturing) industries in which collective bargaining with employee representatives such as trade unions did not exist. Originally they were intended as short-

or medium-term mechanisms for wage regulation, to be abolished at such a time as collective bargaining developed or other conditions conspired to eliminate low pay. Many service industries have gradually been brought within the scope of the Wages Councils, the Catering Wages Act of 1943 being instrumental in developing a wages council system for the hospitality industry. Currently three Wages Councils are concerned with the regulation of wages in the hospitality industry: the Licensed Residential Establishment and Licensed Restaurant Wages Council (LRE), the Licensed Non-residential Establishment Wages Council (LNR) and the Unlicensed Place of Refreshment Wages Council (UPR).

Wages Councils can legally enforce minimum remuneration in the areas for which they are responsible, requiring employers to post up-to-date wages orders in their premises. The Wages Council system is policed by the Wages Inspectorate who can order employers to make good up to two years payment in arrears if they are found guilty of underpayment. In 1986, substantial changes were made to the fairly wide-ranging powers of the Wages Councils. The Conservative Government's Wages Act 1986 removed workers under the age of 21 from the scope of protection. Further, Wages Councils were restricted to setting a single minimum hourly rate (up to a weekly number of hours worked), a single minimum overtime rate (for hours worked over that number) and a maximum accommodation charge for live-in employees. After the passing of the 1986 Wages Act, Wages Councils could no longer fix annual and statutory holidays, additional payments for Sunday work, provisions relating to intervals for rest and deductions permitted for meals provided whilst on duty, separate statutory minima for different job categories and regional premia (Lucas, 1990).

In being restricted to setting only three standards, Wages Councils were required by the 1986 Act to consider, when determining the minimum rate, the likely effect of the rate on levels of employment amongst the workforce, most particularly in areas where payment in general was less than the national average for such workers. As Lucas (1990) notes:

> Therefore, a council covering large numbers of workers in areas of high unemployment and below average pay levels, would appear to have a duty not to make an order incorporating a significant pay rise which would push pay levels to the point which would further jeopardise job opportunities. Thus wages councils might be said to have been given *carte blanche* for keeping rates as low as possible by giving a small or even no increase in certain circumstances.
>
> (Lucas, 1990: 327)

As Lucas (1990) suggests, the priority of the Wages Councils appears to have been shifted from protecting the low-paid to creating employment opportunities. The concept of the safety-net for the low-paid has consequently been substantially diluted. Indeed, in order to introduce the 1986 Act, the government had to dissociate itself from ratification of the International Labour Organisation's 1928 Minimum Wage-Fixing Machinery Convention that in 1980 had over ninety-four signatories.

The effects of the Wages Act 1986 on the activities of hospitality industry Wages Councils and the lot of the workforce are, contrary to the stridency of claims by organisations such as the Low Pay Unit (Byrne, 1986), difficult to assess. Lucas (1989, 1990) notes that Wages Inspectors' own statistics report fewer establishments underpaying workers and this is attributed to some extent to the simplification of Wages Orders which now occupy only a single sheet of A4 paper where previously they could run to a small booklet. However, it is also the case that the numbers of wages inspectors have been drastically reduced (Byrne, 1986). At the same time, the Wages Inspectorate has been experimenting with new methods of assessing underpayment, for example, by distributing questionnaires to establishments covered by Wages Councils. It is unclear as to what effect, if any, these changes have made on the accuracy of statistics relating to underpayment, though the government's own data for 1989 suggests that underpayment is still widespread and may be as high as 30 per cent in some areas. A further complication exists in that workers employed under old orders retain contractual rights to the terms and conditions of employment that prevailed upon their appointment. Workers employed under the more recent orders governed by the new legislative framework can be taken on at lower rates, thus creating a two-tier labour force with one group undercutting the other: hardly a sound basis for good industrial relations as Lucas (1989) notes.

The requirement of Wages Councils to be mindful of the effect of the rates they set on the creation of employment opportunities leads to consideration of the actual effect of this strategy. In an official government reply (House of Commons Hansard, 5 May 1987, Column 334) the then Junior Minister with responsibility for tourism industries, John Lee, responded to a question on the removal of young people from the scope of the Wages Councils as follows:

> Attempts to estimate the employment effects of the reforms implemented by the Wages Act 1986 are not likely to be fruitful, but the removal of statutory minima, which prevent employers from offering jobs at rates which young people would accept, must result in increased employment.

In fact, Lucas' survey of the literature to date suggests that there is little proof that jobs have or will be created as a result of lowering wages. This may be, of course, because the state of the labour market leads to companies paying considerably higher rates than the statutory minima. However,

Robinson and Wallace (1984) report two studies, one in 1978 and the other in 1980, which showed respectively: that for catering vacancies advertised at Job Centres, the statutory minima were the going rather than the minimum rate; and that basic rates of pay in hotels and catering, including a number resulting from collective bargaining, differed little from statutory minimum rates in most organisations. Croney (1988) in interviews with senior executives in four hotel companies found that they too utilised the Wages Council minimum as a benchmark and that actual rates were not substantially higher. Lucas (1989) compared wages orders declaring minimum rates with data from the government's New Earnings Survey and concluded that if female part-time rates were most typical of the industry overall then many workers were being paid close to the Wages Councils' rates.

The 1986 Wages Act has by no means put an end to the debate over the role of Wages Councils in regulating pay in the hospitality industry. From the perspective of individual employees it is difficult to assess the effects of the new methods of setting minimum rates. Studies have repeatedly shown that many workers are in any case unaware of the existence of the Wages Councils and ignorant of their role (Commission on Industrial Relations, 1971). The Trades Union Congress voted in 1986 to pursue policies directed towards the introduction of a statutory national minimum wage, overcoming its long standing unease with institutions that threatened the development of collective bargaining but which protected the poorest paid from low wages. According to Lucas (1989) employers in the hotel and catering industry remain unhappy with Wages Councils. Despite its insistence that it is not an employers' representative organisation, the British Hotels, Restaurants and Caterers' Association (BHRCA) has remained one of the keenest advocates of wages council abolition (*Caterer and Hotelkeeper*, 14 July 1988, 8 June 1989). The BHRCA was involved in an unseemly exchange with the Industry's professional association, the Hotel, Catering and Institutional Management Association, in 1989 when the latter's president proffered the view that the abolition of the Wages Councils would be 'retrogressive' (*Caterer and Hotelkeeper*, 8 June 1989). What does seem clear is that as a result of the 1986 Act, Britain has now some of the poorest wage protection policies in the world (Lucas, 1989). Further, Byrne (1986) points out that coverage of the hotel and catering industry by Wages Councils continues to exhibit substantial anomalies: some 7,000 private hotels, hostels and guesthouses are left outside the scope of the councils and trainee managers in hotels are not protected.

Perhaps the group most affected by the changes introduced in the Wages Act 1986 are the under-21s, estimated by Byrne (1986) to number at least 150,000. The young are particularly vulnerable not only because they fall outside Wages Council protection and can thus be easily exploited but also because their age works against them in other ways. It is not unheard of for employers to take on under-21s for periods of time just short of the length of service required to acquire statutory employment protection, then dismiss them. High rates of youth unemployment encourage exploitation and it has been suggested that many employers are turning from migrant workers to the young as the regulations governing employment of the former have been tightened up (Byrne, 1986; see also Crompton and Sanderson, 1990). Byrne reports that almost all countries in the world operate some form of minimum wage systems and none appears to exclude young workers. The position of youth in hotels and catering appears somewhat bleak therefore, and it is difficult to see the changes engendered by the 1986 Wages Act as little more than government support for the creation of a low wage economy.

Subsidised food and lodging

Much is made of the value to employees of subsidised food and lodging by hotel and catering employers. In fact, the level of availability of food and accommodation is unclear relative to other elements in the total rewards system. The Hotel and Catering Economic Development Committee (1975) estimated that three-quarters of hotel workers were provided with at least one free meal on duty whilst about one in five hotel workers lived in. Nevertheless, regardless of the *extent of availability* of subsidised food and accommodation, the nature and quality of such 'rewards' is highly variable.

As far as food is concerned, many hotel and catering workers have no access to items from the customer menu but have to make do with specially cooked meals of often low grade foods. Whilst for guests, meals may be taken within relatively flexible boundaries and are generally relaxed social occasions, for staff they are often available only at prescribed times and have to be eaten quickly. In their study for the Low Pay Unit, Brown and Winyard (1975) found that just over a third of the fifty-six workers interviewed complained that they were only able to grab ten minutes or so 'when they could' for their meals. Similarly, it was found that virtually all workers had to eat their meals in inadequate and squalid accommodation. More importantly perhaps, the value of free meals to employees is not as great as at first might be thought. For single employees, free meals may represent a genuine supplement to basic wages and represent the alternative cost of feeding themselves. For those employees with unwaged partners and/or families however, the value of meals on duty is substantially reduced since there is no effective unit cost saving – others still have to be fed.

The availability of live-in accommodation can also be a mixed blessing.

Employers in some locales often have to provide such accommodation, either in hotels or hostels otherwise some workers would not be able to afford the cost of living. However, accommodation is often charged for, and housing is not always of a high standard. The Hotel and Catering Economic Development Committee (1975) estimated that much live-in accommodation was shared: in 1973, a quarter of men and one-third of women living-in had to share accommodation. According to sources cited by Dronfield and Soto (1980: 4) some 52 per cent of housekeepers, 43 per cent of chambermaids, 40 per cent of receptionists and 31 per cent of bar staff live in, though details of how these statistics are derived is not provided. Saunders and Pullen (1987) in a study of chambermaids employed in London hotels found that some 30 per cent of room-maids lived-in or were accommodated in a staff hostel. Of those who lived-in, some 56 per cent shared a room. Shamir (1981) found many of his respondents citing the major drawback of hotel residence as being permanently on call, subject to management whims at times of short-staffing. The problem of living-in was exacerbated by constant surveillance of the workforce by resident management. Brown and Winyard (1975) found that chambermaids frequently complained about having to work beyond their contracted hours for no extra pay. In one London hotel where all staff bedrooms were shared, the head housekeeper inspected the rooms regularly, even looking in drawers. A lack of privacy for live-in workers in this hotel was compounded by the absence of communal areas and prohibitions on residents bringing guests back to their rooms: both factors contributed to a sense that a normal social life was impossible. The majority of staff interviewed felt that management preferred staff to live-in since it meant that they were always on call. Knight (1971) found that live-in staff worked longer hours than those who lived at home and whilst recognising the potential for abuse suggested that longer hours were acceptable to such workers because the hotel provided them with their social environment. The persistence of subsidised food and lodging in hotels and catering is normally justified by employers in terms of valuable additions to basic pay. These claims are at best spurious and at worst deceitful as Jordan usefully summarises:

> A change of attitude is imperative in the hotel and catering industry which tends to regard itself as exceptional in the value of the non-money benefits it provides. This is nonsense. There are many other industries and services whose employees live 'on the job' and even more who provide free or inexpensive meals, or perks associated with the products sold or manufactured by the enterprises concerned. These companies provide the accommodation or perks because it is in their interests to do

so and because it is economically viable. So too does the hotel and catering industry. In most industries the provisions of these benefits is not offered as a justification for low pay. Nor should it be in hotel and catering.

(Jordan, 1978: 11)

Tips

In their discussion of tipping, Mars and Mitchell (1976; see also Mars and Mitchell, 1977) acknowledge that *some* hotel and catering workers are in a position to enhance their basic wages from tips – an acknowledgement that rather glosses the fact that many workers are not in a position to derive income from gratuities. Indeed, Dronfield and Soto (1980) estimated that 50 per cent of the workforce have no direct contact with customers and therefore no direct access to tips. The problem with tipping is well summarised by Brown and Winyard:

> The contribution of tips to the income of workers is one of the great unknowns of the hotel and catering industry. . .it is frequently argued that tips represent important additions to earnings. However no firm evidence is ever put forward to support this claim. What we can note here is how very large these tips would need to be to raise the earnings of workers. . .above the low pay target of £30. In 1974, one in five of full-time male workers were earning less than £20. Is it likely that these workers were receiving £10 a week as their share of tips?
>
> (Brown and Winyard, 1975: 12)

In their study of a small sample of full-time hotel workers only three – two waiters and a porter – owned to receiving tips. Moreover, the level of tips was liable to considerable fluctuation – one waitress interviewed claimed that in the week of the interview she received £6 in tips but only a little over £1 in the previous week. This finding emphasises a further point, namely that the extent to which the level of tipping is largely outside of the control of hotel and catering staff. It is true, as will be shown in the discussion of waiting-on-table in the next chapter, that there are certain courses of action that may be pursued by some staff to increase the potential for a large tip. There is little however that can be done to increase the likelihood of tipping *per se*. What is somewhat neglected in existing analyses of hotel and catering work is the extent to which largely extraneous factors can influence tipping. For example, the volume of trade is important here since any reduction in the general level of trade is likely to have a blanket effect on the propensity to receive tips. The structure of the product market is important to tipping. Howe (1977), in her study of New York restaurants, found that the majority of up-market institutions employed only male waiting staff thus forcing women into middle- and lower-class units where both formal rewards (basic pay) and informal rewards (tips) were less than in the male dominated establishments. Other factors tend to contrive to keep certain types of workers – such as ethnic minorities and older employees – away from public service roles and, in particular, tipping occupations or again the market operates to confine such workers to less exclusive units. Howe (1977) found that in one restaurant jobs were segregated by sex, race and age such that all employees, except waitresses, were male, all dealing directly with the public were white, all waitresses were fairly young, and the two lowest grade workers – the busboy and dishwasher – were non-white.

In discussions of gratuities, it is important not to lose sight of the point made by Brown and Winyard (1975) that the extent of tipping is unlikely to compensate for low basic wages. Yet this is exactly what many employers and industry commentators argue. For example, in a review of Thomas and Erlam's 1978 report for the Low Pay Unit, Miles Quest wrote in the *Hotel, Catering and Institutional Management Association* (the UK's professional body) *Journal*:

whether the Unit likes it or not (it evidently doesn't) catering workers have always preferred to be remunerated in different ways because there are advantages to them in doing so. No-one knows the value of tips, for example, but to many tippable front of house staff wages are a comparatively minor part of their total earnings. Increasing the basic wage to £55 would give these workers only a marginal benefit which may well be one reason why so few of them want to join a union.

(Quest, 1978: 14)

Quest brings forward no evidence to support his view of catering workers' preferences for remuneration but the point he is driving at concerns the claims made by pressure groups (like the Low Pay Unit) and trades unions for increases in basic pay as a means of overcoming poor rewards which Quest regards as unrealistic in the light of workers' own dispositions. This point has some academic support. Whilst accepting that many hotel and catering workers find themselves exploited and that employers discourage unionism by a variety of means, Mars and Mitchell (1977) argue that core workers, those who benefit most from informal rewards including tips, are least likely to want an increase in basic pay that brings with it a regularisation and possible elimination of informal rewards. Contrary to this, Brown and Winyard (1975) found that tipping and informal rewards were far from welcome aspects of hotel and catering employment:

All of the workers, trade union officials and the members of the discussion group felt that the system of tipping and the service charge was bad and outdated. 'Degrading' was the term most frequently used to describe the system. Those working in hotels remarked that the tipping arrangements were a major cause of friction between the various departments and all, even those receiving tips, felt that decent basic wages would be preferable to the present situation.

(Brown and Winyard, 1975: 24)

The potential hostility towards tipping is more apparent in commentaries on the use of the service charge.

A service charge is levied on many hotel products and services, most notably meals, a factor common also to restaurants. Service charges, typically 10 per cent, are the legal property of the unit owner who is under no obligation to distribute the proceeds to workers. Indeed, Dronfield and Soto (1980) argue that the service charge is often used by employers to subsidise wages. Non-distribution of the service charge can cause resentment amongst employees as can distribution of the service charge on a 'tronc' system. The tronc system can be used independently of the service charge and the term simply refers to a pool whereby all tips or the service charge are collected together and then distributed to all employees in a given eligible set (usually restaurant workers) on the basis of some points system. Essentially, the points allocated to a particular worker are frequently a trade-off between status and length of service and bear little necessary relationship to the effort–reward nexus. Such a system buttresses hierarchical work structures precisely because it emphasises status as a means of allocation (Chopping, 1977: 160). Whilst it may be conceived of as a fair means of ensuring that all workers receive some gratuities there is no guarantee that the tronc is perceived as a fair means of distribution by the workforce, and particularly those employees at the bottom of the status hierarchy. Far from encouraging co-operation, the tronc system may increase deceit and duplicity, with workers withholding monies from the pool especially since less scrupulous employers use the existence of the tronc as a means of establishing the amount generated by tips and use this information in justifying the payment of less in formal wages.

When all other arguments concerning tips fail (or in some cases before they do so) many employers argue that tipping acts as a motivator of staff, encouraging them to give the best service. Nailon (1978), amongst others, considers this argument to be specious. He argues that tips are not an incentive in the normal sense because the effort and skill a waiter or waitress puts into serving a customer may not be matched by a commensurate reward. Nailon's argument is simply that tipping is only ever likely to be a motivator in circumstances where the employee is secure, although it is conceivable that tips fulfil other needs such as those of self-esteem associated with hard work. What is more certain is that tipping effects and reinforces competition and increases the potential for disharmonious working relationships amongst those sections of the workforce who have easiest access to gratuities (Commission on Industrial Relations, 1971).

The balance of evidence therefore supports the view that tipping is undesirable and degrading. A report on tipping by the Hotel and Catering Economic Development Committee (1968a) summarises well the arguments recorded above. They noted, *first*, that young people found reliance on tipping distasteful and preferred the security of a fixed living wage. *Secondly*, they sought the views of industry management and trade associations who unsurprisingly felt that the standardisation of tipping arrangements was undesirable and impracticable. *Thirdly*, in a joint survey with the Consumers' Association, it was found that the two most common attitudes to tipping amongst the general public were that staff should receive an adequate wage instead of having to place reliance on tips and that tipping was a bad practice because it was expected irrespective of the quality of service. *Fourthly*, a survey of trade unions unsurprisingly produced the view that tipping and service charges should be abolished in favour of a basic living wage whilst a survey of hotel and catering staff suggested that tipping decreased efficiency since management abdicated responsibility to the operative for customer service and this in turn generated labour turnover (presumably though it is not stated through the creation of stress and the desire to seek employment likely to improve remuneration). *Plus ça change*. Despite the efforts of hotel and catering employers to reassure the world at large that wages are improving, there is little in the way of hard evidence to support their claims. Tipping in particular is a seemingly invidious problem that in some occupations at least is at the heart of employee disenchantment.

Fiddles and knock-offs

In addition to tips, some hotel and catering workers also benefit from 'fiddles' and 'knock-offs'. The term 'fiddles' refers to the pilferage that goes on in hotels. A 'knock-off' is a particular form of 'fiddle' involving the purloining of (usually) small items such as soap, linen and towels, though more usually it involves stealing food (Mars, 1973; Mars and Nicod, 1981). Fiddles and knock-offs tend to be institutionalised in hotel and catering operations, that is, management collude in allowing both certain monetary benefits obtained by devious means and the petty theft of physical goods. Management's concern is to set parameters beyond which pilferage will not be tolerated and will incur sanctions (Mars and Mitchell, 1976). In their various studies, Mars and his colleagues have pointed out that this gives management considerable power. For example, troublesome employees can be instantly dismissed for pilfering, despite the fact that such activity is normally tolerated within limits. The sacked employee has no recourse to the law because theft is a legally unacceptable activity though it is a normative feature of hotel and catering work.

The mechanics of pilfering small physical goods or comestibles are fairly straightforward except in organisations where security and checking systems are highly developed. Even these can be overcome however: Mars and Nicod (1984: 112) note that food can be smuggled out of establishments fairly easily, quoting the example of a waiter who helped run two restaurants of his own using supplies removed from the hotel in which he worked via the device of strapping to his leg, underneath his trousers, items such as smoked salmon and steak. The mechanisms for fiddling are more complex. In the work of Mars and his colleagues, fiddling is usually taken to refer to money fiddles, that is the means by which employees secure direct cash benefits for themselves, either at the expense of the customer or the employing organisation. The victim of a fiddle is usually defined by the location of action. Thus, in lounges and dining-rooms or restaurants, it is the employer who is usually the object of fiddling:

> Basically these fiddles involve first getting food and drink past a checker or control clerk and second, serving exactly what the customer has ordered, and then pocketing the payment for it. Since a waiter must eventually account for every cheque he presents to the kitchen or still-room, his problem is to obtain food and beverages without a cheque. One solution is to introduce items which he has purchased outside the hotel so that a profit can be made when they are sold at the hotel's higher prices.
>
> (Mars and Nicod, 1981: 66)

Collusion is common between waiting and kitchen staff. In the case of fiddles against the customer collaboration again is not infrequent. These fiddles are most frequently practised by bar staff and wine waiters (Mars and Nicod, 1984) and vary from simple over-charging and short-changing to product substitution. The latter can operate at two levels. First, a customer may ask for, say, a bottled beer and, providing the order can be prepared in relative secrecy, the bartender or waiter may substitute a draught product (which is usually cheaper) and pocket the difference in price (Mars and Nicod, 1981: 68). The second level at which product substitution can occur is when staff supply their own drink. Further exemplification of the variety of means of obtaining fiddles would be superfluous given the extensive literature generated. In addition to the studies by Mars (1973), Mars, Bryant and Mitchell (1979), Mars and Nicod (1981), and Mars and Nicod (1984) a variety of other works have focused directly or indirectly on fiddling and knocking-off (e.g. Spradley and Mann, 1975; Bowey, 1976). The crucial point is that these activities are regarded as a normal part of remuneration for many hotel and catering workers, though the extent to which entitlement to such rewards is universal also needs to be considered.

Mars and Nicod (1981) argue that nearly all workers in a position to have the opportunity for fiddling and knocking-off are allowed to do so. However, access to the type, quantity and quality of fiddle is highly stratified, the most important agents of stratification being membership of the core or periphery, the class of the hotel (and presumably restaurant) and the extent to which rewards are bureaucratised in the hotel in which the employee works. At a very simple level, core workers are likely to take more valuable items and be allowed greater freedom in operating money fiddles than peripherals. Core workers often operate in collusion with one another in order to secure rewards. Peripheral workers by way of contrast tend to be constrained to taking relatively inexpensive items (see also Paterson, 1981) and may not have the opportunity to run extensive money fiddles. Beyond this, the allocation of core and peripheral status depends on the type of the hotel. Mars and Nicod (1981) argue that in prestigious hotels reward allocation is based on technical skill and professional expertise and rankings are easy to devise according to these criteria, invariably leading to a pyramidal structure with a small core at the apex being allowed significant access to fiddles. In the majority of hotels however, ranking by skill is less in evidence and emphasis is instead placed on speed of service, the ability to cope during critical periods and on personal loyalty and reliability.

Whatever arrangements exist for the allocation of fiddles and knock-offs there are some grounds for believing that, as with tipping, these aspects of informal rewards militate against the development of a collective workplace or occupational ethic, fostering individualism and competitiveness. The allocation of informal rewards by means of the individual contract not only makes ambiguous the level of tolerance management will show in respect of workers' pilfering but engenders a degree of obligation on the part of employees to their employers. For workers with and without (but hopeful of obtaining) individual contracts and informal rewards, the promise of benefits can be an important element in management control of employees, buying worker goodwill and acquiescence on the basis of the likelihood of withdrawal or non-conferral of such rewards in the event of non-cooperation with management. Buying the somewhat ambiguous loyalties of workers in this way can also have other consequences. When many managers change jobs, they can often take a substantial number of their underlings with them. The latter move because of loyalty but also because of an awareness of the effectiveness of the manager or supervisor in securing informal rewards. In order to maintain their individual contracts employees, particularly core workers, will follow their boss from one job to another (Mars and Nicod, 1981: 71; 1984: 106–108). The scope for obtaining informal rewards may be confined to a relatively select group of hotel and catering workers but many workers are resigned to the system of informal remuneration found in hotels and catering. The problem for most hotel and catering employees is that there is little hope of expecting conditions and pay to be formalised in such a way as to provide decent basic remuneration. Thus many throw their lot in with the system as it operates on the basis of 'something is better than nothing'.

Johnson (1983a) criticises the concept of the total rewards system because, he claims, it excludes a variety of important elements such as seasonal bonuses, productivity payments, relocation expenses, free uniforms, free transport to and from work and other similar items which defray workers' costs or enhance their remuneration. In short, Johnson argues that the total payment system is not total at all, a point earlier noted by Henderson (1965: 60) who cautioned that tips, free meals and rooms needed to be distinguished from other wage supplements – fringe benefits such as pensions, paid vacations and sick pay – which are common to almost all industries. In his study Johnson found that (a) those provided with the greatest range of benefits and who gave the highest valuation to total benefits were unit and departmental managers followed, in rank order, by chefs and receptionists, waiters, chambermaids and bar staff, portering staff; and (b) hotel companies provided a greater range and diversity of benefits than did private hotels. Johnson argues that fringe benefits actually increase the earnings gap between hotel and catering employees and workers in other industrial sectors, in general implying that, overall, fewer hotel and catering workers receive fringe benefits than do their counterparts in other industries. There are, manifestly, exceptions to this since some employees (e.g. managers working for companies that operate in the national labour market) have considerable access to fringe benefits whereas others (e.g. operative workers in private hotels functioning in a local labour market) are provided with a minimum range and diversity of 'perks'. Nevertheless, Johnson's data supports the interpretation that, in general, benefits institutionalised in general industry (e.g. pension schemes, sick pay, life assurance schemes) are not as institutionalised in the hotel and catering industry. Those benefits which do receive extensive coverage in hotels and catering are those associated with the industry's 'technological base' – food and accommodation.

The persistence of such discrepancies can, Johnson suggests, be accounted for by employers' unwillingness to provide the benefits more typical of general industry. More than 50 per cent of his respondents said they would have provided such benefits if convinced that they were warranted. High labour turnover, short average length of service and perceived lack of interest on the part of staff were all advanced as reasons for non-provision. Some employees felt that the benefits on offer were so meagre as to be not worth having – thus creating a vicious circle of inaction. Generally, employees gave a low value to the institutionalised benefits of general industry and high value to the benefits of hotel and catering. Johnson suggests that one reason for this is that institutionalised benefits, being widely available, offer no comparative advantage to the worker: if this is so, however, it explains why low value is attached to industry-wide benefits but not why high value is attached to the benefits provided by the hospitality industry. Johnson's answer to the latter is to suggest that because the central products of the industry are related to the satisfaction of basic needs then they are highly regarded because they are readily consumable. The cost of satisfying basic needs of hunger, thirst and shelter is considerable and consumption of these products helps offset the costs of satisfying unavoidable needs. This is a somewhat limp explanation in the light of earlier discussed evidence of the attitudes of workers towards provision of food and accommodation and, ironically, it is difficult to identify why fringe benefits like food and accommodation should be highly prized, except insofar as the general levels of provision are so feeble as to induce the attitude amongst employees that a little is better than nothing at all.

STAYING THERE? ORGANISATION, STATUS AND CONFLICT IN HOTEL AND CATERING WORK

The marginal social status of many hotel and catering workers in terms of factors such as gender, race and class is reinforced by a system of employment which is generally exploitative in respect of remuneration and conditions of work. The importance of status to an understanding of work in the hospitality industry does not end with consideration of the extent of labour market discrimination against certain categories of person. Of equal importance is the extent of status differentiation *within* the industry. This has been seen at one level in terms of the distinction between 'core' and 'peripheral' workers. The situation is more complex than this however.

Henderson (1965) argues that in the USA there are five distinct categories of hotel worker whose status is determined by a combination of skill requirements, earning capacity and relationships with management and customers (see Figure 2.1). The existence of more or less distinct occupational hierarchies has been noted by several sources though perhaps the only other explicit models are those furnished by (a) the British Commission on Industrial Relations (CIR) (1971) (Figure 2.2) which, on the basis

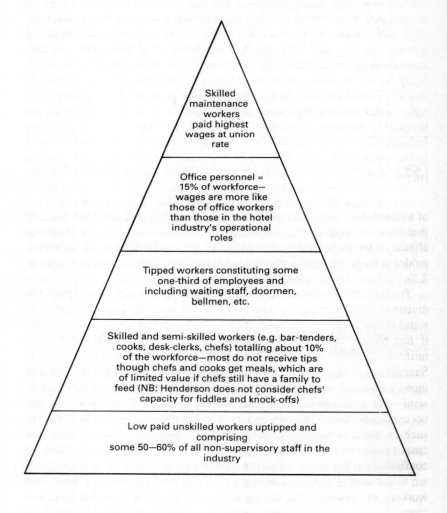

Figure 2.1 Occupational hierarchy after Henderson (1965)

Figure 2.2 Occupational hierarchy after the Commission on Industrial Relations (1971)

of a somewhat limited sample of twenty-five hotels, felt moved to observe that the status consciousness of members of the workforce had far-reaching effects on the performance of work tasks; and (b) Saunders (1981a) whose model is based on more impressionistic evidence from interviews (Figure 2.3).

The difficulty in discussing status differences predicated on *occupational* divisions is that evidence in support of claims made for particular types of status distinction is often vague and frequently contradictory. For example, it has been claimed that a distinction between uniformed and non-uniformed staff persists (Commission on Industrial Relations, 1971; Saunders, 1981a), between staff who have contact with the customer and those who do not (Mars and Mitchell, 1976), between highly skilled and semi- and unskilled staff and so on. Henderson's (implied) view that occupational status is determined by a combination or trade-off of factors such as skill, earning capacity and relationships with management and customers remains unelaborated and illustrates the possible extent of confusion. For example, chefs are uniformed but receive few tips – chefs are still accorded a high status largely because they are seen as skilled craft workers. In other words, in trading-off status-conferring factors in hotel and catering work, as with other forms of employment, it is necessary to

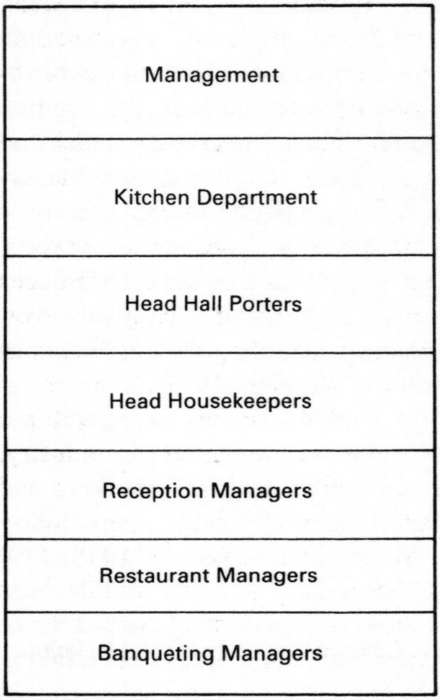

Management
Kitchen Department
Head Hall Porters
Head Housekeepers
Reception Managers
Restaurant Managers
Banqueting Managers

Figure 2.3 Occupational hierarchy after Saunders (1981a)

establish the criteria and contexts which operate to either lend people their status or otherwise detract from it. The existing consensus appears to be that sector specific skills (as with chefs) and transferable skills (as with receptionists and other clerical workers) tend to be the most important status conferrers amongst non-management staff, though formal status positions are equally important – thus head waiters may not correspond in status to head chefs but head waiters are of higher status than relatively junior chefs. The potential absurdity of such debates is further complicated when considering the role of gender and ethnicity in determining status. Women are likely to find themselves in low status jobs or higher status jobs in low status organisations simply by virtue of their gender. Ethnic minorities also tend to be ghettoised in low-status jobs.

Concern with the effect of status differences on workplace relations was a central concern of Whyte (1948). For Whyte, it is the separation of the production and service functions in restaurants that creates a basis for status differentiation and conflict but this is rooted in more generalised forms of status differentiation in terms of class and gender. Whyte is one of the few writers on hotel and catering work to have considered, albeit simplistically, the relationship between class and status. Restaurants (and by extension hotels) occupy positions in a more or less distinct hierarchy predicated on prestige, status, facilities offered and other criteria that lend an establishment a particular 'class'. The class of clientele matches the product hierarchy in a loose sense, prestige establishments operating social and economic barriers to entry for certain categories of person (see Mazurkiewicz, 1983). Similarly, hotel and catering operatives are usually – though not invariably – drawn from the lower socio-economic classes. Resentment on the part of employees can be generated by class differences between higher class patrons and lower class staff. Paradoxically however, it can also be generated as a result of workers regarding certain clients as being of insufficiently high social standing (Chopping, 1977). The contradictions faced by many industry employees are not merely expressed in a general sense but have concrete implications for careers in the industry. Class-based tensions between workers and customers, and workers and each other, often have to be subordinated in order to 'get on' – particularly in occupations involving extensive customer contact. Whyte (1948: 119) noted that working-class women who successfully adopted middle-class values and subordinated themselves to those of higher status found themselves upwardly mobile. For women of a middle-class background, taking orders from people who they regarded as of equal or inferior status caused serious problems of adjustment since clients did not (indeed could not) recognise the employee's status. In a beautiful example of the nature of status and class ambiguities, Whyte notes that:

> in one working class district of cheap restaurants we found restaurant employees universally rated at the bottom of the social pyramid. Regular factory workers considered themselves as occupying a distinctly superior position. On the other hand, in the high standard restaurants of the loop business district, we found groups of employees who considered themselves above factory workers.
>
> (Whyte, 1948: 12)

The complexities of social class influences in hotels and restaurants are echoed in the role played by gender in forming experiences of work. Whyte found that gender differences were a constant source of tension in relationships with customers. Male waiters for example experienced a gender-status 'problem', with well over half of those interviewed expressing deep resentment concerning their position relative to customers:

> it is our impression that the waiters were more seriously disturbed over their role than were the waitresses. This is to be expected, for men, growing up in a man's world, are not accustomed to the continual

subordination that they face from customers, while it is part of a girl's
social training to get the upper hand for herself while appearing to play
the subordinate role.

(Whyte, 1948: 97)

Notwithstanding the inaccuracies, potential or real, of this observation,
Whyte notes that tensions arose when those seen as being of lower social
status because of their gender (female) and occupational position (waitress)
initiated action for those who regarded themselves as of higher status in
both respects (e.g. male cooks/chefs). Having said this, Whyte also
observed tensions between those of the same gender but different occupational status, thus emphasising again the complexity of status-role
interaction.

The investigation of intra-industry status differences is a fertile area for
research if only in order to clarify existing confusion. A crucial area of
ignorance is the extent of interplay between formal and informal status in
hotel and catering organisations for, as Shamir (1978) suggests, whilst (in
particular) most hotels evidence a fairly bureaucratic work structure with
clearly demarcated occupational hierarchies, informal hierarchies are, as in
many organisational settings, of some importance in operational management. Whatever the complexities of status differentiation in the industry, of
great importance is the earlier observation that hotel workers view themselves as lower in status than others in society and this has been seen by
some commentators as not only central to an understanding of workplace
attitudes and the experience of work but to the creation and maintenance of
intra-industry occupational status hierarchies. Chopping (1977) argues that
workers may internalise organisational values, adopting the status of the
establishment in which they work and the mores of self-improvement
common in the industry. Anecdotal examples of the extent to which
hospitality industry employees constantly engage in processes of status
compensation are legion. Hard evidence is less obvious, though Whyte,
Hamilton and Whiley (1964) refer to the psychological adjustment
problems of isolated low-status workers in a hotel they studied who spent a
large proportion of their income on status goods. 'For example,' they write,
'the waitresses were beautifully dressed when in their street clothes. The
bellmen bought the most expensive cars' (1964: 18). The conservative ideal
of self-improvement is most clearly marked in the repeated finding that
many hotel and catering workers aspire to run their own businesses
(Commission on Industrial Relations, 1971; Chopping, 1977). Chopping
(1977) notes that a Hotel and Catering Industry Training Board survey
showed that although two-thirds of those who had held two or more jobs in
the industry had never risen above operative level they felt the opportunity

for advancement was good. The earlier Hotel and Catering Economic Development Committee report (1975) showed that at least one person had been promoted in 77 per cent of establishments sampled, as well as demonstrating that 20 per cent of the workforce desired promotion, 6 per cent thought their chances of obtaining promotion were average and 25 per cent rated the possibility relatively highly. Further, the fact that industrial conflict in the industry most frequently takes the form of labour turnover, workers leaving conflict situations to seek better conditions elsewhere rather than taking collective action to resolve problems, reflects the organisational ethos of hotel and catering organisations in terms of self-reliance, competition and individualism.

This latter point is crucial here since a combination of low pay, and status-based occupational hierarchies is held to be at the root of the individualistic ethos that permeates hospitality work. Most hotel and catering work is competitive in nature, competition not only taking place between different occupational groups in the industry or a unit, but within these groups. It is particularly acute in the tipping occupations, most notably in waiting on table. Bowey (1976) discovered that in one of the restaurants she studied (Cherry's) high labour turnover amongst new waitresses resulted from older waitresses hiding equipment. Possession of equipment is a resource necessary to giving good service – the perception of which by clients is vital to the generation of gratuities. At a higher organisational level, competition *between* departments can lead to inter-departmental conflict. Bowey (1976) quotes one male chef at Cherry's as complaining that waitresses were incompetent, never giving orders clearly. He suggested employing waiters to eliminate such problems. This is not simple sexism. Snow (1981) records chefs making similar complaints about male waiting staff though again, criticisms tended to be based on perceived deficiencies of character, i.e. on appeals to individual psychological traits. Waiters were frequently described as neurotic and overdemanding. One chef illustrated the general trend. He is quoted as saying 'The waiters all argue and run around throwing stuff at each other. . . .A lot of them are Italians and the rest are gay, or poofs, or whatever they call themselves' (Snow, 1981: 48).

Whyte (1948) noted that it is common to find in conflict between kitchen and restaurant that staff of the former fail to appreciate the pressures under which waiting staff are placed (and place themselves) and consequently resort to seeking explanations for behaviour in terms of 'extraneous' variables – gender, sexuality, nationality and so on. Conflict arises because of the need by waiting staff to give good service because good service is equal to maximising good tips. Thus as Bowey (1976) notes, 'nagging' chefs is one of the few ways of attempting to ensure speedy service. In her study of a second restaurant, Plumleys, conflict arose between the Head Chef and Snack Bar Assistant because the latter could exert a twofold influence over the chef's bonus which varied according to the amount of food wasted. The assistant could be (a) careless with waste food which was normally sold to pigswill merchants; and/or (b) give generous portions of food to customers, increasing the likelihood of generous tips but reducing the portion yield and therefore the chef's waste reducing efforts. Snow (1981) found that many workers leave their jobs because of the stress attendant on arguments arising from inter-personal disputes whether between or within departments. Most bickering in departments, Snow claims, arises from conflict over how work should be performed and/or the allocation of work tasks.

Other research directed to the issue of inter-departmental conflict has tended to suggest that neither interpersonal psychology nor factors in the wider social environment are sufficient bases for an understanding of this phenomenon. Dann and Hornsey (1986) pursue the themes explored by writers such as Snow (1981) and Bowey (1976) to argue that four factors are crucial to an understanding of conflict within and between departments in hospitality organisations. The first of these is *interdependence*. Conflict not only arises when individual worker's struggle for autonomy clashes with the desires of others to control them (as is often the case with the chef-waiting staff relationship) but from a failure of reciprocity. Within and between departments there is a need for co-ordination, particularly in food service. Often, despite tensions, bargains are struck between different workers in terms of the performance of favours: when favours are not reciprocated conflict arises. A second consideration crucial to an understanding of inter-departmental conflict is that of the *social environment*. Three elements are important here: the lack of understanding on the part of some staff of the role of those employees who depend on clients for part of their income; stress, which arises from the speed of operation required and which, as shown above, can lead to non-service staff being pressurised; and territoriality – a by no means unusual consideration in studies of industrial workplaces but one which can take on special salience in hotel and catering operations not only in terms of the division of space between departments but within it. For chefs, the kitchen is their domain and waiting staff are often excluded from it on no other grounds than they are waiting staff. Within restaurants, the existence of 'stations', discrete geographical areas comprising a number of tables served by designated staff can be guarded defensively from those who encroach upon another's 'patch', hostility arising from a fear of possible tips being usurped by those engaged upon incursions. A similar phenomenon has been noted in several studies. For example, in Spradley and Mann's study of the cocktail bar, cocktail waitresses were not allowed to impinge either upon the space or the duties of the barman without some reprisals (Spradley and Mann, 1975). Thirdly here, *rewards* are frequently a source of dispute. Tipped staff are often resented by non-tipped staff and conflict can occur over the rights of staff to particular rewards. Finally, Dann and Hornsey return to the theme of *occupational status* as a source of conflict. In their view, occupational groups can form cohesive and status conscious units to the extent that inter-departmental conflict becomes institutionalised.

From the foregoing, it might be thought that inter-departmental conflict exists only between kitchen and restaurant in hospitality organisations. Certainly this is the most commonly exemplified area in existing literature, though Shamir (1975) found that receptionists tended to be regarded as occupying an ambiguous status within the hotel organisation and as such he clearly implies that the ability of receptionists to initiate action for other departments (by virtue of their position as a key link between clients and staff) could cause conflict. Conflict, however, is not the only outcome of competitiveness in hotel and catering work. Despite the 'team work' image of the industry beloved by recruiters, competitiveness leads to isolation in work. Much hotel work is in any case carried out on an individual basis. Food service, front-office, room cleaning and hall portering whilst nominally 'team work' occupations involve tasks that are often taken in isolation and/or are perceived by management as being best suited to execution by one or two workers. The isolation which typifies the performance of many hospitality industry work tasks has long been recognised as reducing group cohesiveness (Commission on Industrial Relations, 1971). Little sustained effort has been devoted to exploring reasons for the highly individual modes of working employed in many occupations. For example, the most common method of room cleaning is the allocation of one cleaner to a set number of rooms rather than employing several cleaners to work through accommodation as a team. In all but the most luxurious of restaurants, the waiter and commis (assistant) system has disappeared and single waiters deal with individual stations without the benefits (or responsibilities) of having an assistant to fetch and carry and aid with service, thus arguably increasing the isolation in which work tasks are performed. The roots of this isolation lie in the conjoining of two hotel management ethics – the supposed need of the customers for unintrusive but *personal* service: finding one maid cleaning your room is far less likely to disturb or irritate than finding a whole team performing the task, despite the fact that the latter may increase the quality of service delivery. The isolation of individual workers is perhaps not as important as the isolation of groups from one another. Often, the occupational hierarchy at the level of a unit corresponds to departmentalisation. Departments tend not only to guard their territory and responsibilities jealously but also operate relatively independently of one another, frequently working on the basis that other parts of the hotel do not exist (Commission on Industrial Relations, 1971). Whilst this does not necessarily imply competition between departments it does suggest a lack of collectivism and one that can be heightened in the largest units.

Existing textbooks on work and industrial relations in the hospitality industry tend to collude in the mythology that conflict in hotels and restaurants is pathological and can be resolved through effective management. The evidence reviewed in this section (and the chapter as a whole) suggests a very different story. Occupational status hierarchies, corresponding for the most part to departmental boundaries in hotels and restaurants, supply a basis for competition and conflict between workers which is supported by highly individual and stressful modes of task performance. The organisation of hotel and catering work in terms of divisions between and within occupational and departmental hierarchies, inflexible working practices, and methods of remuneration all contribute to a 'dog-eat-dog' culture. The experience of work as status-ridden, competitive, conflictual and isolated mirrors the wider social and economic disadvantages faced by the industry's employees. It is not, therefore, sufficient to explain the experiences and problems of the workforce in terms of their supposed social–psychological marginality, or to view conflict and competition in the workforce as the product of essentially unique structural features of the industry. Whilst some researchers have recognised this (Mullins, 1981; Wood, 1988; Lennon, 1989) many others have continued to conspire however unwittingly in perpetuating the myth of uniqueness. In so doing they have paid insufficient attention to the extent to which this myth is, for employers, managers and some workers a self-serving device for justifying the unjustifiable in terms of inadequate basic rewards, feudal management practices and the maintenance of a culture that discourages intervention in the affairs of the industry by others.

3 Occupations in the hotel and catering industry

The purpose of this chapter is to review the literature on occupations in the hotel and catering industry and in so doing to illuminate the issues discussed in the previous chapters. A difficulty that has to be confronted from the start is that studies of some occupations lend themselves more easily to demonstrating certain points rather than others. This largely reflects the piecemeal development of research in the field and the particular preoccupations of the researchers involved, as described in Chapter 1. For example, the literature on waiting-at-table is almost exclusively concerned with the central issue of customer–staff relationships *vis-à-vis* informal rewards. The literature on chefs and cooks provides insights into occupational culture, career and community. The study of accommodation workers is a powerful antedote to the mystique surrounding the work of waiters and chefs, offering as it does insights into the drudgery of much low grade employment in the industry. Studies of management work in hotels and catering have grown considerably in recent years. By focusing on hotel managers, it is possible to gain some insight into how conditions of work in the hotel and catering industry are perpetuated. At the same time, however, discussion of hotel management work demonstrates the extent to which managers themselves might be perceived as victims of the same conditions of work that make hotel and catering employment so unpleasant for operative staff. Hotel and catering managers may have the best deal of all employees in the industry but it is not really *that* much better.

WAITING-ON-TABLE

The moral is, never be sorry for a waiter. Sometimes when you sit in a restaurant, still stuffing yourself half an hour after closing time, you feel that the tired waiter at your side must surely be despising you. But he is not. He is not thinking as he looks at you 'What an overfed lout'; he is thinking, 'One day, when I have saved enough money, I shall be able to imitate that man'. He is ministering to a kind of pleasure he thoroughly understands and admires. And that is why waiters are seldom Socialists, have no effective trade union, and will work twelve hours a day. . . . They are snobs, and they find the servile nature of their work rather congenial.

(George Orwell, 1933)

We must once and for all lay to the ghost that service is somehow equivalent to servile. We must recognize for all time that the profession of a waiter is an honourable profession, that giving good service in a restaurant or hotel is an honourable way in which to earn a living.

(Lord Young of Graffham, Conservative Government Cabinet Minister in a parliamentary speech, 22 May 1985)

Waiting-on-table is the most widely studied hotel and catering industry occupation and, as previously noted, provides the basis for much of what is regarded as the conventional wisdom in the theoretical analysis of hospitality labour. With so much research effort it might be thought that studies of waiting-on-table offer, cumulatively, a plethora of analytic detail about the occupation. They do not. For reasons identified earlier, two key methodological handicaps limit the *collective value* of studies of waiting-on-table. These are, firstly, the types of establishment studied. The published literature covers only a very narrow range of the many varied types of hotel and catering organisation that exist in countries such as the United Kingdom and the United States of America. Thus there is a problem of representativeness. Secondly, the majority of data has been collected using ethnographic techniques, leading to a preoccupation with studies of the relationship between waiters and waitresses and the informal rewards system and, in particular, that competitiveness in waiting work that centres on the practice of tipping.

Most commentators aver that waiting staff can to some degree control the amount of their remuneration by engaging in activities that increase monies from tipping and/or by becoming involved in fiddling and knocking-off. Thus, Butler and Snizek (1976) found that waitresses can exert control over their clients by employing various 'guidance' techniques. The most important of these is *product promotional activity* which entails attempts to maximise the sale of food and drink. The rationale underlying this strategy is that by increasing the size of the customer's bill, the size of any tip will be increased since tip-size, by convention, normally bears a proportional relationship to the bill's total (Debrett's recommend tipping between 10 and 15 per cent for meal service – Donald, 1982). The other two methods of influencing the reward structure are regarded as less likely to succeed but are nevertheless of importance. *Increased ritualisation* involves putting excess emphasis on service acts. *Friendly rapport techniques* entail, in essence, fawning to the customer and striving to reduce the social distance between server and served. Neither activity necessarily serves to increase the chances or size of reward since both are intrusive and are thus high-risk strategies that may result in waitresses being 'stiffed' – receiving little or no tip – a source of criticism by other staff who view being stiffed as evidence of incompetence and inability to control the work situation (Butler and Skipper, 1981).

The activities in which waiting staff engage in order to improve the size of tip is not determined in a wholly arbitrary fashion. Most food service staff develop customer classification schemes which determine the types of customer to whom product promotional activity, friendly rapport and increased ritualisation may be directed with some expectation of success. Bowey (1976) noted that waitresses regarded the most promising customers as those adults in lunch parties of two or more; individuals alone were not regarded as having quite the same potential for tips and involved staff in more work. Parties with children were regarded as being of only limited potential for tips since parents rarely left a pro rata tip on their children's behalf and children also often involved considerable extra work. The use of classificatory schemes by waiting staff was also observed by Mars and Nicod (1984) who found that different types of classification can be operated at any or the same time. Some schemes attributed quite specific labels to individuals (e.g. bastard, bitch – meaning awkward customers; prostitute – a woman whose appearance suggested she was on hire from an escort agency; peasants – persons whose behaviour and/or appearance suggested they were unaccustomed to dining out; snobs – those who knew, or thought they knew, how to behave and thus drew attention to themselves; and pigs – those who ate a lot) (see also Spradley and Mann, 1975 for an American example). Further, Mars and Nicod (1984: 71–72) also found a series of generally applicable industry-wide beliefs about tipping. These are:

1 men are considered better tippers than women (because they are more experienced diners) (see also Howe, 1977);
2 men accompanied by women rather than men are better tippers (because they seek to impress);
3 older persons are better tippers than the young (because of a combination of greater experience and greater affluence);
4 customers with children are poor tippers (because they have less money and do not regard the serving of children as involving extra effort);
5 people on package tours are poor tippers (because budget holidays attract the less affluent);

6 large parties are poor tippers (because as the cost of the meal rises there is a tailing-off in the amount tipped); and

7 the socially insecure are poor tippers (because they are usually inexperienced in dining and therefore are not *au fait* with the correct amount to tip).

Mars and Nicod (1984), in an effort to supply a systematic account of how waiters function in this respect, use the concepts of boundary-open and boundary-closed transactions. Boundary-open transactions exist between server and served where the served prefer to foster intimacy with the server, treating them as friendly or even quasi-members of the family. Boundary-closed transactions reflect a desire by customers to reduce intrusion by waiting staff and a fostering of intimacy between host(s) and guest(s) on the part of the host. Such transactions are typical of business diners. Emphasis is placed on maintaining the ritualised formality of the waiting game, evidenced most in the exaggeration attached to service ritual. According to Mars and Nicod, both types of boundary transactions are governed by common rules which do not vary. These include: always serve a guest before a host, a woman before a man (unless she is the host), and an older person before a younger person; always address a customer by his or her surname or as 'sir' or 'madam'; and always serve from the right and clear detritus from the left (Mars and Nicod, 1984: 58). However, the problems faced by waiting staff are complicated by the fact that, in any single transaction, clients may vary between being open and being closed. Similarly, guests who use a facility regularly may do so in different role guises – as businessman or as a man entertaining his wife. Interactional difficulties can arise particularly in respect of searching for host/guest clues when diners are of the same gender. Mars and Nicod found that this occurred in the case of homosexual males dining together, citing one instance when a guest believed to be a transvestite caused substantial classificatory difficulty. In general, however, Mars and Nicod (1984: 61–62) suggest that the nature of social transactions can be determined by reference to the following patterns of primary cues (i.e. gender, age, race, class and state of health):

1 age: waiters and diners of roughly the same age will tend to experience boundary-open transactions and vice versa;

2 place of origin: those of the same place of origin will enjoy boundary-open transactions and vice versa; and

3 sex: when waiters and diners are of a different sex transactions will be boundary-open and vice versa: there is an assumption by male clients that female waiting staff should be more boundary-open (indeed, there is some suggestion that employers and employees exploit this sexuality element in building up trade).

This process of 'screening' is crucial to the assessment of the kind of service relationship into which waiting staff are likely to enter and therefore the types of activity in which they will have to engage in order to maximise the likelihood and size of gratuities. The level of service received by customers is thus determined as the outcome of a complex of interactional processes centring on the server's assessment of the likely temperament and disposition of clients. In fact the preoccupation in Mars and Nicod's study, evident in similar reports (e.g. Spradley and Mann, 1975), with the actual mechanics of occupational sub-cultures tends to obscure not only how difficult it is to obtain tips, but the extent to which the occupational experience of waiting-on-table is far from uniform. Nowhere is this clearer than with the case of female waiting staff. As noted earlier, many women waitresses may find themselves confined to labour markets associated with the lower end of the product hierarchy and thus unable to progress to establishments associated with better conditions of work, better opportunities to exercise discretionary skills and the opportunity for greater informal rewards. More importantly there are fundamental differences in the terms, conditions and experiences of employment enjoyed by female staff.

One example centres on the generalised exploitation of women's sexuality at work which in the hotel and catering context can achieve extra salience. Dronfield and Soto (1980) claim that:

> Trusthouse Forte tried to train women to be all-round hostesses, combining the images of the sexy receptionist with the caring housekeeper. The plan would allow Trusthouse Forte to cut down on the waiting around time inherent in many hotel jobs. The women would supposedly serve breakfast, check the clients in and out, go upstairs to make the beds, and be ready to serve lunch. After a while the women refused to do the worst jobs and the scheme broke down.
>
> (Dronfield and Soto, 1980: 23–24)

For jobs with high levels of public contact, hotel and catering employers often seek persons who exhibit a reasonable degree of physical attractiveness. Male employers tend to be perhaps more self-conscious in the extent to which they attempt to capitalise upon female sexuality. In the studies by Roebuck and Frese (1976) and Spradley and Mann (1975) of, respectively, an American after-hours club and cocktail bar, sexuality was an integral part of the role of the female waitresses, stopping short of responding to sexual advances from clients – though for reasons, primarily, of avoiding the attraction of management displeasure. Roebuck and Frese (1976) found that barmaids and cocktail waitresses were explicitly selected on the basis of their physical appearance – along with 'class', personal habits and other attributes of social and technical skill. A more obvious case of management exploitation of female sexuality is claimed by Byrne:

> When Berni Inns decided to refurbish the Royal, at Long Eaton in the summer of 1984, they tried to change the staff along with the wallpaper. The company's original plan was that when the Royal closed for refurbishment, all the staff would be made redundant and female staff would only be offered the chance to re-apply for their jobs if they could fit into a size 10, 12 or 14 uniform.
>
> (Byrne, 1986: 19)

Most of the women workers in this establishment were, Byrne claims, middle-aged, long-serving staff popular with regular customers and competent at their jobs who did not, however, fit 'with the dolly-bird fantasies of the Berni Inns Management' (Byrne, 1986: 19). The exploitation of sexuality at the level of the employment decision is often compounded by sexual harassment. A report on the London hotel industry found that some 21 per cent of hotel staff knew of instances of sexual harassment:

> women most likely to be victims are receptionists ('management are always touching the receptionists'), bar waitresses, and chambermaids. . . .One worker from a five star hotel reported that some women workers had been threatened with dismissal in the past for refusing to sleep with management.
>
> (quoted in Byrne, 1986: 18)

A further aspect of the generalised differential experience of women at work is the extent to which women are more rigorously controlled by men. This control can be formal in the sense that men tend to hold positions of authority, or more informal in the sense that within nominally collaborative work teams with relatively little visible role differentiation women are still subordinated to male control. Again in the hotel and catering context, a good example of this is provided by Spradley and Mann (1975) in their ethnographic study of the cocktail waitress. They examine the patriarchal relationships in 'Brady's Bar' engendered by the male proprietor and show how these lead to role conflict. The two male bartenders, custodians of Mr Brady's trust, were also managers to whose authority the female cocktail waitresses had to submit. As bartenders, however, there was scope for disagreement, for the questioning of authority and opinion. To the outside gaze, the relationships between waitresses and bartenders were nominally co-operative. Indeed, for the male bartenders, resort to the use of managerial authority in controlling waitresses was seemingly rare. However, the informal control exercised over women workers was considerable. The bartenders had control over the speed at which the waitresses' orders were filled and in what priority, control that could cause friction at busy times as several waitresses vied for orders. Any mistakes made in filling orders or in respect of other aspects of service had to be shouldered by the waitresses, even if they were due to errors on the part of the bartenders. This 'keeping the peace' was essential to harmonious relationships. Bartenders' control extended to what women waitresses were allowed to drink at the end of the service period and male notions of acceptable entitlement could not be broached without retribution. Waitresses allowed the 'privilege' of assisting the bartender at the bar during busy times had to thank him for the opportunity to participate in the male sphere of operations.

Whilst this may all seem a little bizarre, it begs the question as to whether male waiting staff would receive the same treatment. As Spradley and Mann (1975) point out, the waitresses in their study relied on men not only for technical support to do their work but depended on male approval for their sense of well-being to the extent that pleasing male bartenders became more important than pleasing customers. There are echoes here of Whyte's study (Whyte, 1948). He reports the ways in which women workers frequently coped with the stress placed upon them by (usually) male counter workers or similar by crying. There is of course evidence to suggest that waiting staff in general are often looked upon by chefs and others as something approaching a lesser species. As noted in the previous chapter, Snow found that references to the (homo)sexuality of male waiters acted as a device to further justify contempt on the part of chefs (Snow, 1981). However, the creation of such handicaps is an essentially arbitrary affair. Women workers must *always* carry the dual handicap of discrimination against them, based on their occupational location in the hospitality industry hierarchy and their gender. The effects of this on producing an experience of work different to that of men should not be either ignored or underestimated.

CHEFS AND COOKS

Despite being one of the two principal occupations associated with hotel and catering work (Ellis, 1981), remarkably little systematic analysis of the work of chefs and cooks has been undertaken. Several studies contain incidental comment (e.g. Commission on Industrial Relations, 1971; Bowey, 1976; Snow, 1981; Saunders, 1981a, 1981b; Bagguley, 1987) but seemingly only Chiver's now dated research is devoted entirely to the occupation of chef (Chivers, 1971, 1973). As an occupational group, chefs and cooks are interesting for two principal reasons. First, they have been identified as the victims of hotel and catering managements' attempts to deskill and degrade work in the search for reduced costs. This theme will be subject to examination in Chapter 5 along with the position of women chefs and cooks which is closely linked to the issue of deskilling. The second reason for interest in this occupation, and the one that provides the focus for the following discussion, relates to the position of chefs and cooks in hotel and catering organisations *vis-à-vis* other workers, particularly in respect of claims made for the cohesiveness and solidarity of chefs and cooks as an occupational group. This view derives from the report by the Commission on Industrial Relations (CIR) (1971). It will be recalled that the Commission found the hotel industry to be highly status conscious, hierarchical in organisation and conducive to the encouragement of entre-preneurial, individualistic and competitive attitudes amongst workers. Combined with the personal service nature of employment and the isolation in which many workers undertook their tasks, these factors led to an unstable workforce and stressful working conditions, but also the develop-ment of strong identification with management and the aspirations of management, particularly in respect of the desire for promotion and/or (less realistically) proprietorship of a hotel or catering unit. Whilst chefs no less than other workers exhibited the latter tendency, the CIR argued that they also demonstrated greater cohesiveness and solidarity than other occu-pational groups.

The CIR hypothesised that the greater cohesiveness and solidarity of chefs was attributable to three factors: the collaborative 'teamwork' involved in hotel and restaurant cookery; the craft orientation of chefs and cooks; and chefs' removal from the competitive forum of service that denies them access to tips and other informal rewards. On the last of these there is little information. In theory, chefs have opportunities to run a variety of fiddles and knock-offs in the kitchen, opportunities reinforced by the fact that the geographical isolation of the kitchen and high-trust relationships with management often mean that the latter rarely intrude into the work of the chef. The other two characteristics of chefs identified by the CIR (1971) have found resonance in later studies (e.g. Bowey, 1976; Snow, 1981; Gabriel, 1988).

The crux of the CIR's argument in respect of the collaborative nature of chefs' work is that whereas many hotel and catering employees undertake their tasks on an individual and peripatetic basis, chefs' work takes place in a single location and by definition requires a collective, inter-dependent approach to labour. Further, because in many hotel and restaurant organi-sations the kitchen brigade is controlled by a Head Chef rather than a conventional manager, loyalty is induced not only to the craft but to the occupational group as a whole. That teamwork is an important element of chefs' lives was also suggested by the Education, Training and Advisory

Council (1983) report which found that 85 per cent of those asked said that being a good member of a team was very necessary or essential to their job.

The kitchen is arguably the only true 'product'-creating department in the hotel: the kitchen's output is tangible and real and the kitchen's products (dishes and meals) can be complex to assemble. The basis of food production in traditional kitchens is the *partie* system, the origination of which is normally attributed to the French chef, Escoffier, and involves a division of labour along commodity and dish-type lines (Cousins and Foskett, 1989), though to what extent Escoffier refined rather than devised the working practices associated with the system is unclear. Saunders (1981a) postulates a generic hierarchy for the *Brigade de Cuisine* running from Chef de Cuisine (Head Chef) through the Sous Chef (Deputy Chef) to the 'partie' – the sauce chef, larder chef, pastry chef, fish chef, roast chef, soup chef and vegetable chef. However, a variety of practical interpretations have been put on kitchen organisation and variations in such organisation are clearly a function of the type of restaurant and the market in which it operates.

These differences reflect the essential malleability of the system. It is evident that in many hotels and restaurants, including many smaller operations, the *partie* system persists, however weakly, in one form or another. The *partie* system involves considerable specialisation whilst fostering interdependency. Though the majority of workers may be involved in producing individual tangible dishes (a fish dish, a soup), work in a hotel or restaurant kitchen is organised according to the tacit assumption that the proper meal comprises two or more courses. The specialised tasks of individual chefs and cooks are thus brought together in a whole and the whole is to a very large extent the result of social negotiations over the menu. This point is made by Saunders (1981b) who argues that the work experience of chefs is governed by two mutually influencing factors being: (a) the position of the individual worker within the occupational hierarchy of chefs; and (b) the cycle of meal provision. Both of these are ultimately related to the status of foodstuffs, the status of particular meals and the relationship of the unit to the wider market in terms of staff skill and the technology employed. Whyte (1948) identified five determinants of status amongst the kitchen brigade: The first four are: high skill over low skill; high pay over lower pay; long service over short service; and product finishing over product preparation at the earlier stage. The fifth determinant is probably unique to the activity of food preparation:

the working supervisor of the fish station ranked towards the top of the kitchen in all of these factors [the first four status determinants above], and yet her status in the kitchen was low. Evidently there is another factor powerful enough to overrule all these considerations – *the prestige value of the materials used.*

(Whyte, 1948: 34)

Whyte's point has some significance for an understanding of commercial cookery. Certain meals enjoy higher status than others (arguably the rank order is dinner, lunch and breakfast – though lunch-time is conventionally busier and dinners more expensive – see Wood, 1990b). Also, the position of each of the *chefs de partie* in Saunders' hierarchy mirrors relatively closely the hierarchy of foodstuffs proposed by Twigg (1983), with red meat being most valued followed by white meat, fish, dairy products and vegetables and fruit. Certain other resonances with the claims made by sociologists of food and eating are also evident. Thus the sauce chef is senior because sauces bind dishes together (Murcott, 1982), spoil easily and, in the traditional repertoire of French *haute cuisine* are characteristic features of virtually all dishes. The larder chef is similarly important because s/he is responsible for perishables – for fresh food which is attributed considerable importance in traditional hotel cuisine. The positions of soup and vegetable chef are also consonant with the general (low) value attached to these foodstuffs.

The predication of kitchen organisation on culinary skills directed towards particular commodities and parts of the meal is important not only in defining individuals' place within an organisation or the occupation more widely, but in charting career development. Progress in the traditional chefs' hierarchy is, in simplified terms, usually from apprentice to a *partie* position and ultimately to the positions of sous chef and chef de cuisine – in other words a progress from dealing with the specific to dealing with the general and usually involving some mastery of a large number of *partie* positions. The relatively well-developed career structure for chefs means that, when taken with the mode of work organisation, it is easier for individuals to see their role with clarity which, whilst not guaranteeing co-operative and interdependent working arrangements, is likely to foster individual skill and responsibility that allows for controlled creativity within a bureaucratic work structure.

Further evidence to support the hypothesis that chefs' work is characterised by a high degree of co-operation comes from Chivers' (1971) study of chefs' perceptions of conflict. Chivers (1971: 94) notes that the pressure under which the kitchen is placed, particularly by waiting staff, can lead to losses of temper although he suggests that such outbreaks are rarely malicious, rather they add to the camaraderie of the kitchen since friendship and harmony must survive transient divisions in order for the kitchen to function adequately. Chivers also suggests that temper loss may be a useful strategy for asserting the temporary independence of an individual or (presumably in the case of 'outsiders' such as waiters) the kitchen as a whole. What Chivers does not mention is that the cultural stereotype of the temperamental chef may actually lead to a situation where such behaviour is expected and where the expectation itself glosses real divisions and serves as an institutionalised form of defusing conflict between individuals. Some support for this view comes from Saunders' observation that in traditional kitchens the formal pattern of authority matches closely the informal pattern (Saunders, 1981b). Head chefs often occupy a god-like status, and age and experience rank more highly than informal leadership not backed by these criteria. The clear implication is that there exists less scope for 'dissent' because a professional and highly formalised ethic of behaviour prevails.

That chefs are team-oriented in their approach to work is held to be closely related to their craft orientation and a sense of status superiority. Chivers (1973) confirms this view, suggesting that occupational solidarity is reinforced by dedication to task and a genuine interest in the work and opportunities offered by the use of manual skills. However, being able to exercise manual skills is not everything. The context in which such skills are exercised is important. Chivers (1973) argues that chefs and cooks, like other hotel workers, are located in a wide range of hotel and catering units and this geographical spread militates against collectivism. This spatial constraint to collectivism is compounded by chefs' own perceptions of the range of establishments and their relationship to them. Chivers focused mainly on chefs and cooks in up-market establishments and found that these workers viewed themselves as distinct from those employed in lower-market establishments – the former *were* chefs whereas the latter were merely cooks. What is unclear is the extent to which this is rationalised by chefs/cooks working in less prestigious establishments. The bottom line appears to be that chefs are fairly realistic about their job prospects and are encouraged in this by two simple truths: that there will always be a need for their skills (whatever form particular jobs take) and there exists very clearly demarcated career structures for chefs and cooks in the hotel and catering industry.

In support of this are Chiver's findings concerning the career aspirations of chefs and cooks. Many respondents to his study cited the ownership of a restaurant as a business goal. (Hotels were less popular and Chivers hypothesises that this is probably because chefs and cooks find it easier to visualise themselves as restaurateurs than hoteliers, not having been trained in accommodation management.) However, the extent to which managerial and employer positions were realisable aspirations was very clearly reflected in a second-choice career goal – career cooking – which Chivers interprets as reflecting more realistic assessments on the part of his respondents. A strong craft orientation and status superiority is thus seemingly maintained by chefs precisely because career structures embody relatively precise alternatives in terms of the opportunities to develop and exercise skills and increase status and rewards. A waiter in a small privately owned restaurant working split shifts may, in theory, improve his career prospects by moving to a high-class hotel. However, the waiter is always going to be involved in the same type of work. Being a waiter in one type of operation is not vastly different from being a waiter in any other. For the chef, however, the options are much more clearly defined. A chef, particularly one fairly senior in the kitchen hierarchy, is always going to be an employee whose occupation automatically confers some status irrespective of the organisation. Further, within the hotel and catering industry there exists sufficient sectoral differentiation to present chefs with several quite distinct career options, that, whilst always involving cookery as the central task, vary in quite precise ways in terms of benefits relating to conditions of work and remuneration. Thus, Chivers found high mobility amongst the chefs he studied with a net loss of employees from the hotel and restaurant sector. A third or more respondents in hospitals had experience in the commercial sector whereas only 7 per cent of those in the latter had worked in hospital cooking, suggesting, Chivers argues, a move towards jobs where working conditions were better. It is not simply a choice between institutional and commercial catering, however. Because their skills are less confined to local labour markets, chefs can job hunt in a national market. However, fewer senior positions exist for chefs in the commercial sector, particularly in those high-quality establishments the aspiration towards employment in which is very much a part of the occupational culture. This faces many chefs with career choices that are to a very large extent determined by the state of the market for their skills. For access to incrementally superior and/or better paid posts of responsibility in the commercial sector chefs might have to accept charge of a small unit, the trade-off of which is less opportunity to exercise their skills and diminished opportunities to reach the top of their trade – unless the unit in question is very famous. In the commercial sector, career choice is very much in terms of hoping for a senior position in a high-class establishment, remaining a member of a team in such a unit or a less prestigious establishment, or taking up a senior position in a smaller unit. Chefs could, like other hotel and catering workers, flit from establishment to establishment, but in terms of career development this can be pretty pointless (except when young) since clearly defined options in the market-place exist with genuinely calculable consequences for work experience. The chef's dilemma in the commercial sector is neatly summarised by Bowey:

Careers for chefs are slightly different from those of waiters and waitresses since their earnings are less dependent upon the volume of trade and the generosity of customers in the restaurant. They are taken on as 'commis chefs' and trained as chefs, being promoted to posts carrying higher responsibility as their skills and experience increase. They also move from restaurant to restaurant seeking to move each time to a higher status restaurant where the food preparation is more intricate and therefore the skills learned more valuable. The differentials between the different grades of chef become increasingly more substantial as the skill level of the chef increases. A restaurant builds its reputation on the quality of its food and this depends largely on the abilities of the head chef. The head chef is typically a much honoured, respected and well-paid employee in a restaurant. Like the waitresses, however, a chef who is, say, three grades below the head chef in a high status restaurant may earn more money by accepting a head chef's job in a lower status perhaps smaller restaurant. If he does this he is likely to find himself without the opportunities for practising and developing many of his skills, and his chances of reaching the top of his profession are lessened.

(Bowey, 1976: 136)

Chefs' career options are firmly cemented in a context of highly formalised systems of training. The Education, Advisory and Training Council (ETAC) (1983) in its study found that of seventy cooks/chefs, some forty-one had formal educational qualifications in cookery. Amongst head chefs, thirty-four out of forty-one had such qualifications. Chefs can obtain standard qualifications which are *trade* qualifications – that is, they are universally recognised as appropriate to a career as chef/cook. This system of certification based on what is essentially a national curriculum ensures not only the transmission of basic craft knowledge but also of tacit skills and values, the *culture* of the occupation. Measurement of individual worth therefore extends beyond the actual practice of cookery to a more generalised appreciation of the level of qualification: formal certification links chefs and cooks together in an educational framework that validates their occupation over and above relatively subjective criteria such as craft competency, employment record and so forth.

This process of certification is reinforced by the involvement of chefs in their occupation beyond the workplace. In addition to formal certification, there are many associations for chefs to join and the whole occupation is held constantly in the spotlight through the activities of such associations, through the achievements of individual chefs (for example, in many of the competitions that are held each year) and through the bourgeois concern with food reflected in food guides and specialist magazines. At a less formal level, Chivers (1971) argues that the nature of hotel and catering work encourages patterns of friendship within the trade and this is reinforced by involvement. The occupation is centrally concerned with the craft and craft provides the focus for self-improvement (via sharing experiences and ideas) and advancement via the development of social networks – a feature, to some extent, of other industry occupations also. The attitudes and culture of the occupation are highly generalised: involvement in the craft, national support systems and professional reference points all combine to reinforce a relatively uniform and highly systematic approach to work – perhaps most obviously experienced by the outsider in terms of the perception of chefs as arrogant, superior and self-serving. A concluding quote from Chivers (1971) illustrates the point:

> casual remarks dropped in the course of conversation. . .suggested alleged errors in cooking were mostly the customer's rather than the cook's fault, that head chefs/cooks, not managers, should say how the kitchen is to be organised and operated, that waiters are sometimes 'beggars in uniform'.

(Chivers, 1971: 161)

OTHER KITCHEN WORKERS

In the context of discussion of the more 'glamorous' job of chef, two studies of basic grade kitchen workers are worthy of note. Paterson (1981) studied hospital kitchen maids using ethnographic techniques, principally participant observation. The kitchen in which she worked provided 700 meals daily for all staff and patients and the maids had a dirty job that entailed not only food preparation but the cleaning of floors, surfaces and equipment. In a manner reminiscent of Saunders' claims concerning the role of the menu in determining social relations in the kitchen (Saunders, 1981b), Paterson argues that the structure of maids' working day was fleshed out by the weekly menu cycle. For example, when food had been processed for one day, it was often the case that ingredients were prepared for the following day's menu, the menu dishes indicating the necessary 'food work' that had to be undertaken. Maids' work experience was characterised by a sense of overwhelming drudgery. Dealing with food in bulk led to a fragmentation of perceptions of food production, a disassociation of experience gained in the domestic provision of food made manifest in that the maids brought their own food to eat. Because of role-strain engendered by the conflict between their positions as food producer in the home and hospital bulk food producer, they had difficulty in adjusting to the dissemination of small portions when instinct led them to feel that larger amounts were 'normal'.

The experience of 'food as work' also led maids to develop different criteria of 'good' and 'bad' food, based not on taste but on the relevance of preparation for work control and experience. An example of bad food was lettuce, which being presented unprocessed for consumption, meant that carelessness in the form of presenting dirty or infested leaves could create a negative image of maids' competence and of the standards of hygiene operating in the kitchen. 'Doing lettuce' (i.e. washing and preparing) was therefore regarded as an arduous task, generally eliciting sympathy from colleagues. Good foods were those requiring little or no preparation by the maids or which meant that few items of equipment had subsequently to be cleaned. Paterson's study reveals continuities in the themes highlighted previously. Kitchen maids were at the bottom of the departmental hierarchy and felt this subordinate position acutely, a feeling heightened by arbitrary and erratic supervision (cf. Gabriel, 1988). It was difficult for them to take pride in their work since nobody praised them and most other higher grade kitchen workers treated them as skivvies. Also, because maids were unable easily to reconcile the perceived low standards attendant on the preparation of hospital food with their own personal domestic standards, a good deal of frustration was experienced. As a result of these experiences, a number of coping strategies were evolved, including distancing, marked by protestations that skivvying was 'not really them' and activities such as joking cheekily with amenable cooks – pretending to refuse to undertake instructions and suchlike (cf. Spradley and Mann, 1975, who found that cocktail waitresses also developed central conversational themes emphasising non-work aspects of life and also distanced themselves from their work by having regular styling sessions and wearing perfume). In addition to these distancing tactics, kitchen maids abused the control system almost as a form of compensation for being employed there. Food was taken and eaten and when food was not available this led to annoyance and frustration. The appropriation of knock-offs was not simply related to expectations of total rewards but was also a manifestation of resistance, of fighting back against menial, degraded and monotonous jobs.

Saunders (1981a, 1985) studied kitchen porters. His general conclusions are not at variance with those of Paterson. He argues that kitchen portering serves as a reservoir to take up those into work who have suffered as a result of changes in local industrial employment or some personal reason for which they had to leave other work. The majority of kitchen porters in Saunders' sample were men with few if any school-leaving qualifications. Only 21 per cent were married and 64 per cent had no children. Over half Saunders' respondents said that they became kitchen porters because it was the only job they could get. Their work was predictably degrading, though there are some hints that a minority of workers made something of it.

Interestingly, the work of the kitchen porter is often monotonous and dull and little effort is made to invest in technological aids. Saunders found no evidence of the existence of mechanical or technological aids to minimise the drudgery of the job and the picture he paints would appear to confirm a lack of advance in the treatment of kitchen porters since Orwell's (1933) account of his own experiences in *Down and Out in Paris and London.*

Of course technological investment is expensive and kitchen porter labour cheap and disposable. What arises mostly clearly from the works of writers like Paterson (1981) and Saunders (1981a), however, is the lack of dignity allowed to workers in these low grade posts. These authors direct attention to the routine, everyday aspects of hotel and catering work, processes that have become increasingly common with new forms of food work, notably those that characterise capital intensive chain restaurants. These systems of catering exists alongside the more traditional forms of food provision but there is little evidence to suggest that they provide employment which is any less engaging (Gabriel, 1988).

ACCOMMODATION WORKERS

Of all hotel and catering employees, those engaged in accommodation services work have received least research attention (but see Lennon and Wood, 1989). The term 'accommodation workers' is used here to describe a diverse group of employees including room-cleaners (still usually called chambermaids or room-maids because of the gendered nature of the employment), receptionists, hall porters and housekeepers. The limited literature on the third (Saunders, 1980) and non-existence of any significant commentary on the last means that discussion here is slanted towards the first two, the largest categories of accommodation workers in the industry.

In the Hotel and Catering Industry Training Board (HCITB) (1985) classification of occupations, chambermaids are subsumed in the category 'domestic staff' and number some 81,000 in the commercial sector. Some 97 per cent of workers in this category are female. Chambermaids, like all accommodation workers, are more or less exclusively concerned with the hotels sector. Shamir (1975: 178–183) in his study of London hotels adopts a typical attitude to room cleaning work. Chambermaids, he argues, are amongst the least skilled of hotel staff (in fact the HCITB, 1985, classifies them as unskilled). They are expected by employers to draw upon their reservoir of domestic skills in undertaking work tasks. The assumption that women's socialisation 'naturally' suits them to the maintenance of hotel accommodation is convenient in that it enables employers to: (a) avoid giving anything other than minimal on-the-job training; and (b) hire a group of people who bring to their work a basic training undertaken at no cost to the employer. Shamir argues that room-cleaning is physically demanding and dirty work, repetitive, boring and limited in variety and scope, and undertaken at times when employees are unlikely to encounter customers. Despite this, he contends that it offers workers certain compensations such as a relatively pleasant working environment and freedom from close supervision (a view reiterated by Guerrier and Lockwood, 1989b). The latter permits workers a limited degree of control over work-rates and methods of working plus opportunities to develop strategies to cope with monotony (for example, the use of radios and televisions in guests' rooms).

Saunders and Pullen (1987) questionnaired room-maids in thirty London hotels. Their study goes a considerable way towards confirming industry trends in terms of labour instability, the employment of marginal workers and the selection of hotel and catering work because of the lack of alternatives. The typical room-maid in the Saunders and Pullen survey was female, single, childless and aged between 25 and 44. The majority (63 per cent) were from Europe and those who had been in post for the shortest length of time originally took up their employment because it was the only work they could obtain. Others evidenced considerable stability, with 67 per cent of the total having worked in the industry for more than twelve months and 51 per cent in their existing job for more than a year. Saunders and Pullen confirm Shamir's view that hotel room-maids do a physically demanding and dirty job but offer no evidence to suggest that freedom from supervision allows flexible control over work-rates and methods, or allows for socialisation. Indeed, some 80 per cent of the sample cleaned between eleven and sixteen rooms daily, a workload regarded as unreasonable by many respondents. Again, the theme of isolation is evident here. Shamir sees absence from supervision as freeing workers from management oversight but Saunders and Pullen found that many room-maids experienced their heavy loads as all the more problematic because of an absence of management support and interest, manifest in complaints about short-staffing, the absence of help from other hotel staff and failure to provide sufficient and adequate materials for the performance of work tasks. The picture painted by Saunders and Pullen is at least implicitly confirmed by the Education and Training Advisory Council (ETAC) (1983). Their job profiles and case studies of twenty female chambermaids reveals a wider age range (17 to 68) and a preponderance of single people (though here including widows and those divorced and separated). The average number of rooms cleaned per maid was fifteen and there is the same implication that many women take these jobs because of a lack of alternatives and find their employment a source of considerable misery.

There can be little doubt that many women who undertake room-cleaning jobs do so because of a shortage of alternative employment. In his survey of hotel and catering occupations, Ellis (1981) found that more than 40 per cent of school pupils were likely to be deterred from becoming room-maids because they perceived it as repetitive, unskilled and low in status. The low status of chambermaiding was felt by just under half of Saunders and Pullen's sample who suggested they were treated as less than equal by many other hotel staff. Clearly then, chambermaids rank amongst the lowest of the low in hotel work, treated as a cheap and easily replaceable resource by employers and often spurned by their fellow employees. One point on which existing evidence disagrees is in respect of access to informal rewards. The implication of Shamir's research is that customer–maid contact is limited and thus the opportunity for gaining informal rewards limited. However, Saunders and Pullen found that maids had frequent contact with customers and nearly a quarter of their sample claimed to receive tips from most guests and a further 58 per cent from a few – though the majority only obtained between one and three pounds a week. The most commonly received fringe benefit was discount on holidays. Since Saunders and Pullen undertook their research in London hotels, at the centre of the UK tourism industry, their findings must be treated as potentially untypical, though once again the lack of research evidence highlights the problem of assessing the validity of the 'total rewards package' as an explanatory concept in understanding those influences that shape hotel employees' experiences of their work.

In contrast to chambermaiding, reception work is regarded as semiskilled (Hotel and Catering Industry Training Board, 1985). The work of the receptionist is also undertaken more often than not in full-public view, in the 'front office', and receptionists are usually the first people hotel guests encounter, particularly in those hotels where hall porters are not employed. They thus occupy a 'gatekeeper' role, frequently bearing the responsibility for guests' first impressions of the hotel. In fact, the responsibilities that receptionists bear for the image of the hotel arguably extend beyond first impressions. The varied nature of these responsibilities is rarely reflected in adequate remuneration and reception work, no less than other hotel and catering occupations, suffers extensively from labour turnover. The Education and Training Advisory Council (ETAC) (1983) studied forty receptionists of which twenty-three (just less than 60 per cent) admitted to *regularly* being involved in book-keeping, letter writing, inventory taking, typing, record keeping, answering queries, filing, taking reservations, dealing with mail and lost property, dealing with room changes, taking payment of customers' bills, banking monies, holding responsibility for room keys and producing reports and statistics. Further to these diverse duties, the position of the reception at the 'crossroads' of the hotel ensures that the potential for pressure emanating from the demands of the client are considerable: the visibility of the reception desk ensures that it is the first port of call for any disgruntled guest. Shamir (1975) found that receptionists frequently act as conduits for communicating requests and complaints to other departments of the hotel. In addition to a gatekeeper role therefore, the receptionist is expected to be a mediator. It is these roles, Shamir argues, that can lead the relatively high status of receptionist to suffer in terms of role stress and incongruity. He found that receptionists were perceived by senior kitchen and restaurant staff as low in status and by lower kitchen and restaurant staff as arrogant and self-important. The 'in-between' role of the receptionist both in terms of physical location within the hotel and their position in the hotel's communications system creates the potential for a particularly unrewarding job characterised by conflict, both actual and in terms of role image amongst colleagues in other departments. As with chambermaids, little information is available on the extent to which receptionists benefit from informal rewards and fringe benefits. One general point of note is the extent to which illicit activities ('fiddling' and 'knocking-off') are constrained by receptionists' lack of mobility to access the latter and their high trust relationship with management. Their responsibility for monies often entails close supervision and monitoring thus making fiddles difficult. Where information technology has been introduced the scope for fiddling is further reduced. All in all, the experience of accommodation workers is suggestive once again of the weakness inherent in the concept of informal rewards and their effect on work experience.

MANAGERS

The literature on the nature of managerial work in the hospitality industry is concerned principally with *hotel management*. This should be kept in mind throughout the following discussion. In the UK at least, serious research into the occupation of hotel manager is a fairly recent phenomenon. Apart from one or two early studies (Nailon, 1968; Hotel and Catering Industry Training Board, 1970) most research is of the 1980s. Nevertheless, taken together with American evidence, there is a large measure of agreement as to the principal characteristics of management work in hotels.

The first thing to note is that people come to hotel management careers via a range of routes. Baum (1989) in the context of the Irish Republic identified three principal sources of hotel managers: those who come to the industry with formal hotel school training; those who train for management within the industry after starting either in craft positions or being given a traineeship; and those who have an early career in another industry followed by late entry into the hotel industry. The last perhaps is most typical of owner-managers but in general there is good reason to suppose that all three routes are typical of career paths in a large number of countries.

Secondly, as noted before, hotel management like other occupations and the industry itself is notoriously insular. Those who follow a formal course of training in hospitality management are generally separated from general business studies students, and hotel and catering education which normally incorporates periods of industry placement serves as a form of pre-entry socialisation into the occupation of hotel management (Mars, Bryant and Mitchell, 1979). The need for specialist training is coming under increased critical scrutiny (Baum, 1989; Lennon, 1989; Wood, 1988) but has usually been justified in terms of the need for managers in the hospitality industry to possess vital technical skills, particularly in the field of food and beverage management, that allows them the opportunity to control other powerful work groups such as chefs (cf. Guerrier, 1987). Over-emphasis on the need for such skills was criticised as early as 1970 by the British Hotel and Catering Industry Training Board:

> Throughout the industrial survey it was continually impressed on us that managers must, above all else, possess a high degree of technical competence. This we accept, but only in the sense that any manager needs technical knowledge to a degree which enables him to meet market wants, set standards and ensure that they are maintained.
>
> (Hotel and Catering Industry Training Board, 1970: 11)

That such technical competence is perceived as necessary is without doubt. The Education and Training Advisory Council (1983) found that over half the managers in their sample were frequently or sometimes involved in food preparation, cooking and service. However, Baum (1989) suggests that:

> While the business environment in hotels does have very distinct features, there is a danger that the emphasis which the industry places on uniqueness should not be at the cost of the application of the more general principles of good management.
>
> (Baum, 1989: 139)

Relatedly here, the insularity of hotel management education is reinforced by a tendency for those who commit themselves to a hotel and catering career early on to never leave the industry. In Baum's sample, two-thirds of hotel managers in Ireland had no working experience outside the hotel industry (Baum, 1989), a finding confirmed by Guerrier (1987) in the context of British hotel managers.

A third consideration is that most senior hotel managers obtain their appointments at a relatively early age (Commission on Industrial Relations, 1971). The first part of a hotel manager's career is likely to find him or her in very junior positions, often being little more than a dogsbody. Formal qualifications do not seem to affect either position on entry or promotion prospects and career patterns (Guerrier, 1987; Baum, 1989). In their study of UK managers, Riley and Turam (1988) argue that vocational education and time spent working in the industry gaining experience are alternative uses of time that make little difference to long-term prospects.

Fourthly, and following from this, hotel management positions are gained as a result of substantial mobility. Guerrier (1987) notes that as assistant managers gain seniority they are usually given some functional responsibility, the main ones in a hotel being front of house (reception and rooms) and food and beverage. Experience in both of these is usually essential to promotion. Such experience need not be gained in a single institution however. Rather it is usual for managers at this stage of their career to move frequently between hotels 'collecting' experience of both specific functions and of different types of hotel. In the three companies Guerrier examined, the career histories of managers interviewed showed a pattern of lateral moves from hotel to hotel within the same company. Similarly, Riley and Turam (1988) found mobility a crucial feature of management career development though in their case, some 43 per cent of career moves examined involved a change of company, with the change to hotel (general) manager involving a change of company in 41 per cent of cases. High mobility amongst managers is also confirmed by the trade journal *Caterer and Hotelkeeper* (23 March 1989) in a study showing that hotel and catering managers both changed their jobs more frequently and earned less than their counterparts in nine other industrial sectors. The attainment of a General Managership of a hotel is not necessarily an end to mobility. Though Guerrier (1987) found from her small sample that the average age of attaining a General Managership was 30, many of these people were promoted from a senior assistant's position to the General Manager position in a small company hotel with little prestige. For those staying with the same company, it appears this is a cross to be borne. Promotion to General Manager is firstly to a small unit and subsequently – to use Guerrier's naval metaphor – to larger and more prestigious ships in the line. It is perhaps therefore unsurprising that many managers change company to gain a unit manager's post since mobility offers opportunities to 'short circuit' traditional patterns of promotion. Also, Guerrier noted that in the companies she studied, pay was linked to the size of hotel. If this is, as seems likely, a general feature of company owned hotels then it places a further incentive on managers to move in search of career acceleration.

Certainly, little appears to constrain hotel managers' mobility. Guerrier noted that children are more likely to be the primary consideration in job moves than spouses, many of whom are in any case often involved in the running of the hotel (if they are women). A more important barrier is the possibility of an end to mobility within a single company. Guerrier (1987) points out that by the time a manager who has spent his or her life with a single company reaches their mid-40s there are fewer properties to manage. Indeed, given that even general managers move with frequency, options within a single company expire quickly. Moving to another company is one option as is promotion to a head office (regional or specialist management) position. Guerrier suggests, however, that the ethics of hotel management prevent many managers moving to Head Office posts as a matter of pride.

The fifth characteristic of hotel management positions is the degree of latitude individual managers are given in the running of their units, a freedom reflected in the manner in which hotel management work is conducted. Nailon (1968) found that hotel managers engaged in a much larger number of activities than counterparts in other industries, saw less of their peers and were rarely involved in group situations. They spent less time alone because of the time spent in direct supervision of staff and contact with customers. Managers were usually engaged in the continuous monitoring of their unit through brief contacts with personnel and regular movement about the establishment. Subsequent research has tended to confirm this picture. Baum (1989) found management to be dominated by operational demands. Guerrier and Lockwood note that:

> The traditions of hotel management emphasise the hotel manager as the person who is always around to greet guests as they arrive. The Victorian hotelier was almost like a host welcoming a guest into his own home . . .the 'greeting' and 'being there' aspects of the role remain important.
> (Guerrier and Lockwood, 1989a: 84)

Guerrier and Lockwood (1989a) found that managers expressed a preference for active management and disliked the 'sitting behind a desk' aspects of their job and doing paperwork. This attitude was encouraged by cramped accommodation that made it difficult for the management team to meet and make contact. They write that managers:

> saw their jobs very clearly in terms of being out and about in the hotel. This very often involved working long hours – an average of 12–14 hours a day was not seen as unusual and with very few and irregular days off, if any. Rather than seeing this as a potential source of dissatisfaction, they saw it more as perfectly normal for the industry.
> (Guerrier and Lockwood, 1989a: 85)

Similarly, Worsfold (1989) quotes a respondent to the effect that:

> It's pointless the general manager sitting behind his desk all day, he needs to be out and about encouraging his staff. . . .If he's going to be stuck in an office all day then he's going to be away from that team and not know what's going on in his hotel.

(Worsfold, 1989: 150)

The 'being there' aspects of a hotel manager's role are perhaps in normative terms an important indicator of how successful any individual is in the eyes of staff and superiors. Analyses drawing on Mintzberg's ten managerial role categories and their contribution to managerial effectiveness are instructive here. Mintzberg (1973) identified ten managerial role categories: figurehead, leader, liaison, monitor, disseminator, spokesman, entrepreneur, disturbance handler, resource allocator and negotiator. In a small-scale study of seven American managers of a single company, Ley (1980) observed the work of management personnel and classified their activities according to Mintzberg's schema. Following from this, the ratings of these managers' effectiveness as perceived by corporate superiors was obtained. Two managers were graded highly effective, three effective and two less effective. These gradings were then compared to the role ratings. Ley argues that the highly effective managers allocated *less* time to the leadership role than the two less effective managers, and more time on entrepreneurial activities than managers with lower effectiveness ratings. In a much larger study of American general managers, Arnaldo (1981) secured 194 responses involving self-classification of activities according to Mintzberg's model and a note of the time spent on each plus a rating of the importance of individual roles. No corporate ratings of effectiveness were available here but it is worth noting that in terms of time allocated, the most important roles were leader, disseminator and monitor whilst in terms of importance they were leader, entrepreneur and monitor.

It is clear then that hotel managers set great store by leadership and also on entrepreneurship – though the extent to which the latter is realised may be problematic. Notwithstanding the likelihood of corporate perceptions of effectiveness differing from those of unit managers, the latter do appear to share a common perception of what a 'good' hotel should be and what good managers should do. In Guerrier's terms, (Guerrier, 1987) this emphasises the importance of the occupational community's self-perception which is likely to be reinforced by the views of colleagues and subordinates. The ability of managers in the hotel industry to get involved in basic operative work is something likely to invite the respect rather than disapprobation of these groups. Yet, as several researchers have noted, there is something absurd about this approach. Baum (1989) argues that there is little evidence to show that 'being there' styles of management are costed relative to the benefit which may accrue from them. Guerrier and Lockwood (1989a) go as far as to suggest that the culture of hotel management emphasises 'being there' as the most important aspect of hotel management and achievement of results as secondary. This is encouraged by the nature of hotel management apprenticeships which encourages managers to respond to problems by being downwardly mobile:

> Having sorted out the immediate problem, however, the manager does not pause to analyse the problem but passes on to the next operational crisis. The hotel culture sees this activity based behaviour as the 'right way' and will reward it with praise and career progression, so passing the approach higher up the organisation.
>
> (Guerrier and Lockwood, 1989a: 86)

'Being there' styles of management give rise to procedures characterised by informality of communication between management and operatives and a paternalistic and authoritarian (or at least directive) approach to staff, although hotel managements understandably tend to dissent from these views. On the issue of paternalism/authoritarianism Guerrier and Lockwood (1989a) found that managers saw the development and care of their staff as a central part of their role but noted that they did little to convert this into direct action. In the same study, staff saw management as being rather critical, autocratic and controlling. Worsfold (1989) found that managers were aware of participative styles of management but none of his sample had adopted such a style. This point is reinforced by Croney (1988) whose interviews with the corporate executives of hotel groups revealed claims to a philosophy of management style typically emphasising consultation, involvement and communication. In the four groups studied, there was an overall tendency to see participation as management-led, though in some instances authoritarian paternalism was ameliorated by a more co-operative approach, differing in at least one important respect – the willingness to accept the legitimacy of trade union representation, a tendency absent in two of the groups. The attitudes of management at unit level in all groups studied evidenced a unitary outlook as opposed to a pluralistic perspective, i.e. a tendency to view organisations as unified bodies in which the interests of management and workforce are shared, managerial authority supreme, and conflict pathological rather than arising from a fundamental diversity of competing intents.

Finally in this list of the characteristics of hotel managers and hotel management there is, as ever, the issue of pay. The role of management in controlling informal rewards was discussed earlier. Management are no less susceptible to the benefits of knock-offs and fiddles than those employees whose access to such benefits they control. Like the rest of the hotel and catering workforce, their basic remuneration is relatively poor. A survey for the trade journal *Caterer and Hotelkeeper* (23 August 1989) compared hotel and catering managers with managers in nine other industrial sectors and found that the average salary of the former was £12,897 compared to an overall average of £16,845. Hotel and catering management was lowest by £3,000. The survey also found that the average hotel and catering manager had spent only 4.4 years with their present employer, the lowest in the data set, compared to an average of 8.3 years. Hotel managers are thus in some ways subject to many of the same pressures that the rest of the workforce experience at managers' hands. The work is hard, often not obviously effective and rewards are, to the outsider at least, somewhat limited. Hotel management careers are easier for some than for others however. The majority of hotel general managers are men and yet the hotel and catering industry management cadre is increasingly made up of women. According to the Hotel and Catering Industry Training Board (HCITB) (1984a) report *Women's path to management in the hotel and catering industry*, some 55 per cent of industry managers are female. Given that 73 per cent of the entire industry workforce are women, the report argues that females are under-represented at managerial level. The extent of this under-representation is highlighted by the fact that over two-thirds of students on hotel and catering management courses in the UK are women (Guerrier, 1986). In reality, women managers are concentrated in certain sectors and positions in the industry, evidencing once again the effects of labour market segmentation. The HCITB (1984a) report calculated that women constituted 59 per cent of managers in industrial catering and 70 per cent in private institutions (e.g. schools, college halls of residence) but only 29 per cent of managers in restaurants and 39 per cent in hotels. In general it is thus the welfare rather than commercial sector in which women are most likely to achieve a management position. However, in the latter, women tend to be concentrated in 'staff roles' rather than 'line management'. That is, women are most likely to be found in ancillary management roles associated with, for example, sales, marketing, training and personnel (HCITB, 1984a; Guerrier, 1986) rather than in food and beverage management or general management. Indeed, Guerrier (1986) surveyed the 1983 World Hotel Directory and found that of the 300 major British hotels included therein, only one was managed by a woman, though the number of women general managers throughout the British *hotel* industry has subsequently seemingly increased (Stacey, 1987). Data on other sectors, particularly restaurants, is notable by its absence.

WOMEN MANAGERS

Common areas of agreement exist as to the reasons for the under-representation of women at managerial level in hotels and catering (Guerrier, 1986; Hicks, 1990; HCITB, 1984a; Larmour and McKenna, 1983; McKenna and Larmour, 1984). These are:

1 gender differences in rearing and education and the orientation of girls to caring careers which involve an extension of (male defined) roles for women;
2 women's career decisions relative to traditional career paths to general management in hotels and catering;
3 the requirements of the role of hotel line manager *vis-à-vis* conventional requirements of sociability;
4 the attitudes and aspirations of women; and
5 organisational discrimination against women, normally in the form of male impedence of career progress.

The first of these points was considered in detail in Chapter 2. It is thus to the four remaining issues that the remainder of this discussion turns.

Career paths to hotel management

As noted earlier, Guerrier (1986) found that general managers in the hotel industry tend to need mobility and experience of food and beverage and accommodation/front of house management in order to achieve their position. However, food and beverage management tends to be a male preserve and women often find themselves in departments of low status such as housekeeping, the low status definition of which often derives from nothing more than the preponderance of women in such departments. How food and beverage management has become a male preserve is difficult to establish. However, one clue is to be found in the HCITB (1984a) report on female managers which found both that more men had craft qualifications than women and more men had worked their way up to management from the lower occupational echelons. The HCITB argues that it is common to find that men who have done this have held a considerable number of positions. Women by contrast follow a more formal route involving fewer positions. What is meant by 'formal route' in this context the HCITB does not make clear but it seems not unreasonable to assume that barriers to women 'working their way up' are greater than for men because of the confinement of women to predominantly part-time, low status and non-food and beverage jobs. Taking the argument one step further, it could also be that colleges constitute the main supply of potential women managers. Women thus enter the industry (with formal qualifications) at an age when ambitious upwardly mobile and relatively unqualified males have already acquired several years head start.

Not only is it difficult for women to acquire the necessary experience even to begin to qualify for general management but they must also contend with the industry's 'old boy network' which is frequently instrumental in mobility, i.e. in gaining jobs within any one unit or within units in a chain. Career moves within the industry tend to be handled informally and in a personal manner, and managers higher in the organisation may sponsor individual mobility. Since the majority of managers are men it is unsurprising that they tend to sponsor men in preference to women, with the result, as Guerrier (1986) implies, that women do not acquire the mobility deemed as necessary for the attainment of senior positions. Similarly, the traditional path to hotel general management predicated on mobility does not easily facilitate the aspirations of women who also desire a family life and/or may require to take a break in order to raise children. It is more difficult to re-enter hotel management than many other forms of management because absence leads to a break in a career route characterised by the acquisition of experience through mobility. It is unsurprising to find that the HCITB (1984a) survey of women managers discovered that most of those in senior positions were both unmarried and childless.

The conventional role of hotel manager

In her study of women hotel managers, Guerrier (1986) highlighted a rarely recognised problem facing all managers but of particular relevance to women – namely that much of the work of hotel management is carried out in a semi-social setting (see also Nailon, 1968; Venison, 1983). In such jobs, promotion decisions may be affected by what Guerrier calls 'extra-functional variables', for example, sex, race and education. For women, jobs where contact with the public is involved may be particularly problematic. This is not simply because male managers and clients expect women to be servile and compliant with the demands of men but they also expect them to be attractive. As suggested earlier, physical appearance is an issue for *male* employers and clients and can give rise to such incidents as the Berni Inns sacking of women for not fitting the company's uniforms (see Chapter 2). As far as hotel management is concerned, managers must be acceptable to the predominantly male clientele and thus women have to contend with the twin difficulties of sexism and maintaining their authority. As Guerrier summarises:

Hotel companies may prefer men to women in certain management jobs because of their greater acceptability to (predominantly male) clients, as they might prefer an older man to a younger man. And a woman who is appointed to the job of hotel manager may find it harder than a man to acquire the status and credibility she needs with clients.

(Guerrier, 1986: 235)

Guerrier argues that the vicious circle of discrimination against women managers is compounded in the case of the requirement of the visibility of the post holder because it is often antithetical to the strategy adopted by token women in organisations, that is to become socially invisible, keep a low profile and willingly accept low profile jobs and promotions.

Attitudes and aspirations of women

The family aspirations of many women, for example in terms of bearing and rearing children, rarely coincide with the levels of support and provision required to allow women to break from their careers without disadvantage – even when women themselves want to. Indeed, the whole edifice of work organisation discriminates against women in this as in other respects. In the hotel and catering industry the problem is compounded because of the high level of mobility required in order to reach senior management. The HCITB's finding that many female hotel managers were single seems to be true of successful business women in general (Larwood and Wood, 1977). However, Guerrier (1986) notes that many women opt for college courses in hotel and catering management because it represents a resolution of pressures in the form of interest in management with interest in the traditionally female field of domestic science and cookery. In this sense, many women are arguably misled early on in the process of career choice and do not realise the extent of either the general or industry specific discrimination they will face. When they do discover the extent of discrimination and lack of opportunity, many withdraw altogether or to the point where they limit their aspirations and resign themselves to lower levels of achievement. Certainly, once women have some experience of hotel and catering management education their expectations seem to diverge from those of men. The HCITB (1984a) reports that both male and female students had similar aspirations concerning the post they would hold five years after leaving college, but women had lower expectations of their employment prospects upon their graduation, expectations which for the most part appear to have been realised. The HCITB also administered attitudinal tests to its women respondents and found that many shared male stereotypical views as to the nature of women as lacking in confidence to push themselves, insufficiently ambitious, more influenced by their emotions (which affected their behaviour as managers), less worthy as employees because of their physiological capacity for child-bearing and not aggressive or competitive enough.

Discrimination against women

Many of the discriminatory practices directed towards women have been identified under the previous headings in this discussion. Some form part of that wider social and industrial edifice of prejudice against women that ultimately limits them in all but a small number of cases to subordinate and ancillary roles. In this category falls the absence of adequate support facilities for women seeking to bear and raise children. Not all women wish to raise children, however, nor constantly find themselves in the position of having to contemplate this course of action. All women face more general forms of discrimination that derive from the patriarchal structure of social relations in society and are mediated in the work context by the nature of the industry and organisation in which they work. In the hotel industry, the stereotype of the hotel manager, the entrenched nature of career paths and the essentially male control of service provision all present women with formidable barriers to career progression.

Other forms of subtle or obvious discrimination against women managers in hotels and catering not already mentioned include the nature of training. The HCITB (1984a) report on women managers found striking differences in the in-company training of men and women. A small number of women managers had received no training at all despite the availability of programmes. Where they had undergone such training it differed considerably from that of men in that women had taken (been pushed into taking?) courses in the ancillary management functions in which they are slowly coming to dominate (e.g. sales, marketing and personnel) rather than courses in operational management. Yet, as the HCITB shows, the majority of women on hotel and catering management courses express a considerable interest in a career in operational management.

A further problem that women managers have to overcome (more so than their male counterparts) in order to be successful is that of convincing their (usually male) superiors that they are committed to the organisation. Stacey (1987) cites one woman with experience of food and beverage management to the effect that 'You have to work ten times as hard to prove yourself'. Stacey's journalistic piece leaves more questions open than it answers but an example of the pervasiveness of male 'matter of fact' attitudes towards the role of women managers in hotels and catering is evident:

Guests may express surprise when a woman duty manager is sent to sort out a problem. But Tom Eckstein, personnel executive with recruitment consultants LMS says the old excuse 'the customer expects a man' no longer applies. . . . He sees a growth in women managers in personnel and training and sales and marketing, rather than in line management. But it's partly up to women themselves to put themselves forward. . . . David Coubrough managing director of Portfolio, another recruitment consultant, believes that women themselves draw back from being ambitious. A salutary example is given by Joanna Foster of the Industrial Society which is thinking of organising a course, like some it has done for other industries, for women in catering management. A job advertised at £19,000 attracted no women applicants. When readvertised with a salary of £14,000 women applied.

(Stacey, 1987: 12)

Clearly this was not intended as a piece of investigative journalism. The motivations for Eckstein's comments (let alone justifications) receive no attention. Nor do Coubrough's views of women's lack of ambition receive critical attention. In fact, this article, published in the hospitality industry's professional association's house magazine, typifies only too well the problems with all discussions of women's lack of progress in terms of their own attitudes and aspirations – namely that to adopt such a stance is really to indulge in the politics of victim blaming. Blaming women themselves for their lack of progress conveniently diverts attention from the sexism of male-dominated social institutions and the lack of effort on the part of these institutions to take affirmative action to ensure equality in the treatment of male and female employees. Similarly, as Guerrier (1986) notes, blaming women in this context ignores the fact that any real lack of aspiration or ambition is a response to the perceived lack of opportunities rather than some form of innate disposition.

CONCLUSIONS

In distilling common themes from the literature on hotel and catering occupations three areas in particular spring to mind. The first is the pressure that hotel and catering workers at all levels operate under. This pressure may emanate from a need or desire to ensure adequate remuneration from informal rewards, from the erratic nature of demand for hotel and catering services, from the unreasonable demands of hotel and catering supervisors and managers or from the sheer drudgery of much of the work. Whatever its origins, stress is an ever-present feature of hotel and catering work and occurs in an environment of uncertainty. This leads to a second consideration, namely the extent to which occupational groups feel undervalued by both the general public and each another. The mutual suspicion that exists between different occupational groups in hotels and catering is often intense and contributes to the pressures felt by many workers. A third and much more general point is also a more obvious one. It is that there exists a need to adopt a wider perspective on hotel and catering occupations that takes into account divisions between workers based on factors such as gender. In most studies of hotel and catering occupations, women tend to be invisible and their experiences treated (usually implicitly) as being the same as those of men. The evidence considered in this and the previous chapter suggests that this is not the case. Given the number of women who work in the hotel and catering industry, there is more than ever a need to target differential as well as common experiences of men and women.

Finally, it is worth entering a further caveat about the limitations of a wholly occupation-based approach to the study of hotel and catering work (see Chapter 1). Clearly, some industry occupations, noticeably management and cooking, have particular patterns of recruitment and socialisation, career progression and strategies of professionalisation. A sense of occupational community is also evident. Some workers are clearly better off than others in terms of their conditions of employment and experience of work. Having said this, the literature reviewed in this chapter deals with only a small part of the hotel and catering industry. Many of those engaged for 'positive' reasons in certain occupations and who derive positive experiences from their work are not, in reality, necessarily better off in any absolute sense. It is easy to be seduced into a trap of simplistic relativism, to point out that one occupational group is better placed than another in the industry, enjoying better remuneration and conditions of work. It is also necessary to recognise however that, when compared to other industries, managerial and skilled workers in hotels and catering are subject to many of the processes of stress, conflict, low rewards and degradation experienced by the vast majority of the semi-skilled and unskilled workforce. The privileges of status and rank in the hotel and catering industry are still privileges but in many cases it is doubtful whether they are worth having. By focusing too readily on occupational differentiation in the industry, it is easy to obscure the many experiences shared, in varying degrees, by all members of the workforce, and in particular the experiences of exploitation and insecurity in employment faced no less by bosses than by their subordinates.

4 Issues and controversies in hotel and catering work I

Personnel management, labour turnover and the role of trade unions

This is the first of two chapters devoted to enduring issues and controversies in hotel and catering work. To refer to something as 'controversial'
is perhaps to dignify it with too great an importance. Controversy all too
often exists only in the minds of academics. This would be largely true of
topics like high rates of labour turnover, deskilling and work flexibility in
the hospitality industry (the last two are discussed in Chapter 5). In contrast,
the areas of personnel management and procedures and unionisation in
hotels and catering arouse strong feelings amongst academics, employers,
trade union leaders and officials and the workforce itself. Whatever the
case, all the topics examined here illuminate earlier themes and consolidate
understanding of the nature and experience of hotel and catering work.

PERSONNEL MANAGEMENT

Despite the existence of many textbooks on personnel management
designed specifically for hotel and catering students, very little has been
written on personnel practices in the industry. This is somewhat surprising
since many characteristics of work in hotels and catering have been
attributed to the lack of education in personnel management and/or the
inadequacy/total absence of professional personnel management in the
industry. The Commission on Industrial Relations (1971) found that few
hotel companies had an industrial relations or personnel policy. Johnson
(1978) argues that the personnel function in hotel and catering organisations is frequently marginalised. Often, the responsibility for personnel
lies with the unit manager who has little or no training in the field and
whose other responsibilities are so wide as to preclude effectiveness in all
areas. Indeed, a common phenomenon in the hotel and catering industry is
recruitment through internal contacts and word of mouth, though it is
difficult to assess whether this is a cause or consequence of limited
attention to the personnel function. In most circumstances then, personnel

matters take a lower priority than other management functions. A further difficulty in developing systematic procedures, Johnson argues, arises from the plethora of advice on personnel management that managers have to contend with. In many cases, advice from government agencies, professional and business organisations and textbooks appears contradictory and confusing and support for systematic personnel strategies from senior management in hospitality organisations is often lacking. Johnson suggests that many of the labour problems faced by the industry could be overcome if senior organisational and unit controllers took the personnel function seriously.

In a later study by Kelliher and Johnson (1987) reporting two surveys (the 'Ealing Study' and the 'Leeds Study') less than half (42 per cent) of the establishments surveyed in the Ealing Study employed a full-time personnel manager. The likelihood of finding a member of the hotel management team whose primary responsibility was personnel was closely related to the size of the unit, 96 per cent of hotels with more than 200 bedrooms employed a personnel manager, usually with executive status and often with a team of back-up specialists. In smaller establishments, personnel was delegated to a wide variety of people including the Managing Director, the Head Receptionist and, in one case, the General Manager's Secretary. In medium-sized hotels, responsibility for personnel tended to be devolved to assistant managers who performed the role along with other duties. The Leeds Study of ten hotels revealed that half of all personnel managers had never held a personnel position prior to their current job *or* had any formal training in personnel. Despite this, many felt confident in the role, often because they were able to rely on personnel instruction manuals issued by their companies. Many managers relied *very* heavily on these manuals, adhering to them rigorously rather than adapting procedures to meet their own circumstances, with the result that personnel management was highly simplistic and reactive in practice rather than strategic and systematic. The limited impact of personnel management in hotels is attributed by Kelliher and Johnson to the narrow way in which the personnel function is defined. The main activities of those employed in hotel personnel management were found to be recruitment and training, with 71 per cent of all the Ealing Study respondents identifying recruitment as the major personnel function and 63 per cent identifying training as a major activity. Again, training was seen to be more important by those in larger units. Welfare was considered an important personnel task in both small and large hotels but received less emphasis in the medium-sized unit, a polarisation the authors attribute to the paternalistic management style of the former (cf. Lowe, 1988) and the more sophisticated practices of the latter.

Further research by Croney (1988) both partially confirms the work of Kelliher and Johnson (1987) and highlights their naivety. Croney found that company support for personnel or human resource management at executive level bears no relation to the extent to which personnel management is practised at the unit level. The physical and communication distance between 'Head Office' and company units is such that the latter can largely negate corporate philosophies. Croney studied pay systems, recruitment and selection and employee participation in the management process in four hotel groups. In all cases he found considerable divergence between statements of corporate philosophy and/or the views of executive management, and the views and practices of managers at unit level. In the context of recruitment and training, even where formal personnel philosophies or procedures had been laid down at corporate level, most units followed informal procedures, laying particular emphasis on the role of line managers. Personnel managers' roles were frequently confined to effecting the decisions of hotel departmental heads and the preliminary interviewing of candidates for vacancies. More importantly, two of the hotel groups studied did not lay down any formal or systematic procedures for unit personnel management, devolving such responsibility to the units themselves. All but one of the hotel groups expressed positive corporate sentiments about the desirability of employee participation in the management of labour and pointed to the mechanisms that existed for facilitating involvement. Most of these schemes were management initiated and controlled, designed to foster a sense of common interest and not concerned with collective bargaining. At unit level, the implementation of employee participation schemes laid down by corporate management was undertaken with varying degrees of enthusiasm and compliance with company procedures and often initiated reluctantly and less frequently (if at all) than required by company guidelines.

In the light of the evidence from Croney's study it is unsurprising that Kelliher and Johnson (1987) obtained the results that they did. What is surprising is that they and others persist with the notion that better personnel management would reduce the extent of labour problems in the hotel and catering industry. Even Boella (1986), perhaps the UK's foremost exponent of the application of personnel techniques in hotels and catering, points out that the industry has been extremely backward in the application of professional personnel management to commercial hospitality operations. He argues, unconvincingly, that textbook development in this field has increased awareness of the role of personnel by the application of social scientific concepts (for a partial critique of this view see Wood, 1988). Even if it has, the personnel function remains largely ignored in hotel and catering organisations and there is little evidence to support the prognosis that it will become either more important in the future or more significantly, that the presence or absence of professional personnel management makes any fundamental difference to workers' experience of their employment.

LABOUR TURNOVER

⋊Labour turnover in the hotel and catering industry has been the subject of several detailed studies (Mars, Bryant and Mitchell, 1979; Johnson, 1980, 1981, 1985, 1986) as has labour mobility and labour movement more generally (Knight, 1971; Hotel and Catering Economic Development Committee, 1969; Riley, 1980, 1981a, 1981b, 1981c: Hotel and Catering Industry Training Board, 1983). All commentators are agreed upon one thing: labour turnover in hotels and catering is exceptionally high relative to other industries. Commonly quoted figures are an industry average of 70 per cent, though much higher unit rates are common, including figures of up to 300 per cent (Hotel and Catering Industry Training Board, 1983 and the University of Surrey, 1985: quoted in Byrne, 1986). Whilst agreement may exist on the level of labour turnover, there are two distinct views as to just how significant a problem it constitutes. The first sees labour turnover as problematic for the industry, the second regards high turnover as an unavoidable and even necessary and desirable feature of hotels and catering.

⋊ Researchers in the first tradition have identified several factors contributing to high labour turnover. Mars, Bryant and Mitchell (1979) report a study of twenty-one firms in nine principal categories of establishment. For them, labour turnover is 'probably the most common of the vicious circles encountered in hotel and catering work' (1979: 73) and in the first instance is best understood in terms of management attitudes. Their survey showed that managers of units with 'least troublesome' (*sic*) levels of labour turnover were, at best, disposed to trying to reduce it whilst those managers with high rates of turnover viewed the phenomenon as an industry-wide problem arising from factors external to their control. In the case of the former, several members of the sample were managers of small hotels who viewed control of labour turnover as a matter of personal skill and management style. A minority of managers viewed levels of labour turnover as a function of employment strategy. Mars, Bryant and Mitchell cite the example of an employer who successfully improved labour stability by employing those who evidenced stable social integration in preference to the 'marginal workers' supposedly typical of the hotel and catering workforce, for example by choosing married men with families rather than young singles (1979: 80). A further contingent of the sample were managers working in large units or in executive posts, many of whom expressed the view that excessive turnover was due to a failure or absence of personnel management policies, views which frequently led to expressions of sympathy with the aims of trade unions.

The work of Mars, Bryant and Mitchell has received empirical and theoretical support from other sources. Johnson (1981) also regards high turnover in the hotel and catering industry as problematic, affecting the quality of products and services, incurring significant replacement and recruitment costs and thus likely to affect profitability. He too argues that management fails to treat labour turnover as a priority problem, regarding it as 'normal' for the industry, but goes further in arguing that many managers frequently attempt to cast labour turnover in a *favourable* light by pointing to the flexibility it gives them in operational matters and the way in which turnover ensures recruitment of new blood. This last point gains credence in the light of hotel tycoon Lord Forte's remark that:

> The industry has been criticized for having a high turnover in staff, but this does not imply staff dissatisfaction. Statistics are distorted by the seasonable nature of a lot of our employment. Many people in our business only want to work for a part of the year, or part of the day or night, and the hotel and catering industry is thus ideally suited to them.
>
> (Forte, 1986: 122–123)

The concern expressed by Johnson and others about employers' attitudes to labour turnover is evidently well founded. The existence of indifferent management attitudes to labour turnover are, however, not in themselves *sufficient* for the explanation of labour instability. Rather, what is more important is how these attitudes translate into action.

In this respect, three factors are important. First is the tendency of hotel and catering managers to abdicate responsibility for their staff. Mars, Bryant and Mitchell (1979) suggest that the system of informal rewards (and especially tips) in the industry gives rise to a situation whereby the employee is working more for the customer than for management, increasing the stress on employees who find they have to function without management support. As a result workers may move on in the hope that the grass will be greener elsewhere, or alternatively they are prepared to tolerate job moves which may act as a temporary relief from frustration. Secondly, management attitudes operate at a far more concrete level. Management is heavy handed and dismisses employees for the most trivial of reasons. When taken with low pay and poor conditions, this drives workers from job to job in search of ever incremental improvements in their lot (Byrne, 1986). Thirdly, the dynamics of work groups themselves can influence labour turnover, whether because of competition between employees or a host of other reasons. Friction between workers is not unusual as the earlier discussion on inter-departmental conflict showed. Both Bowey (1976) and Mars, Bryant and Mitchell (1979) identify cases where conflict between workers in the form of harassment can make some employees' positions untenable. The latter cites the case of a manager who, experiencing high turnover amongst grill-bar staff, investigated to find that new female workers taken on as a result of expansion were being harassed by older female employees. The older workers had been in charge of the bar prior to expansion and resented the new appointees. When all the older women had left (an instance of turnover not explained by Mars and his colleagues!) they were replaced by a full-time manager and turnover was reduced.

The above accounts tend to ignore external factors influencing labour turnover, thereby reinforcing insular and personnel-oriented strategies to the 'problem' of labour instability. Perhaps the best example of this approach is the work of Johnson (1980, 1981, 1985) who focuses on labour turnover as a unit problem amenable to essentially unit-level solutions deriving from improved management technique, in the earliest of his reports remarking that 'the problem of high turnover in the hotel sector as a whole is nothing more than the sum total of the problems facing each and every individual unit' (Johnson 1980: 34). Johnson has provided some original insights into the nature and causes of labour turnover in hotel and catering organisations that are worthy of detailed consideration.

He begins by noting that in most hospitality organisations staff can be divided into two or three main groups on the criterion of propensity to leave (Johnson, 1981). At one extreme are the hard core of staff, stable and settled at work with long service to their credit. At the opposite extreme are the transient workers, those who frequently change jobs and rarely survive in a single organisation for any length of time. A third group of staff Johnson terms 'opportunists'. These have survived an induction period but have not yet joined the hard core. Traditionally, Johnson argues, the labour turnover problem has led researchers to focus on the transient workforce as the most economically damaging category of staff. Whilst not denying the importance of these workers in terms of mobility, he argues for more consideration of the processes that may influence the opportunists either to become part of the core or join the transients. He perceives the opportunists as caught between conflicting forces – encouragement to stay by hard core personnel and encouragement to seek alternative employment opportunities by transients. Johnson postulates that the strength of the opposing forces is directly proportional to the size of the core and transient groups, a hypothesis that leads him to recommend building up as large a core of staff as possible as a strategy for reducing turnover. Since hard core staff will most likely come from the opportunists it is necessary, Johnson suggests, to provide opportunities within the organisation for advancement, including training schemes, job rotation and worker participation – in other words to make fuller use of internal labour markets.

Sadly, Johnson's theoretical suggestions remain largely unelaborated. In a later study the preoccupation is still with turnover as an essentially unit level problem. Johnson (1985) found a strong positive correlation between labour turnover rates and staff:room ratios in a small sample of hotels. To a large extent, he argues, staff:room ratio is influenced by the quality of the hotel (e.g. its star rating) and indeed, a hierarchy of turnover rates was evident in the hotels surveyed. Thus the five-star hotel in the sample had two staff per room whereas the ratios for the three and four star units were 1:1.63 and 1:1.44 respectively, whilst the average annual turnover rates for the five-, four- and three-star units were 34 per cent, 89 per cent and 115 per cent. Possible reasons for the inverse relationship between star rating and turnover are advanced by Johnson and include the suggestion that job satisfaction is greater in higher class establishments, and status and total rewards may also be higher. More important, if staff:room ratio is regarded as a crude indication of average employee workload then the higher the workload the higher is turnover likely to be. Johnson suggests that occupancy rates did influence turnover in some instances (the higher the occupancy, the higher the turnover). This was damaging because when workers left a greater load fell on those remaining which led to further turnover. In other cases Johnson found that peaks of turnover occurred *after* peaks of occupancy indicating, he suggests, that employees who leave as a result of extra workload take some time to find a new post and/or work out their period of notice.

Perhaps Johnson's most interesting finding from this study concerns the nature of turnover amongst core and peripheral workers. In his earlier research Johnson (1980) identified the phenomenon of pulse turnover – long periods of stability in hotels' labour forces followed by periods where turnover rates increase dramatically. This turnover, he argues, was explicable in terms of the departure of core workers triggering the departure of peripherals – those dependent on the core worker(s) for preferential terms under individually negotiated contracts governing access to informal rewards – who either join the core worker in his or her new place of employment or become so unsettled as to leave for another establishment altogether. In his 1985 study, Johnson found that increases in occupancy and workload were insufficient to cause direct turnover amongst core workers since at times of crisis, the bargaining power of core workers was increased. Increased workloads do nothing for peripherals, however, only increasing their stress whilst leaving the effort–reward relationship untouched. In these circumstances, peripheral workers can leave in search of new employment, substantially eroding the power base of core workers whose value to management lies in their ability to negotiate individual contracts with subordinates and manage peripherals at times of crisis. When the power of the core worker declines to this extent, s/he is in danger of being diminished to peripheral status and thus leaves in order to restore core status elsewhere – what Johnson refers to as inverse pulse turnover.

For Johnson then, labour turnover is to be understood as a problem that can be tackled by managerial action at unit level. Like the Hotel and Catering Economic Development Committee (1969) and Mars, Bryant and Mitchell (1979) before him, Johnson regards excessive labour turnover as a blight. This puts him and others at odds with a second group of analysts who do not regard high turnover as particularly problematic, instead viewing it as both desirable and vital to the development of employee skills. Their position is neatly summarised by Bowey:

> High labour turnover should not always be seen as a major problem for this industry. It is, in some cases, a useful process by means of which a restaurant manager, particularly in a large restaurant, can adjust to seasonal changes in trade so maintaining a balance between the number of customers served. In this way, labour costs are lower and efficiency is higher than if he tried to maintain a constant labour force.
>
> (Bowey, 1976: 133)

Bowey goes on to argue that labour turnover not only allows management flexibility but facilitates skill acquisition. This is because careers in the restaurant industry are not normally perceived by employees in terms of promotion within a single establishment but in terms of a series of job changes whereby each post to which an employee moves is hoped/believed to be to a higher status establishment than before. From the skill angle, Bowey argues that the increased ritualisation associated with higher status establishments offers waiting staff the opportunity to gradually increase their repertoire of skills as well as the effort–reward relationship whereby more tips and other informal rewards are earned for less effort because the better clientele of the higher status establishments expect more personal attention in a more leisurely and relaxed atmosphere. Thus volume of trade and speed of service is lower but clients pay more and thus tip more.

Riley also begins from the premise that:

> No myth about the hotel and catering industry is more difficult to dispel than that of the all-pervading evil of high labour turnover. . . .The facts are indisputable: labour turnover is exceptionally high. . . .It is that around these enormous percentage figures has grown the belief that labour turnover is unexceptionally damaging.
>
> (Riley, 1980: 52)

Like Bowey, Riley argues that labour mobility plays an important role in the development of employee skills and that two sets of features emanating from industry structure encourage mobility. The first set contains those residing in the external labour and product markets which tend to draw individuals away from units. These essentially enabling or motivating factors include the nature of demand for labour, fluctuations in the product market, transferability of skills and the disproportionately high demand for managerial skills. Demand for labour, Riley argues, is a direct demand – wanted for what it can produce without intervening machinery. Demand for labour is thus linked directly to customers' tastes and purchasing power, with higher skills being demanded by greater purchasing power. From this, Riley adduces a hierarchy of skills closely corresponding to the product hierarchy, the graduation of which encourages mobility. The hierarchy is not rigid since the product market changes; consumer tastes and spending power change, individual units change their character, both these factors leading to overall changes in the product market if they occur on a sufficiently large scale. Transferability of skills is also an enabling factor in mobility since many skills are not only transferable between units but also between sectors (thus chefs can move between units but also between commercial and institutional sectors). The stimulus to acquire more skills and develop existing ones is further enhanced by the opportunities at managerial or proprietor level within the industry. Such occupations being multi-skilled in nature encourages mobility in the lower echelons of the labour market and there is, as noted earlier, no shortage of hospitality industry employees who aspire to run their own businesses or attain a management post.

The second set of structural features influencing labour mobility contains those relating to the internal labour market – these influences tend to force people out from within by limiting the scope for personal development, thus making mobility the only alternative for those seeking to develop their skills. The most important of these influences is the scope, or lack of it, for training within any single unit. Within any one unit there is an upper limit to training capacity and skill acquisition which to a large extent is set by the unit's market position, its size and the capacities and talents of management. An additional constraining factor on the development of skill at unit level is the rigid occupational structure. This inhibits the opportunity to develop skills within a unit and in order to gain diversity of experience mobility is necessary.

Riley's arguments are problematic at a variety of levels. For example, he tends to treat the workforce as more or less homogenous in terms of their aspirations and abilities. Not all workers are desirous of improving their skills: many are content with one particular job or type of job or are simply thankful for *any* job. More importantly, many workers are confined to local labour markets. The fact that most hotel and catering product and labour markets are essentially local in nature has two consequences. On the one hand it can mean that skill acquisition is limited by the structure of the local product market, on the other that mobility is a prerequisite to skill acquisition rather than a partial or total consequence of it. Thus the ability and willingness to leave an area in pursuit of 'necessary skills' is crucial to acquisition – people must have both freedom from constraints on their place of work *and* the possibility of bettering themselves. This view is supported by Knight (1971) who came to the conclusion that the hotel and catering workforce is perhaps best seen as 'a number of geographically separated localities with limited mobility between these areas' (Knight, 1971: 169). In fairness to Riley, for anybody familiar with the hotel and catering industry it is obvious that within specific geographical areas mobility does occur, often on a substantial scale. Whether this is invariably for the purpose of skill improvement is more doubtful.

A more fundamental objection to the Bowey/Riley perspective on labour turnover is the tendency to overestimate both the skill content of hotel and catering work and the scope and capacity for the application of skills. In terms of objective technical skill content the majority of hotel and catering jobs require only a limited amount of manipulative expertise – the exceptions to this being chef work and, arguably, those posts concerned with information technology (e.g. receptionist). At the same time, if, as Riley suggests, product, labour and skill markets are arranged hierarchically it is logical to posit that only a handful of workers can reach the apex of the hierarchy and the motivation for mobility in search of skill acquisition is thus diminished except in so far as these may involve changes of occupation or entail deliberate strategies to seek managerial appointments. One further criticism here arises from the work of Johnson (1985) and others (e.g. Mars, Bryant and Mitchell, 1979). This is to the effect that it is manifestly the case that there are, at unit level, influences which can be identified as reducing labour mobility. Mars, Bryant and Mitchell (1979) offer a case study of an eighty cover restaurant, Le Pays du Nord, where the proprietor had attempted (successfully it seems) to minimise labour turnover by (a) making arrangements for chefs appointed to the restaurant to move on at a mutually convenient time to a job of equal or more prestige; (b) avoiding recruitment of 'socially marginal' workers, instead favouring unemployed actors and actresses between jobs (though why such people should not be regarded as socially marginal is a mystery); and (c) practising multi-skilling through the flexible deployment of staff throughout all the restaurant's operations. This allegedly increased productivity and allowed payment of better than average wage rates. The authors do not tell us of the nature of the arranged movement of chefs but the example is not wholly satisfactory since chefs, being the most highly skilled hotel and catering workers, have perhaps more opportunities for mobility than most of their industry colleagues.

That a fundamental difference of emphasis exists between the two positions described above is beyond dispute. For example, Johnson (1981) recognises that taken to its logical conclusion, Riley's arguments (Riley, 1980) would suggest that active encouragement be given to labour turnover. Johnson and others reject this view on the grounds that reductions in labour turnover are achievable as a result of better management at unit level. Yet, it is evident from the work of Johnson (1981, 1985) and Mars, Bryant and Mitchell (1979) in their case study of the Le Pays du Nord that far from actually being able to reduce labour turnover by introducing new management attitudes, the best that can be achieved is greater control over the rate of leavings. This is a somewhat tenuous point but one that appears to have been underplayed in existing discussions.

The 'problem' of labour turnover in the hotel and catering industry remains a thorny one. Further research might abandon managerialist notions that labour turnover can be at least ameliorated by employing better personnel techniques or forecasting strategies. There is little suggestion that better management of labour turnover is, to the employer, any more cost or human resource effective than simple replacement of departing workers. Similarly, given the local nature of most hotel and catering labour markets, explanations of labour turnover rates in terms of drives to skill acquisition must be treated with equal caution. However, there are some grounds for believing that in the case of certain hotel and catering occupations, the *belief* amongst hotel and catering employees that skills can be enhanced by mobility within local or national labour markets is worthy of further investigation. Of some interest in this context would be more information on the circulation of labour. Whilst many people leave the industry altogether in any given period of time, many join allied industries such as retailing. Similarly, many persons who leave one sector of hotel and catering work take up employment in another. The Hotel and Catering Industry Training Board (1984b) found that the hotels and guest houses sector of the industry tended to be a predominant source of recruitment to other sectors. A more detailed analysis of intra-industry labour circulation might explore the motivations and circumstances of employees engaged in such movements.

An allied consideration here is the composition of mobile labour groups, particularly at the operative level. If the majority of labour markets for operative staff are local in character, then high rates of turnover amongst operatives merits analysis in terms of the history of personal mobilities. This view is reinforced by the suggestion that high rates of labour turnover can possibly be accounted for in terms of small numbers of workers moving frequently:

> Staff turnover seems to be, at least in part, a problem associated with individual workers. While 53 per cent of experienced catering workers have never held any job for less than 2 years, and a further 24 per cent none for less than 18 months; some 3 per cent have held no job for longer than 6 months. The high rates of staff turnover reported by some employers would seem to be associated with a small minority of employees experiencing a large number of short stays.

(Knight, 1971: 166)

Knight's statistical inferences are perhaps a little ambitious. However, discussion of labour turnover at both unit and sectoral levels in terms of core and peripheral workers has arguably disguised the relative heterogeneity of these groups. It would be interesting to establish the nature of movements in a local labour market, abandoning research programmes of turnover in individual hotels in favour of more complex longitudinal studies of particular locales and sectors.

It is important in ending this discussion to reiterate that for the most part, hotel managements and many hotel and catering workers do not appear to regard labour turnover as especially damaging. The two sides of the debate that characterise discussions of labour turnover have generated two different research agendas. For writers such as Johnson (1985) and Mars, Bryant and Mitchell (1979) the agenda is limited by research ideologies that attempt prescriptive 'solutions'. In the light of this, the views of writers like Bowey (1976) and Riley (1980) are liable to be more productive since they cast their analytic nets wider and carry less pre-formed assumptions as to the desirability or otherwise of high rates of labour turnover. In short, there have to be better reasons than already exist for regarding high labour turnover as a blight before research is directed towards problem-solving.

TRADE UNIONS

Given low pay and poor conditions of employment, it remains to outsiders one of the great enigmas of the hotel and catering industry that workforce unionisation is low – at least in the commercial sector. Figures for the latter reveal that overall union membership is just 6 per cent of the total labour force, some 57,000 employees in all (Byrne, 1986). The total is distributed amongst four unions: the Hotel and Catering Workers Union (HCWU – now simply referred to as the Hotel and Catering Union – a section of the General, Municipal, Boilermakers and Allied Trade Union – GMBATU or GMB) with 33,000 members; the TGWU (Transport and General Workers'

Union) with 12,000 members; the Union of Shop, Distributive and Allied Workers (USDAW) with 6,500 members (1984 figures) and the National Union of Railwaymen (NUR, now the National Union of Rail, Maritime and Transport Workers, or RMT) with 5,000 members (also 1984 figures) (Byrne, 1986). There are many reasons for low union density in the commercial hospitality industry. For convenience, they may be grouped under four headings: isolation and the ethos of hotel and catering work; structure of the workforce; the attitudes of employers to trade unionism; and the role of trades unions in the hotel and catering industry.

Isolation and the ethos of hotel and catering work

Riley (1985) argues that, historically, the development of UK accommodation services in the nineteenth century followed travel patterns with the consequence that London, semi-rural and coastal areas provided the focus for industry growth. Because of this, hotel workers were isolated from the mainstream of the urban working class and the subsequent development of industrial unionism. This geographical separation was reinforced by cultural separation. Early hotels embraced the values of domestic service. The practice of living-in, the long hours of work and close contact with management and guests encouraged insularity and separation from the wider community and isolation from traditional union values of solidarity, opposition to management and a dichotomous class view of society. Despite the fact that many of the outward trappings of domestic service have receded and the pattern of location of hotels become more widespread, Riley argues that the domestic service ethos persists and the dependence of workers upon management for preferment and the negotiation of individual rewards militates against opposition to management values. Similarly, close proximity to social superiors, whilst frequently generating resentment, also induces a desire to emulate. The dependence of many workers on clients for part of their remuneration gives rise to instrumentalism and thence to competition for resources and rewards. All these factors, discussed in earlier chapters, are compounded in organisations where the informal rewards elements of the payment package are well established, since it is in these organisations that employees tend to associate trade unionism with a 'debit effect', a phenomenon that will be returned to in the discussion of trade unions below. Riley (1985) argues that the individualistic ethics of the workforce are complemented by a view common to both workers and unions that service employment is not necessarily compatible with trade unionism (see also Macfarlane, 1982a, 1982b and Wood and Pedlar, 1978). For trade unions, he suggests, the value attributed to an occupation is important to solidarity. Traditionally, trade unions are linked to industries that produce material items. Thus, service work is not highly valued. Further, making things is inseparably associated with a masculine ethos. Pronounced masculinity is a defining characteristic of industrial trade unionism and service industries may be seen as effete in traditional union terms.

The issue of geographical separation and isolation in inhibiting successful union organisation should not be overlooked. The hotel and catering industry comprised as it is of many small and geographically widespread units makes recruitment difficult in at least two senses. First, the financial cost associated with organising labour can be prohibitive. Secondly, the small size of units is not always compatible with trade unions' conventional modes of organisation. For example, one small hotel or restaurant may not justify a single union branch and the natural response to this is to organise several units into a branch. This may present workers with difficulties as mundane as securing transport to union meetings. Trade unions' failure to develop an administrative structure suitable to the organisation of the industry will also be returned to later in this discussion.

Structure of the workforce

Whilst the ethos of individualism and competitiveness endemic to hotels is a major barrier to effective unionisation, the structure and organisation of employment in the industry is also an important variable in this context for, as noted earlier, the emphasis within the industry on individualism is buttressed by lack of security in employment and the structure of employment opportunities.

First, part-time workers are traditionally viewed as difficult to recruit and organise (Mars and Mitchell, 1977; Byrne, 1986). Frequently, part-time workers are employed on shift systems, feel themselves (or are made to feel themselves) outsiders and do not always have regular contact with their colleagues. Lack of cohesion within the workplace can lead them to question the value of unions as well as reducing any sense of solidarity – often an important precondition for effective union organisation. Motivation to join a trade union may be further diminished because of (in Britain at least) a legislative structure that denies part-timers many rights that accrue to full-time staff: part-time workers employed for less than sixteen hours a week are disenfranchised from many employment rights, and this is hardly a basis for fostering collectivism.

Secondly, many part-time workers are women and women have often felt neglected by the trade union movement. Until recently, it was part of union mythology that women are often unwilling to join unions and to act collectively (Mars and Mitchell, 1977). Byrne (1986) points out that in order to combat feelings of neglect, unions such as the GMB (parent organisation of the Hotel and Catering Workers' Union) have campaigned to ensure that part-timers are incorporated within the collective bargaining process by the creation of set objectives for part-time employees. What is unclear is the extent to which these strategies further ghettoise part-time workers, and in particular women. Many female catering employees are on record as having mixed views about unions. In one of his case studies of the catering industry Gabriel reported that:

> The women's complaints against the managers' arrogance were compounded by the feeling that they were entirely ignored by the union. They all belonged to one of the general unions as part of a closed-shop agreement.
>
> (Gabriel, 1988: 84)

This grievance took specific forms as the following quotations show:

> Working in catering you feel sometimes that your job lacks dignity. Kitchen ladies and catering staff generally are treated as inferior people by everyone. The unions don't do enough to improve our conditions or status. Within the union we are second-class citizens.
>
> (Gabriel, 1988: 85)

> Because we are part-time and all women they don't take us seriously. They don't come to talk to us and we never seem to get anywhere with them. They never follow up our suggestions; they say 'We'll see what we can do' when problems arise but never do anything.
>
> (Gabriel, 1988: 87)

If part-time workers present unions with problems of organisation then the same is true, thirdly, of seasonal and casual workers. Seasonal workers have no obvious rational reason to join a union for a short, set period. Casualisation is one of the biggest problems facing unionisation in the hotel and catering industry, being one of the forms of 'flexible working practice' that appeals to employers. Casuals have many advantages. They are often available for work at short notice and can therefore help employers plug gaps caused by fluctuations in the demand for services. Often, casual workers like many part-time workers earn less than is required for the payment of National Insurance contributions and are not registered for tax purposes. On both counts, casuals can undercut the wages of permanent full- and part-time staff and are reluctant to engage in wage bargaining with union involvement. Also, as Byrne (1986) notes, some companies who *do* enter into union agreements allow bargaining only for permanent staff thus maintaining the possibility of a two-tier workforce with one group being able to undercut the pay of the other.

A fourth problem that makes for difficulties in unionisation is labour turnover. Agreements between hotel and catering managements and trade unions often confine the latter to certain areas in worker representation. A central issue is often pay and bargaining rights: recognition of the union to participate in collective bargaining is frequently made conditional upon it maintaining a specific number of members within a company/unit. The high rates of turnover that prevail in the industry can make maintenance of a core membership difficult. Employers can play on this by encouraging mobility either directly (mobility within the company) or indirectly (by adopting the stance described earlier whereby labour turnover is regarded fatalistically and thus few efforts are made to sustain a core of workers). High labour mobility can also make it difficult for a union to build up a team of shop stewards. Many hotel companies stipulate that only those who have worked for a unit (or sometimes the company) for a set period of time – often one year – will be accepted as shop stewards.

Many barriers to unionisation can be seen to derive from the structure of the hotel and catering workforce. In the remainder of this discussion, attention focuses on the two slices of bread in the unionisation sandwich: employers and the unions themselves, with a view to examining the effects of the activities of each on the propensity or otherwise of hotel and catering workers to join a trade union.

Management and employer attitudes towards trade unionism

Despite frequent protestations to the contrary, there can be little doubt that the attitudes of most hospitality industry employers towards trade unions are hostile. The point is well illustrated by reference to the National Economic Development Office's report *Manpower policy in the hotel and restaurant industry – research findings* (Hotel and Catering Economic Development Committee, 1975). This report by the Manpower Working Group (*sic*) of the Economic Development Committee for Hotels and Catering, carried a foreword by the Director-General of NEDO that contained the following remarks:

> Some management representatives nominated by the BHRCA to represent the hotel and restaurant sectors of the industry have asked it to be made known that their acceptance of the report is subject to certain comments and reservations. . .they note that the report recommends that 'staff should be encouraged to join a trade union where they wish to do so' in order to encourage the development of collective bargaining. They cannot accept that management should be expected to do more than respect the right of staff to join a trade union.
>
> (Hotel and Catering Economic Development Committee, 1975: ix)

The sentiments of the BHRCA – British Hotels, Restaurants and Caterers' Association – are echoed and extended by Lord Forte of Trusthouse Forte plc in his autobiography:

> I will not allow the unions to bully our management or staff, or tell us how to treat our employees. Moreover, I do not recognise or approve of the concept of two sides of industry. It is the manager's sole responsibility to see that his staff are properly looked after and happy in their work.

(Forte, 1986: 123)

Later in his book, Forte argues that unions' interests do not necessarily coincide with those of employees, that trade union activity can subvert management communications with staff and that union tactics can on occasion be underhand and akin to bullying. It would be difficult for even the most objective of academic commentators to describe Lord Forte's attitudes as encouraging, yet management attitudes towards unions are not always as honestly expressed.

Macfarlane (1982a, 1982b) draws on the work of Bain (1970) to analyse employer strategies towards unions. Bain studied white-collar trade unionism and found that white-collar employers advanced a number of reasons as to why trade unionism was inappropriate to their organisations. These included, *inter alia*, the view that the company was better able than any outside organisation to look after its employees; that the terms and conditions of employment observed by the company were comparable to or better than those negotiated by unions; and that unions were simply inappropriate to the firm or industry in question and would have serious consequences in terms of the restrictions that would be placed on management's decision making capacities. Further, trade unions would entail the introduction into the organisation of a basis for divided loyalties amongst employees and increase the scope for conflict between management and staff. Bain found that on the basis of these beliefs, many employers pursued strategies to discourage employees from joining a union. These included methods of 'peaceable competition' such as granting salary increases during a trade union recruitment campaign, creating special benefit schemes, consolidating and extending the rewards of loyal employees and establishing company unions. Alternatively, employers used methods of 'forcible opposition' – for example, passing over union members for promotion or pay rises, attending union recruitment meetings in order to note the names of those attending and the outright dismissal of key union members. Bain also found that employers adopted restrictive policies in their relationships with union officials, particularly in respect of conceding recognition of unions in terms of the representativeness of the union organisation. As noted earlier, such representativeness is normally established by the maintenance of a minimum membership of the union, the level of which is a matter for negotiation between employer and union. Employers can thus adopt 'difficult' attitudes in the agreement of such a level (Macfarlane, 1982a: 35–36; see also Macfarlane, 1982b).

There are many instances from the hotel and catering literature that support Bain's findings and consolidate Macfarlane's claim that the hospitality industry exhibits many characteristics of white-collar employment. The Commission on Industrial Relations (CIR) (1971) found that trade union officials felt managements to be generally hostile to trade unionism, and the Commission itself encountered one strongly anti-union manager and four others who are recorded as having reservations. The Commission noted that 'Those who were against unions mainly seemed to fear strikes and demarcation disputes and the loss of total control over their staff' (Commission on Industrial Relations, 1971: para. 167). Similarly, Wood and Pedlar (1978) in their study of a strike at the Trusthouse Forte owned Grosvenor Hotel in Sheffield argue that the manager:

> pursued a policy of subversive rejection under a guise of neutrality. Episodes such as the payment of Christmas bonuses and other rewards to 'loyal' employees; the ending of live-in accommodation and the widely differing values put upon this; the inviting in of the lady dismissed from the Town Hall for refusing to join NALGO point to something other than neutrality.
>
> (Wood and Pedlar, 1978: 34)

Wood and Pedlar (1978) also draw on Bain's work and point out that in the case of the Grosvenor dispute, 'peaceable competition' and 'forcible opposition' overspilled into actual discrimination. In fact, outright attack on union members and union officials is perhaps not so uncommon a tactic as one might suppose. In their account of their Savoy Hotel strike of 1946 Dronfield and Soto (1980) note that the leader of the unofficial shop stewards' committee involved in the dispute, Frank Piazza, was suspended from duty some eight days after the dispute was ended with the involvement of the union in March 1947. Subsequently he was dismissed and after a drawn out dispute including further strike action, the union (the General and Municipal Workers Union) acceded to an offer by the Savoy to reinstate all strikers who had come out in sympathy for Piazza except the man himself (Dronfield and Soto, 1980: 29–30). Another more general example of victimisation of a union member is cited in Byrne (1986):

> Paul, a HCWU member, working for Berni Inns, had left his workplace momentarily to check the safety of his bike, which was parked outside,

because he was worried about vandalism in the area. On his return, the Assistant Manager acted in an extremely abusive manner, swearing and accusing him of having been out for a quick pint. When the worker tried to respond he was sacked. The union organised a meeting with the company under the auspices of ACAS [Advisory, Conciliation and Arbitration Service]. The outcome was that, not only did the worker receive compensation, but the company, in a tacit admittance of guilt, transferred the Assistant Manager.

(Byrne, 1986: 52-53)

Evidence from Croney's study of the 'fit' between labour and industrial relations policies of hotel groups at corporate and unit level reinforces the foregoing evidence (Croney, 1988). The study covered four groups. The corporate response to trade unionism in Groups One and Two was hostile. In Group Two Croney's respondent noted that when the company acquired a new hotel in which there existed a union agreement, the agreement was terminated and union recognition withdrawn (Croney, 1988: 55). In contrast, the corporate managers of Groups Three and Four evidenced a sympathetic approach to unions. In Group Three a collective agreement existed between the company and the Hotel and Catering Workers' Union covering recognition and procedures in a document accessible to all unit managers. A similar agreement with the same union existed in Group Four. However, at unit management level, Croney found a somewhat different picture as far as hotels in all groups were concerned. A positive approach to 'human relations' was offered by a manager in a hotel unit of Group One though there was an acknowledgement of the fact that trade union membership was not encouraged. In a unit of Group Two the manager confirmed company hostility towards trades unions and clearly viewed those who wanted to join a trade union as trouble makers (Croney, 1988: 59). In units of Groups Three and Four the existence of collective trade union agreements was irrelevant since neither of the units studied had union members on their payroll. Indeed, the manager of the unit in Group Three asserted that management–employee communication was directed to ensuring that employees were aware of management's view and authority.

Managers have vested interests in perpetuating an environment in which their power and authority goes largely unquestioned. To a large extent, the work of researchers like Croney (1988) demonstrates that despite corporate policy, the flexibility allowed unit management permits individual managers to pursue their own, often contrary strategies. This creates a further dilemma for unions keen to recruit hospitality industry workers, for it raises questions about whether they would better direct their efforts towards executive or unit management level.

The activities of trade unions

Dronfield and Soto (1980) have argued that the history of trade union organisation in the hotel industry prior to 1945 was one of failure, with membership never exceeding 2,000. The success of hotel and catering unionism has, arguably, been only more marginally successful in the period since. It is undoubtedly the case that the behaviour of unions themselves has been a major contributing factor to their poor showing in hotels and catering. The key to understanding these problems lies first in analysis of trade unions' handling of industrial disputes, for as the Commission on Industrial Relations (CIR) (1971) noted:

> In the past, trade union growth in hotels, albeit on a very small scale, has mainly come about through the use of industrial action, and recognition of a trade union has usually been obtained when an hotel has been involved in an industrial dispute.
>
> (Commission on Industrial Relations, 1971: para. 171)

In the post-war period, the first major hotel dispute of any significance took place at the Savoy Hotel in 1946–47 in the context of rapid growth in membership of the London Catering Branch of the General and Municipal Workers Union (GMWU, later to become GMBATU which spawned the Hotel and Catering Workers Union or HCWU) from five hundred members in March 1946 to 13,000 members a year later. The London Branch operated on the basis of building up strong workplace organisation in the belief that successful unionisation and union effectiveness centred on direct action led by shop stewards with close day-to-day contact with members (Dronfield and Soto, 1980: 28–29). Its strategy was to focus on one establishment where they had or could build strong membership and organisation and then take action to gain union recognition. In October 1946 the union membership of the Savoy Hotel came out on strike for recognition and there was sympathy action in the rest of the company – at Claridges and Simpson's in London – and in other non-company hotels and some small restaurants. There was also support from non-industry workers who refused to cross picket lines. The management of the Savoy capitulated after eight days and recognised the union but insisted that the dispute be called off before any terms of agreement had been settled. The union agreed and it took till the following March for an agreement to be worked out. Shortly after agreement had been reached, the Savoy suspended the leader of the unofficial shop stewards' committee, an action met by a second strike. The GMWU attempted to resolve this dispute through legal and quasi-legal channels, convincing the strikers to return to work. The basis of the return to work was agreement between the British Hotels, Restaurants and Caterers' Association and the union that the shop stewards' leader, Piazza, should be reinstated after two weeks suspension, a decision in fact ignored by the Savoy who converted suspension to dismissal. A subsequent strike ballot was organised in which the membership again voted for action. Two days before the strike was due to begin however, the Ministry of Labour set up a Court of Inquiry and asked the union to defer the strike: the union's preference for using legal channels won over and the Savoy membership was asked not to strike. The workers, ignoring the request, came out on unofficial strike and were all promptly sacked, the union being forced to make the strike official the following day. Support was widespread but not as effective as in the earlier dispute. This latest dispute – in November 1947 – met with some resistance from the Savoy. On the 24 November, the Court of Inquiry confirmed an earlier decision of the National Arbitration Tribunal to reinstate Piazza which the Savoy ignored. Four days later, the Savoy offered to reinstate all strikers except Piazza to which the General Secretary of the union, now handling negotiations personally, agreed without consulting the striking workers or officials. Subsequently, the union suspended the London Catering Branch official, all members of the branch committee and all but one of the regional committee. By December 1948, union membership had slumped to about 2,000 workers – mainly in hotels where unions had some experience of negotiation with management (Dronfield and Soto, 1980: 29–30).

The Savoy dispute demonstrates differences in strategy between senior union executives and 'grassroots' officials and members. The GMWU attempted to work within the law, using time-consuming legal channels that sapped the morale of the workers, allowed employers to recover from initial shock tactics and, more importantly, led to a turnover in membership that reduced the union's strength. The Savoy dispute indicates that resistant management and inflexible executive-level union activity can have a profound impact on union membership and success. Success in unionising the hotel industry has, as a result of the actions of unions themselves, been characterised by glaring own goals. Perhaps the most illuminating of these is the fiasco that occurred in the Torquay hotel industry in the late 1960s (Commission on Industrial Relations, 1971; Mars and Mitchell, 1976; Airey and Chopping, 1980).

Torquay, the popular coastal resort in Devonshire famed for its palm trees and situation on a charming bay and known because of its warm south-westerly location as the 'English Riviera', seems an unlikely location for hotel and catering disputes. Indeed, the Commission on Industrial Relations (CIR) (1971) noted:

In Torquay, there is a higher proportion of GMWU members amongst hotel workers than in any other urban area in the country, and the union say that there were 531 members there in September 1970. In this area the union branch and the Torquay Hotels Association have operated a joint negotiating committee since 1968 which meets every quarter. . .to discuss a number of matters. . .including. . .a sickness benefit scheme and sleeping accommodation standards.

(Commission on Industrial Relations, 1971: para. 160)

This seemingly idyllic picture of management–union relationships in fact came about as a result of damaging inter-union competition and not a little Machiavellian strategy on the part of employers. The actual history is rather confused but the key events appear to have been as follows (see Mars and Mitchell, 1976; Commission on Industrial Relations, 1971; Airey and Chopping, 1980).

The recruitment of Torquay hotel workers by the TGWU in 1966 and 1967 led, in August 1967, to strikes for recognition in the Palace and Grand Hotels, strikes which appear to have been resolved (Commission on Industrial Relations, 1971: para. 161). In early 1968, recognition was sought for TGWU members at the Torbay Hotel and in January members were brought out on strike for recognition and the TGWU blacked the hotel, preventing oil supplies from being delivered (Commission on Industrial Relations, 1971: para. 162). According to Mars and Mitchell (1976) the strike for recognition at the Torbay Hotel was at least in part inspired by the action of employers who, concerned not only with the growth of unionism in general in the area but with the particular role of the TGWU, sought to involve the GMWU, the union *employers* preferred but also the union recognised under earlier inter-union and union-employer agreements as the appropriate union for hotel and catering workers (Mars and Mitchell, 1976; Commission on Industrial Relations, 1971; Airey and Chopping, 1980). This type of employer strategy is not unusual. In circumstances where unionism seems unavoidable, employers will often strike bargains with favoured unions. These 'sweetheart' agreements may or may not be contrived with the connivance of the union in question but usually represent to the employer the lesser of two evils. In the case of the Torbay Hotel, Mars and Mitchell suggest, management invited the district organiser of the GMWU to recruit in the hotel and the organiser did in fact succeed in obtaining some members. It was recognition of the GMWU and not the TGWU that contributed to the Torbay dispute which, however, seemingly fizzled out because the employers were able to ride out the strike, operating with the help of some non-striking workers (Mars and Mitchell, 1976: 21). This was seemingly not before several other hotels in the area had been involved in the dispute and the owners of one of these, the Imperial, issued a writ against TGWU officials and subsequently obtained a court injunction preventing the TGWU from placing an embargo on the delivery of oil supplies (Palmer, 1968; CIR, 1971).

The damaging competition between the TGWU and the GMWU in Torquay seems to have led to an improvement in the relationship between the two unions, though it was not until the early 1970s that a formal agreement between them, regulating recruitment areas, was achieved. This came about as a result of the activities of the so-called International Branch of the TGWU, which had its origins in a community group for Portuguese political refugees. Concerned with the plight of Portuguese catering workers, this community association gathered together some fifty hotel and catering employees to join the TGWU, which they did in 1972. Within months, their membership had risen to over 1,500, attracting many Spanish, Greek and Turkish workers (Macfarlane, 1982a). The success of the TGWU affiliated International Branch was seemingly due to flexibility of organisation: branch meetings were held in several languages and at times when reasonable attendances could be guaranteed. The strategy of the International Branch was to concentrate on particular companies and undertake intensive recruitment drives, in the latter case relying on the fact that often, specific migrant groups were concentrated in specific companies (Dronfield and Soto, 1980; Macfarlane, 1982a). Once membership had been built, efforts were made to achieve recognition for the union. These strategies proved relatively successful, particularly with the Grand Metropolitan group of hotels, then the second largest hotel company in the country. After recruiting sufficient members at several Grand Metropolitan hotels, demands for recognition were made but allegedly met with threats of hostility to union recruiters and migrant workers (in the case of the latter these supposed threats took the form of suggesting that work permits would not be renewed). Eventually, a shop steward was sacked at one of the hotels which brought about a two month dispute, the resolution of which was in part seemingly influenced by the signing of another sweetheart agreement between Grand Metropolitan and the GMWU, giving the latter full recruitment rights. TGWU membership was rapidly eradicated in the wake of this agreement. The bitterness that followed led to the signing of a 'spheres of influence' agreement in 1973 between the TGWU and the GMWU, designed to eliminate competition for members and foster instead co-operation in unionising the industry. The 'spheres of influence' pact was essentially a carve-up of who could recruit where and in what company/ sector of the industry. The TGWU secured the right to recruit in several large London hotels and many restaurants and restaurant chains in London whilst the superiority of the GMWU elsewhere remained guaranteed (Johnson and Mignot, 1982). The spheres of influence agreement can be seen as an attempt by the central union authorities to reassert control over the rank and file (cf. Macfarlane, 1982b). The International Branch were reportedly unhappy with the agreement's restriction on their recruitment activities. In 1976, the TGWU reorganised its branches around individual companies and establishments and the International Branch did not survive, its members being siphoned into new branches (Macfarlane, 1982a). According to Dronfield and Soto (1980), the TGWU's arguments for this change were based on the claim that the International Branch had become too unwieldy and trade union organisation along racial lines was divisive. As with the spheres of influence agreement however, it appears that the reorganisation of branches was a way for the TGWU to reassert its authority as a result of losing control over a form of worker organisation it experienced as threatening.

Subsequent to the spheres of influence agreement and prior to the disbanding of the International Branch a number of other disputes similar to those described at Torquay and in London with Grand Metropolitan took place (see for example Macfarlane, 1982a, 1982b; Dronfield and Soto, 1980: 32–33). One study that deserves particular attention is that by Wood and Pedlar (1978) of the strike at the Grosvenor Hotel, Sheffield, between 15 December 1976 and 2 June 1977. These authors studied the Grosvenor strike from the perspective of all four groups of interested participants by means of interviews, the transcripts of which were resubmitted to the interviewees for verification and, as necessary, redrafted/corrected. Around this fourfold account the authors construct a chronological history of the dispute – the 'factual account'. From an illustrative point of view, the details of the strike are in fact of less interest here than the beliefs expressed by interested parties about the behaviour and alleged behaviour of other participants.

The first participant was the strike committee who claimed that a change of management in 1975 was at the root of disharmony. Specific grievances included demands by management for extra effort on the part of employees (instead of taking on extra staff); a stop to overtime pay and its replacement by a scheme whereby employees were expected to take time off in lieu at times stipulated by management; low wages; a refusal to pay a £6 a week pay rise; uncertainty over the destination of the service charge; and in order to keep their jobs, the stipulation that chambermaids take one day off per week without pay. When a decision was taken to approach a union, the TGWU was chosen in preference to the GMWU since the latter was the union favoured by the Grosvenor's proprietors, Trusthouse Forte (THF). Despite 102 out of 120 full-time employees being recruited to the TGWU, the Grosvenor refused to recognise the union. The strike committee claimed that management began a vendetta when live-in accommodation was withdrawn in September 1976: a ploy to split up union members in the eyes of the committee but justified by management on the grounds of the accommodation being required for renovation prior to letting to guests.

After a meeting between management and the union in October 1976, the strike committee was optimistic that progress towards resolving grievances had been made: a draft procedural agreement had been posted, though including management's view that membership of the union should be at 50 per cent before a closed shop and wage bargaining could be included in the agreement. On 13 December a spontaneous and arguably disorganised meeting produced a secret ballot showing a vote of fifty-five to twenty-seven in favour of a strike. Throughout this period of the dispute, the TGWU had sought the help of the Advisory, Conciliation and Arbitration Service (ACAS). The draft agreement of October, on which it had not proved possible to make progress because of management's insistence on the closed shop and pay bargaining elements, had led ACAS to be once again called in – it in fact set a meeting for 20 December that subsequently came to nothing since management did not change its position. On 15 December however, two days after the vote, a strike began and the hotel was enthusiastically and controversially picketed. On this day a letter was despatched by taxi to the homes of all strikers offering an unconditional invitation to return to work. A few staff accepted, but the hotel management in any case brought in assistance from other hotels. At Christmas time, when the strike was still young, those employees still working were given a £5 bonus and taxis to and from work, actions the strike committee argued were unprecedented and designed to subvert the dispute. After Christmas, difficulties developed as the union leadership refused a national blacking of THF – inaction that seemed to cause a lowering of morale. Many workers drifted away from the picket line into other jobs.

On 24 December, with the agreement of the non-striking employees a second letter was despatched to the strikers offering reemployment with THF provided they accepted that the TGWU was not recognised by the Grosvenor, that they would not take part in further unofficial industrial action (the company regarded the strike as unofficial because the union was not recognised) and upon acceptance of a three-month probationary period after which previous service with the company would be regarded as continuous. Again, a few workers accepted this offer, which was open until 29 December, after which those still on strike were deemed by the company to have been sacked – some forty-one or forty-six workers in all depending on whether the hotel management's figure or that of the strike committee was accepted.

The second viewpoint considered by Wood and Pedlar is that of the manager, who saw the dispute as occurring because of the failure of the union to control its members. For some months before the strike there had been talks between management, union and ACAS on union recognition but deadlock centred around the issue of the closed shop which the manager claimed, on the basis of his own survey of employee opinion, that no worker wanted. According to the manager, the early weeks of the strike were chaotic and marred by threats of violence from pickets, many of whom were, he claimed, non-employees. The manager claimed that morale amongst non-striking employees improved as a result of something approaching a 'Dunkirk spirit', an attitude picked up by Wood and Pedlar in their interviews with non-striking staff. Management had also organised a secret ballot of the non-strikers, held under the auspices of the Electoral Reform Society, and asking 'Do you want to be represented in negotiations with the management by the T & GWU?'. Of the 134 staff not on strike some 106 voted, ninety-seven 'No' and only nine 'Yes', a result that the manager felt vindicated his position. At the same time, he did concede that there had been a tightening up of efficiency under the stewardship of the hotel by THF but denied his actions were confrontational. The manager adamantly denied that the conversion of employee accommodation was a recent development; planned for some two years, it had just happened to coincide with increased union activity. In general, the manager felt that the dispute at the Grosvenor was part of a concerted effort by the TGWU to organise THF hotels, deliberately planned to disrupt the lucrative Christmas trade. In support, he cited the case of a similar dispute taking place at the THF owned Randolph Hotel in Oxford.

The Electoral Reform Society Ballot result was announced on 14 February. Prior to this, a second abortive meeting under the auspices of ACAS had been held by THF and the TGWU (on 19 January) and many of the non-striking employees had on 27 January sent a letter to the TGWU Official proferring mass resignation from the union. They also petitioned the union's leader, Jack Jones, asking that the pickets be removed. At about this time Parliament became involved and the Prime Minister refused a request that THF be boycotted by Ministers and Departments whilst suggesting that THF should recognise union membership. A further meeting supervised by ACAS was held between the two parties to the dispute: it was again abortive, THF withdrawing because they felt unfairly represented. A further meeting after the Electoral Reform Society Ballot of 14 February was similarly inconclusive.

The point of view of the union official was that contact with the hotel management had been difficult from the start and it was only until ACAS stepped in initially that the hotel would discuss recognition of the union's members: prior to this, the overtures of the official had been ignored, letters not replied to, telephone calls not returned and so on. This led the official subsequently to feel that the strike was, at least in part, attributable to the active hostility of the company towards the union and his feelings were confirmed by the attitude of the hotel manager and the never-ending meetings between union and company over the recognition issue, meetings which at their heart were concerned with THF's resistance to the idea of the closed shop. So anti-union were the company, he suggested, that they ignored the advice of ACAS to the effect that the second letter sent to striking workers offering a return to work on condition of non-participation in any further unofficial industrial action was a potential breach of the law, as to accept it would be to form part of the contract of employment. The union official felt that the dispute was winnable but that attitudes had been hardened by the standard of media reporting. Further, victory in the dispute could, in the view of the official, be achieved only at a cost of great inconvenience to the public, and to public opinion of the union.

The final viewpoint considered in the study was that of the non-striking employees – in essence three workers who seemingly made themselves accessible for interview: the Head Housekeeper, the Head Waiter and a room-maid. These staff objected to the way in which the original strike ballot had been organised and in particular the fact that not all those eligible to vote had been able to do so. It was argued that the TGWU did not understand the hotel and catering industry and that the strike weapon was inappropriate in any case for a service industry and constituted a misuse of power. The strikers were seen as dupes, not understanding why they were on strike and generally misguided, whilst the shop stewards were viewed as incompetent, having mishandled the genuine grievances of the staff. These three workers felt that, not withstanding the unpleasantness engendered by the picket line, life and work at the hotel had improved since the strikers had gone out.

On 30 May, the Grosvenor dispute technically ended with an agreement acceptable to the strikers and other parties. This entailed *ex-gratia* payments to strikers calculated on the basis of weekly hours worked, favourable consideration for strikers in any application they made for vacancies with the company and recognition by THF that the TGWU had the right to represent on an individual basis any members employed by the company. The strike at the Grosvenor illustrates many of the points raised earlier in the discussion of trade unionism in hotels and catering. Wood and Pedlar (1978) argue that the TGWU showed a lack of leadership. However, the authors demonstrate well the full range of problems that characterise industrial relations in the hospitality industry: management intransigence and manipulation, union incompetence, the reluctance of many workers to strike and so on. Wood and Pedlar's methodology also highlights the tendency for disputes to centre on recognition issues.

In the hotels sector at least, recognition disputes or issues attendant upon them are still at the root cause of industrial relations problems. The trade magazine *Caterer and Hotelkeeper* (15 December 1988) reported that the TGWU was picketing the Churchill Hotel in London in protest against poor conditions of employment and draconian management. The management unsurprisingly denied both charges stating that (a) the TGWU were employing 'bullyboy tactics'; (b) the picket did not consist of *bona fide* hotel staff; and (c) the hotel would not recognise the TGWU but workers would be allowed to elect their own representatives to sit on a committee with management. In the following year, *Caterer and Hotelkeeper* (1 June 1989: 13) reported that the TUC (Trades Union Congress) had withdrawn its one hundred room booking from the Imperial Hotel, Blackpool. The TUC who were holding their annual Congress meeting in Blackpool during September were unwilling to stay in a hotel that under its new proprietors – Trusthouse Forte again – had failed to honour an agreement with the GMB that operated under the previous owners. Three other THF acquisitions were also reported as having been 'blacked' for similar reasons. An earlier and slightly different case is perhaps more disturbing, though it did not lead to a dispute. In 1987, the Scottish based Stakis hotel group gave notice to the Hotel and Catering Workers' Union that it intended to withdraw from the main part of a longstanding agreement with the union. As reported in the *Guardian* newspaper (17 April 1987) the agreement covered 4,000 workers and withdrawal stemmed from attempts by the union in the previous year to resist attempts during wages negotiations to (allegedly) worsen the conditions of workers. The company claimed that the union represented only 15 per cent of staff and had in fact failed to negotiate the previous year's pay deal. The story was taken up the following day in the national (Scottish) newspaper the *Glasgow Herald* (18 April 1987). Here, the HCWU was reported as claiming that Stakis were tearing up a national agreement covering all its 3,500 employees to which the company allegedly responded that only 574 members in the company were represented by the union and that company proposals on pay and conditions had been accepted by a majority of its staff consultative committees. In this case, the withdrawal from negotiations over pay and related conditions was seen by the union as an attempt to exploit the Wages Act of 1986 by paying workers under the age of twenty-one less than other employees.

From the foregoing accounts it is clear that trade unions in the hotel and catering industry have far from acquitted themselves well in their approach to the problems of hospitality industry workers. Riley's point that, in many ways, trade unions are ill-equipped for effective action in the hotel and catering industry, both in terms of an ideological bias towards manufacturing and in the ways in which union organisation reflects this bias seems justified (Riley, 1985). The issue of the suitability of existing forms of union organisation to effective involvement in the hotel and catering industry has attracted some attention. Mars and Mitchell (1976) point out that the GMWU is a general union organising many industries and various skills, and is accordingly bureaucratically rigid. They claim that conflicts between the central and regional power bases of the union limit consistency in approaches to the recruitment of hotel and catering workers. Similarly, Airey and Chopping (1980) note that:

> One reason frequently mentioned for the lack of interest in and acceptance of trade unionism is that the structure and organisation of a general union does not match the needs of industry. To overcome such problems it is often suggested that a special union to look after the needs of hotel workers is required. Employers are vociferous in their condemnation of the inadequacies of the knowledge of trade union officials about the trade. Officials who lack the expertise to discuss operational problems cannot, they claim, negotiate sensibly on questions related to hotel practices.
>
> (Airey and Chopping, 1980: 65)

Since Airey and Chopping wrote, of course, the GMWU (now the GMB) has established the Hotel and Catering Workers' Union (HCWU) as a distinct section within the GMB for representing hospitality industry employees. The GMB has pursued a gradualist strategy over a long period in order to build its current membership. In 1977, David Basnett the leader of the (then) GMWU launched a recruitment campaign specifically designed for the industry. This strategy produced a notable response, membership increasing in the hotel and catering industry from 9,000 in April 1977 to 28,000 in September 1979 and just over 30,000 by February 1980 when the HCWU was established (Johnson and Mignot, 1982). The gradualist and non-confrontational approach of the union is reflected in a variety of ways: workers caught up in recognition disputes can be found new jobs by the union's 'Job Shop', thus discouraging industrial action. The emphasis on gentle persuasion rather than confrontation is further evidenced by the maintenance of the 'Fairs List' which identifies unionised hotels.

In contrast to the GMB/HCWU, the TGWU, whilst still active in the hotel and catering industry, has not made special provision for hotel and catering workers. Indeed, Johnson and Mignot (1982) argue that the TGWU has seemingly never developed a distinct strategy to recruit in the hotel industry. The hotel industry is not provided with a distinct section within the union but incorporated in the 'Food, Drink and Tobacco' division. Whilst it would be unfair to generalise from so little evidence as to the activities of the TGWU, it does seem that the history of relative militancy in this union has achieved rather less than might have been attained by utilising the gradualist approach of the GMB in the hotel and catering field. At the same time however, the 'softly softly' approach can be seen as relatively ineffectual. Much of the activity of the GMB seems like a holding operation, successful in hotels and hotel groups where a foothold has been gained but defeatist in respect of avoiding downright confrontation with employers. It is probably fair to say that trade unions in the hotel and catering field have yet to find a strategy suitable to mass recruitment and that success in this will to some extent depend on how the union organises its activities in the area and represents itself to both hostile employers and reluctant workers.

This can be seen in an aspect of trade union organisation and ethos that may militate against recruitment on any scale, namely the trade unions' focus on the formal aspects of rewards, a desire, central to the *raison d'être* of trade unions to establish systematic pay scales and methods of remun- eration. As suggested earlier, the existence of informal rewards in many hospitality industry organisations means that workers tend to view the policies of unions in this respect as a 'debit effect', directed towards reducing employees' access to what are often regarded as vital sources of income. The issue of the debit effect has been explored by Johnson (1983b) who utilised a variety of research methodologies in order to assess the variety and extent of rewards in hotel companies, compare provision in unionised and non-unionised hotels and establish the attitudes of workers to these rewards. Certain benefits were common to both unionised and non- unionised hotels namely: the provision of accommodation (both live-in and external, e.g. hostels); clothing allowances; discount holiday schemes; employee introduction bonuses; loans; meals on duty; occupancy bonuses; productivity bonuses; and provision of uniforms and uniform cleaning (it is not made clear by Johnson how some of these 'benefit' the employee). Not all workers received these benefits or stood an equal chance of doing so. Indeed, access was influenced by such factors as length of service, age, sex, job title and job status – in other words elements that to some extent form the basis for individual contract making. Benefits most commonly found in unionised hotel companies included discount buying schemes; travel con- cessions; life assurance schemes; suggestion bonuses; long-service pay- ments; pension schemes and sick pay schemes. According to Johnson, employees increase their chances of receiving these items simply by working for a unionised company, their chances for the first four items being doubled and for the remaining components by about one and a half times. Benefits most commonly found in non-unionised companies included annual bonuses and Christmas bonuses. Employees working for non-unionised companies seemingly double their chances of receiving these rewards.

Johnson makes two points attendant on these findings. First, many of the items offered by both unionised and non-unionised hotels are derived from the technological base of the industry, i.e. because of the nature of the industry they are easy for any company to provide at limited cost (for example, accommodation and meals on duty). Conversely, rewards offered by unionised hotels are not related to the technology of any industry but instead are concerned with security of payment, whilst the benefits most frequently offered by non-unionised hotels are loyalty-type bonuses often paid to keep key staff at crucial times. Secondly, Johnson argues that, contrary to established wisdom, both core and peripheral hotel and catering workers could benefit from unionisation. Whilst he accepts that core workers because of their superior bargaining power are more likely to benefit from technological and loyalty benefits, he sees no reason why the benefits of unionism should be confined to peripherals in weak bargaining positions. In short, he views the institutional benefits that would derive from collective bargaining as likely to enhance the position of both core and peripheral workers without necessarily impinging on the former's ability to negotiate better total rewards through exploiting technological and loyalty benefits. However, Johnson's findings from his interviews with workers reveal a somewhat less optimistic perspective.

His sample polarised into two groups, one sceptical about the benefits of union membership, the other more receptive. Using criteria of length of service, job title and status it was possible to equate these two groups with core and peripheral workers respectively. Core workers expressed anti-union views, emphasising the limitations they felt that unions would place on the opportunity to secure technological and loyalty benefits. In this instance, the emphasis placed by unions upon formal pay and rewards can be seen to have induced negative feelings in those who saw aspects of their livelihood threatened. Peripheral workers expressed sympathetic views towards trade unions, seeing unions as likely to bring about improvements in basic pay. But, as Johnson notes, both types of employee failed to recognise the influence of unions upon institutionalised benefits – the emphasis on basic pay of both groups revealing a narrow appreciation of the full range of benefits potentially attendant upon unionisation. This lack of understanding, Johnson suggests, is the cause of the debit effect amongst hotel and catering employees, since in reality there is little reason for any worker to assume that unionisation will adversely affect their rewards.

A further aspect of trade union organisation that may have an effect on recruitment and retention of members centres on the role of shop stewards. Mars and Mitchell (1976) and Jameson and Johnson (1985; 1989) argue that shop stewards are crucial to the development of effective workplace unionisation and the wider success of trade union activity. Jameson and

Johnson (1989) found that the hotel shop stewards they studied lacked any deeply held convictions about trade unions. This leads the authors to construct a somewhat bizarre argument. They suggest that shop stewards' relationship and commitment to trade unionism and how this relationship acts to constrain union growth is the 'most crucial aspect for our understanding of industrial relations in the contemporary hotel industry'. Further, whilst other barriers to trade union development are important, the barrier of shop stewards' attitudes towards unionism is the most important. 'Unless this barrier is overcome', Jameson and Johnson write, 'the other barriers are almost irrelevant' (1989: 173). The sheer absurdity of this argument points to the dangers of going too far in blaming unions for the low level of union organisation in the hotel and catering industry. Jameson and Johnson suggest that for trade unions to grow effectively in the industry shop stewards' motivations towards unions are critical. This completely ignores the effect of labour turnover and other variables on the maintenance of the workforce and is a little like arguing that a commitment to the truth necessitates believing everything that one is told. This is not to say that the role of shop stewards is unimportant in developing and maintaining workplace unionism but rather to reject the view that effective stewardship is the only truly significant barrier to unionism. Jameson and Johnson (1989) seem too ready to make their facts fit their theory. They claim that hotel workers do not join unions for instrumental reasons and that the HCWU in particular has failed to recognise this. Jameson and Johnson give no significant insight into the reasons why hotel workers *do* join unions, however. They also argue that unions in the hotel industry, and the HCWU in particular, concentrate too readily on recognition agreements involving formal procedures between corporate management and union officials and, by concentrating on the creation of a favourable attitude amongst employers, have tended to ignore building up grass roots union membership. They go on to suggest that the HCWU has adopted strategies utilised in other industries and these have failed because they do not take into account the particular needs of the hotel and catering industry. The second and third of these points assume, respectively, that a grassroots membership can be built up in spite of high rates of labour turnover and the predominance of non-unionised hotel and catering establishments and that the hotel and catering industry is in some way unique. More importantly the authors do not produce a shred of evidence in support of any of their claims, so keen are they to press the point that effective shop stewards are crucial above all else to the development of workplace unionism. Jameson and Johnson's claims are an abject example of mistaken logic combined with too easy seduction into the politics of victim blaming: there is a certain truth in attributing the failure of unionisation in the hotel and catering industry to the activities of unions themselves but it must be recognised at the same time that the failure of unions is at least as great as the failure of employers and of industrial relations legislators to tackle a structural problem that transcends the hotel and catering industry and embraces many of those who work in low pay industries. Certainly some doubt remains about the real commitment of trades unions to the industry. Trades unions in Britain no less than society more generally tend to look upon service industries with suspicion if not disdain. Having said this, the supposed instrumentalism or hostility to unions of staff should not be used as an excuse for low unionisation or the reduced efforts of trade unions to organise the industry, since such a view embodies the notion that trades unions are necessary only in problematic circumstances. In fact, alleged workforce resistance to unionisation can equally be interpreted as lack of opportunity to join a union rather than lack of interest (Commission on Industrial Relations, 1971). Unions therefore need to consider very carefully the resources – both physical and intellectual – that need to be committed to the hospitality industry if they are to enjoy greater success than has hitherto been the case.

CONCLUSION

This chapter has examined some of the recurring issues and controversies in the literature on work and industrial relations in hotels and catering. There is almost something ritualistic about the extent to which the relative merits of high labour turnover and the pros and cons of unionisation are debated amongst academics and industry interest groups. Whilst it is not entirely accurate to suggest that the hotel and catering industry is the only industry that suffers large scale labour turnover and law unionisation in the light of poor pay and conditions of work, it is certainly the case that for many industries labour stability and at least moderate union involvement in industrial relations is taken for granted. This is not true in the main of the issues discussed in the next chapter. Deskilling has been a latent issue in much of the literature on hotel and catering work, though it has not formed the basis of any sustained analysis (the most important and obvious exception to this is Bagguley, 1987). Work flexibility has recently been 'discovered' by hotel and catering analysts in much the same way as it has by mainstream industrial sociologists. More important here is the observation that with the issues of deskilling and work flexibility, the analysis of hotel and catering labour approaches the mainstream research concerns of industrial sociology, providing the prospect for at least some integration of the analysis of hotel and catering work with other forms of labour.

5 Issues and controversies in hotel and catering work II
Deskilling and work flexibility

As noted in Chapter 1, one of the most important debates in industrial sociology in recent years has concerned the deskilling and degradation of work. This chapter explores these debates in the context of hotels and catering. It is difficult to give anything other than a flavour of the issues involved. Beginning with a discussion of deskilling, the chapter moves to consideration of overlapping debates centred on the concept of flexible working practices. For those unfamiliar with the arguments there are a number of excellent reviews available including, in no particular order, Littler (1982), Wood (1982), Rose (1988) and Thompson (1989). The originator of the deskilling and degradation thesis, Harry Braverman (1974) was seeking amongst other things to restate Marxist priorities in the socio-logical and political analysis of work in his text, *Labor and Monopoly Capital* and it is with Braverman's arguments that the discussion begins.

THE LABOUR PROCESS APPROACH AND DESKILLING DEBATE

In its purest form, the labour process as defined by Marx comprises three elements: purposeful human activity directed to work; the objects on which work is performed (natural or raw materials); and the instruments of work. Following Marx, Braverman (1974) argues that work under capitalism is geared to the creation of profit rather than satisfaction of human needs, thus generating a conflict of interests between labour and capital. In order to realise the full potential of labour in these antagonistic circumstances, it is necessary for owners and managers of capital to secure maximum possible control over the labour process. Braverman argues that over the course of the twentieth century Taylorism (scientific management) has played the central role in the extension of capitalist control over the labour process. This is because scientific management stresses the divorce of conception from execution in work. Managements become responsible for the

planning, design and organisation of labour processes whilst workers are
confined to the performance of manipulative operations. The consequence
of this extension of scientific management is the degradation and deskilling
(though Braverman never uses the latter term) of labour processes, with
jobs becoming increasingly specialised and routinised. The content of work
is cheapened and the financial cost of labour to the capitalist is reduced as
the single most important bargaining counter held by many workers – their
skill – is destroyed or reorganised (the latter as a result of the creation of
demands for new skills defined by and under the control of the capitalist).
The process of deskilling is complemented by the application of technology
to labour processes, technology frequently incorporating systems of control
designed by those who own the means of production and which require no
or few skill inputs from machine minders.

As with most writings on industrial sociology, Braverman's examples
are, in the main, drawn from manufacturing industries though he does
comment on the nature of services and service labour. He defines services
in the following, characteristically rhetorical, way:

> But what if the useful effects of labor are such that they cannot take shape
> in an object? Such labor must be offered directly to the consumer, since
> production and consumption are simultaneous. The useful effects of
> labor, in such cases, do not serve to make up a vendible object which then
> carries its useful effects with it as part of its existence as a commodity.
> Instead, the useful effects of labor themselves *become* the commodity.
> When the worker does not offer this labor directly to the user of its effects,
> but instead sells it to a capitalist, who re-sells it on the commodity-
> market, then we have the capitalist form of production in the field of
> services.
>
> (Braverman, 1974: 360)

Braverman appears to be arguing that the only 'true' form of service labour
is where the effects of labour themselves are the commodity for sale.
Support for this interpretation comes from his view that the concept of
service labour is essentially artificial, most forms of service work being
more typically akin to manufacturing work than is commonly supposed.
Thus the work of chefs and other restaurant workers is not unlike that of
manufacturing employees in that it takes form in a tangible product:

> restaurant labor, which cooks, prepares, assembles, serves, cleans dishes
> and utensils etc., carries on tangible production just as much as labor
> employed in many another manufacturing process.
>
> (Braverman, 1974: 360)

Braverman's remarks are redolent of earlier observations by Whyte (1948) and Levitt (1972) concerning the combined production and service chara-cteristics of service operations and service work (see Chapter 1). But Braverman means more than this, for his comment is intended to cover not only the chefs and cooks producing 'tangible goods' but all those engaged in restaurant labour including food service staff. Food service staff may be engaged in many of the activities listed by Braverman but they may also be reduced to the role of those for whom the 'useful effects' of labour are the commodity sold by the capitalist (i.e. food service skills). Either way, the imprecision in Braverman's analysis is outweighed by a clear view of service labour as more or less equivalent to manufacturing work. In an extreme form, this can be seen in his analysis of chambermaids' work. He comments:

> Chambermaids are classed as service workers, but their labors are not always different, in principle, from those of many manufacturing workers, in that they take shape in a tangible result. When. . . chamber-maids. . .make beds they do an assembly operation which is not different from many factory assembly operations. . .the result is a tangible and vendible commodity.
>
> (Braverman, 1974: 361)

This brief summary of the main strands of Braverman's principal thesis and his limited consideration of service work clearly indicates that service work is to be viewed as essentially similar to other forms of labour in terms of the content, form and extent to which it has been degraded and routinised, although Braverman regards the extent of deskilling in service occupations as 'lagging behind' that in manufacturing. The many criticisms and revi-sions of Braverman's thesis that have followed in the wake of *Labor and Monopoly Capital* have been well rehearsed (Wood, 1982; Rose, 1988; Thompson, 1983, 1989) and comment here will be restricted to three main areas.

First, it has been argued that Braverman's analysis is historically inade-quate insofar as there is a tendency to assume that prior to industrialisation there existed some halcyon era of work dominated by craft skill, an era in which workers exercised greater control over their own labour. However, as writers like Littler (1982: 27) have argued, varying degrees of autonomy and control existed in pre-Taylorist industrial workshops and the view of 'petty commodity handicraft production' advanced by Braverman is some-what romanticised. It is also inaccurate, for as Rose (1988: 317) has noted, the majority of the pre-industrial workforce were employed as farm labourers and domestic servants, not craftspeople (see also Kumar, 1978).

A corollary of this is the observation that Braverman's rosy picture of the pre-Taylorist workshop as a repository of skill reflects his belief in the moral and intellectual superiority of traditional craft labour (Rose, 1988: 320).

A second criticism of Braverman's thesis has centred on his assumption that the application of scientific management to the labour process has been both universal and unproblematic. The suggestion is that Braverman and his followers fail to recognise the extent to which workers may resist deskilling initiatives and/or managers may choose to pursue strategies that allow workers relative autonomy and the retention or acquisition of both existing and new skills (Wood, 1982; Thompson, 1989). Braverman, it is alleged, both represents the working class as passive and acquiescent in the light of managerial efforts to gain control of the labour process and ignores the development of collective movements such as trade unions and working-class political parties as a means of resisting such initiatives. At the same time, it is held that Braverman overstates the cohesion of the dominant capitalist class, presenting it as unified and omniscient with coherent shared objectives, a view which again bears little empirical scrutiny. Braverman's critics have pointed to the many different forms of control that may be exercised in the workplace and the various forms of legitimation of industrial power that combine to produce diverse modes of work organisation (cf. Thompson, 1989).

Thirdly, critics have taken issue with Braverman's conception of skill and his unwillingness to accept the possibility of counter-tendencies to deskilling. Braverman tends to valorise traditional craft skill favouring what Beechey (1982) has called the 'male artisan/mechanic' conception of skill. This ideal type of 'craft skill' is of particular relevance for analysis of some service industries, dominated as they are by female employees, as well as for unwaged female labour in the home. The concept of craft skill seems particularly narrow and inappropriate in such cases, especially where the term is used to exclude certain types of work. For example, Beechey argues that:

> There are, for instance, forms of labour which involve complex competencies and control over the labour process, such as cooking, which are not conventionally defined as skilled (unless performed by chefs within capitalist commodity production).
>
> (Beechey, 1982: 64)

Much of the work associated with the hotel and catering industry is commonly defined as 'women's work' and seen as an extension of women's domestic tasks and responsibilities. Only when tasks such as cooking are translated from the home where they are performed by women to the market place where they are performed (or at least controlled) by men do they begin to be taken seriously as 'skilled' work. As Beechey correctly implies, there is a tendency for Braverman to assume that technical skill is absent from certain forms of service work. Braverman argues that for services:

> Except for the special case of police and firemen, the incidence of developed skill, knowledge and authority in the labor processes of society is naturally very small in these categories, and can be found only in that small layer of housekeepers and stewards who have the function of superintending institutional labor, and among the tiny number of cooks who practice the art on the chef level.
>
> (Braverman, 1974: 367–370)

The dismissiveness of this comment highlights two factors: the extent to which Braverman operates a particularly narrow definition of skill; and the tendency to make certain questionable assumptions about service work in terms of the differential value attached to male and female employment.

These issues draw attention to the extent to which skill is socially constructed. This view of skill comes in a 'weak' and 'strong' form (Littler, 1982: 9–10). The strong version of the social construction of skill thesis avers that definitions of skill may be created and sustained for reasons of industrial politics irrespective of the technical content of a given job. Most jobs therefore unnecessarily bear skill labels and might, theoretically, be performed by any persons who could gain access to a particular occupation. The weak version of the social construction of skill thesis is that nearly all skilled jobs can be said to have some objective skill content but that it is the collective strength and action of workers that lead some occupations to be regarded as skilled and other jobs as semi- or unskilled. Whilst Braverman recognises that skill labelling occurs, he views this as a process that merely obscures real levels of deskilling. He concedes that industrialisation brings into being many new occupations at least as skilled as traditional crafts, these being created mainly as a result of scientific–technical change (Braverman, 1974: Chapter 8). However, as Rose (1988: 318) notes, Braverman alleges that these occupations are gradually deskilled, at the same time holding to the view that little or no work is ever upgraded in skill terms. In this he is at odds with the majority of his critics and a good deal of hard evidence. Rose rather acidly remarks:

> There are numerous examples of both kinds of occupation: nurses, electronics engineers, typists. I have just seen the results of an enquiry among several thousand employed people in Britain. Those who claim that their tasks have been subject to simplification or other kinds of

'degradation' in the last five years are far outnumbered by those who claim to have experienced a growth in the skill and responsibility expected of them. This does not mean that these jobs are becoming 're-skilled', in the sense of becoming like craft work. They are probably not. It merely suggests that the process is an infinitely more complex one than Braverman suggests.

(Rose, 1988: 318)

The social construction of skill thesis is but one alternative or complementary viewpoint to Braverman's degradation thesis and one, as is clear from the above, that Braverman regarded as essentially flawed. Indeed, he was singularly reluctant to accept alternative points of view couched in terms of what he regarded as an academic social science ideologically supportive of the capitalist orthodoxies of advanced industrial societies. Nevertheless, in addition to the degradation and social construction theses, Littler (1982: 13–14) identifies three other views of skill current in post-war industrial sociology. These are:

1 the human capital view of skill as upgrading and increased specialisation (associated with the work of Becker, 1964);
2 the idea of a transition in industrial societies to flexible multi-skilled supervisory or maintenance job tasks where as a result of automation, workers have no direct role in the productive process but instead supervise, control and maintain production processes – a view most closely associated with the work of Touraine (1962); and
3 the idea that the application of technology to work not only lodges skill in machines but increases work complexity such that labour processes involve both deskilled and reskilling.

In the context of the critical response to Braverman (1974) elements of (2) and (3) have assumed some importance. Motivated by the view that there is no central tendency towards deskilling in capitalist labour processes, but rather levels of deskilling may vary across and within industries and over time as a result of processes of worker resistance and management control strategies, there has been recognition of counter-tendencies to deskilling, notably in terms of reskilling and the redistribution of skill in certain areas of work (Friedman, 1977; Edwards, 1979; Jones, 1982).

A useful summary of this view is offered by Attewell (1987) who rejects Braverman's view that technology eradicates skill, pointing out that automation most easily replaces already deskilled and repetitive labour and is thus more likely to replace unskilled rather than skilled workers. Of course, this position tacitly concedes that some forms of work must have been deskilled for automation to be attractive to employers. Attewell (1987) drawing on earlier work by Lee (1981) goes on to argue that the reorganisation of labour processes in expanding industries can lead not only to the persistence of highly skilled jobs filled by existing craft workers but the opening up of low skill jobs to previously unskilled workers who may view their new jobs as promotional upgrading (enskilling). Attewell argues that 'mechanization and work reorganization often occur when growing demand necessitates greatly increased production or because of shortages of skilled labor' (Attewell 1987: 330). His point is that employers' activities may consciously or unconsciously lead to certain forms of skill upgrading. Further, employers' intentionality need not, as Braverman and his supporters often maintain, lead to the 'rational' choice of minimising production costs by opting for a low skill, low wage workforce. Sometimes, they will choose high technology solutions involving higher paid and higher skilled workers. These processes may be mixed so that both types of worker co-exist in a single enterprise or industry. Attewell also points to the potential for reskilling, drawing on his study of the insurance industry:

> During my research, management reorganized the work process, transferring the simpler tasks of examiners (e.g., coding bills, identifying family members, and methods of payment) to the lower paid DPE [data processing and entry] clerks. . . .The examiners were left with a higher skill mix of tasks, since their least complex tasks were removed. The DPE clerks were also upgraded: their repetitious data entry work was now mixed with the (simple) intellectual labor of organizing claims. All this flowed from the profit motive and not from managerial altruism. Thus the redistribution of tasks is one countertendency to deskilling that follows logically from capitalist profit making. . .but that works in the opposite direction from deskilling.
>
> (Attewell, 1987: 325)

Attewell's implicit rejection of the idea that the transfer of examiners' skills to DPEs was not deskilling is problematic insofar as the putative 'mix' of reskilling and deskilling was still seemingly detrimental to one of the groups. One of the problems that arises from his claims about skill and indeed permeates the whole of the labour process debate is just exactly how 'skill' should be defined. If, over time, skills are redistributed or diminished, do they fall into complete disuse and eventually disappear forever? This question may seem naive, obvious and even trivial but the complete eradication of certain forms of skill is a central theme of Braverman's work and deserves more attention than has been accorded by labour process analysts. Although the message from Braverman's critics is that an idealised notion of craft skill is not the best yardstick by which to judge the general concept of skill, the degradation debate is weakened in common-sense terms by the failure of many commentators to commit themselves to detailed consideration of what is actually meant by skill. Most would probably subscribe to Beechey's view:

> First, the concept of skill can refer to complex competencies which are developed within a particular set of social relations of production and are objective competencies (in general terms, skilled labour can be objectively defined as labour which combines conception and execution and involves the possession of particular techniques); second, the concept of skill can refer to control over the labour process; and third, the concept of skill can refer to conventional definitions of occupational status.
>
> (Beechey, 1982: 63–64)

The problem with this approach lies in the concept of 'objective competencies'. Clearly it is a widespread belief (and not only amongst sociologists) that such 'objective competencies' exist. Whilst in practice some broad agreement may be possible on what does or does not constitute 'objective skill' in any given context, given that most sociologists do accept that skill is socially constructed to a greater or lesser extent the danger arises that academic pluralism disguises a fundamentally arbitrary approach to the nature of skill itself.

This indeed appears to be the case. Thompson observes that 'systematic definitions of skill are surprisingly hard to come by in the literature on deskilling'(Thompson, 1989: 92). Even Braverman avoids a positive definition. Thompson notes that:

> the general picture built up in the assessment of changes in the labour process is that skill is largely based on knowledge, the unity of conception and execution, and the exercise of control by the workforce. . . . But in most cases skill is measured less by a formal definition than by historical context and comparison.
>
> (Thompson, 1989: 92)

Putting the least charitable gloss on these remarks, it seems that sociologists might, quite literally, not know what they are talking about! Certainly, much of the deskilling debate has done less than justice to the study of non-craft labour processes, the role of women in the labour process and the nature of labour processes in service industries. It has also perhaps placed inadequate emphasis on the nature of unskilled work. Whatever concept of skill is employed, there are many jobs which it would be possible to define consensually as lacking any significant technical skill content. The study by Attewell (1987) discussed earlier (see pp. 130–131) illustrates that some forms of work amenable to automation may have already been deskilled. By the same token however, upgrading may occur for those whose work has never been regarded as skilled nor could legitimately (i.e. consensually) be viewed as such.

DESKILLING IN HOTEL AND CATERING WORK: SOME EVIDENCE

Discussion of deskilling in hotel and catering work has often been submerged in general commentaries on industrial relations in the industry. There is an implicit view that many forms of hotel and catering work have been deskilled in the period since 1960 and indeed, in Bravermanian terms, practices likely to lead to deskilling were advocated by the British Hotel and Catering Economic Development Committee (HCEDC) during the late 1960s. The Hotel and Catering Economic Development Committee (1968b) was concerned to show how the cost of labour-intensive services could be calculated and suggested savings by using non-personal methods of service that included: limited menus; moving to buffet/grill forms of service operation; the phasing out of porters (with shoe cleaning to be achieved by supplying guests with appropriate materials in their rooms!); and the placing of tea-making machines in rooms to eliminate the need for room service. In order to improve productivity at minimum cost, methods of working in hotels were to be analysed in order 'to establish the best method of working and the most suitable facilities. When this had been done the work content should be measured and true standards established' (1968b: 16). Taylorism indeed! By the early 1970s a trend towards deskilling was observed by both the governmental Commission on Industrial Relations (CIR) (1971) and the Department of Employment (1971, 1976).

From their survey of trends at that time the Department of Employment (1971) found evidence of a move towards greater standardisation, with personal services being either reduced or provided by non-personal means, particularly in middle-range hotels: standardisation trends were seen as less likely to affect the most luxurious and the smallest hotel units. Developments in pre-prepared frozen dishes combined with a strategy to simplify and standardise menus were seen as a means by which caterers would be likely to reduce dependency on skilled chefs and cooks whilst speeding restaurant service and reducing the time spent in kitchens on preparation and cooking, allowing the latter to be undertaken by less skilled staff. The Department of Employment (1971) noted that fewer hotels expected to maintain a full kitchen brigade by 1973 and were instead likely to rely more greatly on general purpose chefs and cooks, sous chefs and chefs tournant than on specialised chefs de partie. Similarly the Department of Employment (1976) report on the catering industry noted that multi-firm units operating in the popular restaurant market (i.e. with products aimed at

low-spending consumers) had developed standardised restaurant operations characterised by centralised organisation and cost control procedures.
Menus and food service and preparation methods were designed primarily
to reduce costs by reducing the need for skilled staff. Again, the biggest
changes had taken place in kitchens where rising costs, high labour turnover and staff shortages had led to increased use of convenience foods
(notably frozen foods and packet soups) and technology such as convection
ovens and microwaves. The report on hotels (1971) pointed out that deskilling would affect not only chefs and cooks, but other kitchen staff as
well:

> In the middle range of skill less will be needed in future while at the top
> and bottom additional skills will be required. Increased scale of activity
> and new food production and processing developments will necessitate
> more managerial, planning and presentational skills in head chefs, while
> technological advances in the manufacture of wash-up and waste dis-
> posal equipment will require higher operational skills in wash-up staff
> and kitchen porters.
>
> (Department of Employment, 1971: 36–37)

Both reports suggested that actual deskilling in the restaurant kitchen would
involve a redistribution of skill to the food factory where the production of
prepreared dishes would require the skills of chefs and cooks. A similar
redistribution of skill within hotels more generally was also envisaged. The
Department of Employment (1971) suggested that increased competitiveness within the industry when combined with higher costs and staff shortages would lead to a breakdown in traditional departmental boundaries and
the adoption of more flexible organisation practices.

In the early 1970s, then, standardisation, technological change and
deskilling were already observable: pressures of costs and staff shortages
being reflected in greater product standardisation and the simplification of
restaurant operations via the proffering of a restricted menu involving only
limited cooking and waiting skills. Many respondents to the Department of
Employment (1971) hotels survey reported that they, in any case, always
offered a no-choice menu. Full floor service was available in around only a
quarter of hotels sampled and limited floor service was available in a
further 30 per cent. More recent commentaries by Humphreys (1985) and
Pine (1987) have pointed to the increasing development and deployment of
integrated catering systems that not only reduce labour costs but go some
way to eliminating the need for employees to work the erratic hours
(normally in the form of split shifts) characteristic of the hospitality
industry. In a study of contract catering, Kelliher and McKenna (1987)
argue that the introduction of cook-freeze and cook-chill technology

necessarily entails a reduction of hours worked and the deskilling of traditional cooking functions with a concomitant downward pressure on staff wages. This would appear to be confirmed by a number of reports. For example, the *Caterer and Hotelkeeper* of 29 October 1987 noted that the National Health Service was facing a crisis because it could not secure the staff necessary to work with cook-chill technology as a result of there being no opportunity for weekend work or overtime (one of the principal aims of cook-chill systems is to reduce such opportunities by preparing food for consumption in advance and storing it whilst employing those engaged in food preparation during more conventional working hours). However, it would be foolish to assume that the deskilling of cookery has progressed uniformly across all sectors or indeed within them. The Education and Training Advisory Council (ETAC) (1983) found that a very high proportion of staff involved in food preparation used certain fresh products as opposed to convenience ones (1983: 19). The persistence of the small restaurant offering *haute cuisine* testifies to the continuing existence of 'traditional' forms of public cookery alongside the more standardised cuisine found (by no means exclusively) in chain hotels and restaurants. This draws attention to an important point made by Saunders (1981b), namely, that whilst wider adoption of kitchen technologies may have reduced dependency on skilled staff and/or led to some deskilling and redistribution of skill, it is the menu itself that provides managements with the greatest opportunity for deskilling the workforce.

To a very large extent, the menu is determined by the market to which any catering unit is directing its efforts. An understanding of the market can eventually lead to the manipulation of taste, reinforcing particular modes of provision such that they become accepted as 'normal' or 'standard' (Wood, 1990b). The form the menu takes will normally be dictated by cost considerations, including the cost of skilled labour and appropriate technologies. In highly competitive and standardised markets, limitation of the menu has gone in hand with the increasing use of standard recipes whereby permutations of dishes and courses are planned and designed at Head Office level for execution at unit level by chefs and cooks. Menu limitation almost invariably entails simplification of dishes themselves. Less complex items are favoured over those difficult to prepare, a trend logically extended to 'fast food' where menus and menu items constitute an easily comprehended repertoire of reassuringly familiar items, reassuring because of the ever closer approximation of available foods to those consumed in the home (Wood, 1990b; Delamont, 1983). Shamir (1976) found that managers favoured increased use of convenience foods not only because of the high cost of skilled labour but because they felt they could get away with it – customers reportedly being unable to tell the difference between convenience and other foods. The power of the menu to determine the social relations of production in restaurants and kitchens is therefore considerable. The menu is the starting point for both job and product analysis. Any casual consideration of the nature of supply in certain sectors of the hotel and catering industry reveals the extent to which certain categories of operation – burger restaurants, carveries, steakhouses, pizza and pasta restaurants – offer roughly similar menus and the concept of product differentiation and competition is an essentially mythical one.

The influence of the menu extends beyond the kitchen. Dronfield and Soto (1980) argue that the introduction of point-of-sale food preparation and service outlets such as coffee shops and carveries reduces the need for skilled staff since the style of these operations permits the employment of less skilled staff in preparing, often by the use of regenerative technology (e.g. heating or reheating preprepared foods), and then serving food to clients. Similarly, several commentators have pointed to the elimination of full-blooded silver service and its replacement by a diluted craft or plated service, thus dispensing with the need for staff to acquire and use silver service skills. The Department of Employment (1971: 37) reported a 'wide-spread conviction' amongst hoteliers that guests preferred more informal service even at the expense of skilled waiter service. This process is not confined to highly standardised chain hotels and restaurants. In the world of *haute cuisine*, fashionable styles of cookery such as *nouvelle cuisine* have been represented as a means by which deskilled chefs can reassert their craft control via running their own restaurants (Mennell, 1985). Here, plate service has dominated as the chef's right to arrange the food according to his or her own desires has relegated waiters to mere fetchers and carriers.

Outside the direct sphere of food and beverage management, evidence of deskilling has been identified in other departments. In accommodation, traditional room services provided by floor waiters have been replaced by what Riley (1984) has termed 'touches and things'. Hotel bedrooms increasingly contain tea- and coffee-making facilities, mini-bars and so on. However, whilst tea- and coffee-making facilities in bedrooms are now standard, mini-bars are rarer and room service may be making something of a comeback in certain hotels. Shamir (1976) noted that managers had one major reservation about the total abolition of room service and this was that it removed an important selling point. In other accommodation services, notably reception, the introduction of computerised reservation services arguably eliminates the need to exercise all but the most elementary clerical skills since knowledge, control and technique are invested in machines that merely require operators to input and extract information. The evidence for deskilling in the hotel and catering industry is therefore contradictory and complex, as is the case for other industries, and a 'straight' deskilling thesis cannot be strictly applied.

DESKILLING IN HOTELS AND CATERING: SOME PROBLEMS AND ISSUES

Contrary to folk wisdom, hotels and catering are not *simply* labour intensive. As Airey and Chopping (1980: 48) observe, the industry is both labour and capital intensive and reduction of labour intensity can be achieved by (a) substitution of capital for labour; and (b) substitution of the consumer's labour for that of the worker. Both trends were noted in the evidence for deskilling contained in the previous section. There are, however, problems with assuming an overall trend towards deskilling in hotels and catering. Some of these are fairly obvious: the hotel and catering industry is a relatively heterogeneous grouping of industrial activities operating in associated but well-demarcated product markets. In some areas the introduction of technology is not possible because of the lack of investment finance and/or the absence of any need for technology. A good example would be the small hotel and boarding house sector. At the other end of the scale, luxury hotels and restaurants trade on their ability to give a high quality or personal service and a high standard of physical product whether this be food or accommodation. Labour savings are thus difficult and the economic disadvantages and costs of technological rationalisation may be greater than the costs deriving from maintaining a substantial workforce. As these two extremes show, it simply is not possible to make any credible generalisations about deskilling in the hospitality industry, though in certain sectors such generalisations are easier – for example in highly capitalised fast food restaurants or heavily standardised and branded chain hotels. Even here however, care is needed to identify not only the extent of deskilling but also the counter-tendencies to it.

To a very large extent this can be seen by returning to the example of chefs and cooks. There is some doubt as to whether *in general* chefs and cooks, those workers singled out as most susceptible to processes of deskilling, actually view their work as undergoing a process of degradation. Chivers (1971, 1973) whose study, it is worth noting, pre-dated Braverman's own, found that chefs and cooks viewed technological innovation as a help rather than a hindrance as it speeded up operations, reduced wastage and increased their control over the cookery process. Greater concern centred on the use of convenience foods, between half and a third of Chivers' sample fearing that increased use of convenience foods would entail a loss of skill, and between a quarter and a half that their use would affect the quality of dishes. A similar hostility to the use of convenience foods was observed in a later study by Shamir (1976). Chivers found that while the operational advantages of convenience foods were appreciated, genuine fear centred on the possibility that the quality of dishes would suffer as a result of their utilisation. The now widespread use of convenience foods seems to lend weight to the fears of those chefs surveyed by Chivers. However, two qualifications are needed. First, in those hotels where deskilling was seen (by, for example, the Department of Employment, 1971) to be biting particularly hard in the increased use of convenience foods, there has been a tendency for convenience products to be utilised as part of a wider culinary system that still employs fresh foods. The Education and Training Advisory Council (1983) evidence (see p. 135) is suggestive here of the possibility that there are fewer circumstances than might be supposed in which convenience products have completely replaced fresh foods. Further, it is also the case that in many hotels, different types of food and beverage operation co-exist within the unit, one highly standardised and the other more traditional in its provision of one form or another of *haute cuisine*. Secondly, whilst a trend towards greater standardisation and the use of technology including convenience foods is noticeable in both hotels and restaurants, the persistence even within 'middle markets' of demand for 'good food' has ensured the survival of restaurants offering relatively sophisticated cookery and hence a labour market able to sustain a body of chefs and cooks able to deploy extensive culinary skills.

Moving on a little, the issue of convenience foods has rather obscured other aspects of labour process changes in commercial cookery. In 1981, Snow found that chefs regarded convenience foods as a positive development that helped them cope with fluctuations in demand. The ten-year lapse since the work of Chivers (1971) might of course suggest that some groups of chefs and workers at least had been socialised into accepting convenience foods as a 'fact of life' and/or that in not regarding themselves as having been subject to extensive deskilling were evidencing 'false consciousness'. Equally however, it is possible that the regularisation that technology brings to the kitchen (for example, in terms of coping with fluctuations in demand), when combined with elimination of drudgery, is prized more by chefs and cooks than the potential for deskilling. Certainly, the potential for deskilling in the hotel and catering industry and particularly in cooking seems to have had little effect on the very high standard of training that chefs receive. The issue of management control over the work of chefs is a more problematic issue and comment is difficult for lack of evidence. Most contemporary literature still paints the picture of the chef as a powerful member of the hotel/restaurant team who experiences minimal interference in the operation of his or her department. Similarly, senior chefs have always held a range of responsibilities that require them to exercise clerical and management skills suggesting that the issue of *direct control* at unit level over the realm of chefs is a non-starter in conceptual terms. Having said this, departmental heads in hotels have arguably always been allowed considerable latitude in the running of their departments. It is at the higher, strategic, level that decisions about product orientation, market position and employment policy have had an impact on the design and redesign of hotel and catering work. Thus the introduction of technology to the hotel and catering workplace is rarely a matter for unit or departmental heads alone and the latitude allowed unit heads, say, in determining their own employment strategies based on prevailing local markets, is a function of prior decisions about the labour cost percentage target and permitted variance made by executive management. In short, there is little to be gained in an understanding of deskilling by concentrating on the level of the unit alone though it is here that evidence for adjustment and resistance to control initiatives may be sought.

For example, Bagguley (1987) whilst not arguing for a straight de-skilling position presents an analysis of occupational restructuring in the hotel industry that rests on that version of the feminisation of labour thesis which argues that women are drawn into particular occupations once these have been deskilled (see Chapter 2). Drawing on the 1981 UK Census of Population data, he argues that women have come to dominate the chefs and cooks category after a period (1951–1971) in which the proportion of women cooks fell by over a half and the percentage of male cooks nearly doubled. During this period, the mechanisation of routine tasks such as potwashing led to a decline in women's employment. Since 1971, Bagguley speculates, the wider introduction of technology such as prepre-pared foods has deskilled chef/cook jobs with the result that more women have been drawn into these occupations and/or more routine and deskilled jobs have become available that have been filled by women. The difficulty with Bagguley's analysis is that reports such as the Hotel and Catering Industry Training Board (1985) workforce survey show that men still dominate the chef/cook category – though only just. More importantly, the tendency for Bagguley and others to conflate the chefs/cooks category may disguise the fact that women are more likely to be cooks than chefs. Within the commercial hospitality industry, female cooks co-exist alongside male chefs, constituting a two-tier occupational labour force, the former charac-terised by (perhaps) more limited skills, greater part-time working, less job security and lower pay. The point is a speculative one requiring substan-tiation but there are dangers in accepting the oft vaunted common-sense view that occupational segregation in the chefs/cooks category is confined to a sectoral division between male chefs in the commercial sector and female cooks in the institutional and welfare sector (cf. Gabriel, 1988). Management control strategies over labour processes in the hotel and restaurant kitchen vary greatly and the widespread introduction of technologies combined with changes in labour utilisation may affect work experience in different ways. Specifically, the apparent unwillingness of (one suspects) predominantly male chefs to concede that their jobs have been deskilled may result, to a large degree, from the extent to which men continue to dominate the most interesting and skilled jobs in commercial cookery, whilst more mundane and routine tasks have been deskilled as a result of technological advance and redistributed to a second tier of female labour. The latter in turn may, in the sense proposed by Attewell (1987), be largely new entrants to commercial cooking work who in a general sense have been enskilled by the reorganisation of the labour process in hotel and restaurant kitchens.

The maintenance of skill labels in professional cookery, whatever the realities of deskilling, is a matter of some interest. Bagguley (1987) implies that the absence of collective organisation of worker interests in hotels and catering suggests a lack of resistance to managerial initiatives to deskill. Yet resistance and conflict take many forms, in hotels and catering labour turnover constituting one indicator of discontent and conflict. At the same time, the extent to which skilled, semi-skilled and managerial workers in hotel and catering units are closely enmeshed in a shared ideological and operational culture and are relatively independent of close scrutiny by executive management means that the scope to mediate at unit level the strategies of executive management is considerable, at least where control has not been built into the physical design of the capital and technology of the operation. Where the latter does exist and where relationships between management and workforce have been predicated on different criteria, the scope for resistance to deskilling initiatives may be limited. McKenna's study of the introduction of cook-chill methods of catering into National Health Service and Schools Meal Service catering is instructive here. McKenna (1990) found that contract caterers viewed cook-chill as a valuable means of reducing staffing levels and emphasised the extent to which cook-chill increased specialisation and the division of labour by separating the location of food production from service points. He concludes that whatever problems may be attendant on defining skill, managers and others implementing cook-chill systems responded to his survey in a way that demonstrated that 'as far as they perceive the traditional notion of "skill" in catering, cook-chill eliminates the need for skilled labour in aggregate terms' (McKenna, 1990: 394). More than this, McKenna writes, the retraining of staff is, in the views of catering managers, retraining 'to use a deskilled operation' (McKenna, 1990: 394). Most managers also had little hesitation in proclaiming that cook-chill systems increased efficiency, increased cost savings and increased managerial control over the labour process. McKenna's study offers a fairly cut and dried example of 'real' deskilling but remains, however, one small island of information in a sea of relative unknowing.

BEYOND DESKILLING? WORK FLEXIBILITY IN HOTELS AND CATERING

Partially dependent for its impetus on developments in labour process analysis and constituting to a very large degree a rejection of the deskilling thesis, the debate over the nature and extent of flexible working has come to occupy a central position on the industrial sociology research agenda in both Europe and America. Sociologists in general do not like the positive claims made for flexible working and regard the intellectual foundations of the debate as being empirically 'shaky' (Thompson, 1989: 224).

In essence, the flexible working debate is concerned with a supposed shift in the organisation of work towards a reuniting of intellectual and manual skills in employment. For some commentators, this trend arises within the context of mass production where flexible working and production methods are developed in response to highly differentiated and fickle markets. A stronger reformulation of this view asserts that demand takes the form of highly specialised niche markets for customised products that can only be met by the adoption of advanced technology based on employee knowledge of production and process concepts that cross traditional boundaries of hierarchical work organisation (Thompson, 1989: 219). Both of the above variants are couched in tones that assume worldwide changes in the organisation of work, at least in the long term. In Britain, the debate has tended in contrast to focus more on the adoption of flexible employment practices as a management strategy or policy tool for coping with cost structures. The form of this discussion derives from the key studies of Atkinson (1984), the National Economic Development Office (NEDO), in a study undertaken by the Institute of Manpower Studies (1986) and the British Advisory, Conciliation and Arbitration Service (ACAS) (1988). The latter reported that the most common reasons cited by employers for introducing flexibility were 'to increase productivity' and 'to reduce labour costs', with 'to meet fluctuating demands for the product or service' coming a close third.

It is conventional to identify four basic types of flexibility in working (Atkinson, 1984; National Economic Development Office, 1986; Lockwood and Guerrier, 1989; Kelliher, 1989). *Numerical flexibility* involves adjusting the number of workers or number of hours worked in response to demand. This can be achieved via utilisation of temporary, part-time and casual workers; increased overtime; changes in shift patterns; and variable working times (e.g. annual hours contracts). Numerical flexibility may be advantageous to a company facing low skill requirements and where little training or induction is required (National Economic Development Office, 1986; see also Kelliher, 1989). *Functional flexibility* involves attempts to obtain greater flexibility in the utilisation of skills particularly in ways that allow job holders to develop skills and competencies that allow them to move between a variety of jobs and tasks at either similar levels (horizontal flexibility) or different levels (vertical flexibility) – most commonly referred to, though not always accurately, as multi-skilling. A cost element is associated with any attempt to move towards functional flexibility in contexts where skills are traditionally organised since employees may require (re)training. *Pay flexibility* entails adjustment in the form and delivery of rewards that encourage functional flexibility and reward scarce skills and/or individual employee performance. Pay flexibility may be manifest in systems that include merit and productivity awards that reward skills on the basis of their value to an employer at a given point and, where a policy of functional flexibility is pursued, multi-skilled staff being paid enhanced rates for their skills. Finally, there are *distancing strategies* whereby employers contract-out certain types of work in order to attempt some re-distribution of risk and uncertainty elsewhere.

The National Economic Development Office (1986) report found that flexible working strategies were not an important priority for service sector firms because they either already existed by tradition or could be employed relatively easily. There is some evidence to suggest that this is an appropriate conceptualisation of the extent of flexible working practices in the commercial hotel and catering industry. In short, flexible working practices are not new to the industry, the use of part-time casual and part-time workers and multi-skilled staff being a common and arguably a defining feature of labour organisation in some sectors, most notably small hotel businesses (Lowe, 1988; cf. Kelliher, 1989). Until relatively recently, discussion of flexibility as a matter of work design by employers has been confined to 'multi-skilling' strategies, defined in terms of encouraging the mobility of staff through a variety of occupations in a unit in order to combat monotony at work, enrich work experience and stabilise the workforce. The Commission on Industrial Relations (CIR) (1971) advocated multi-skilling as a means of overcoming the rigid hierarchy of occupations in hotels, increasing worker satisfaction and inducing greater flexibility in the management of labour in the face of erratic consumer demand.

Perhaps the most detailed early reports of multi-skilling in the hospitality industry are those by Mars, Bryant and Mitchell (1979) whose study of the Le Pays du Nords (see Chapter 4) restaurant revealed higher productivity and payment of higher than average wages as a result of the introduction by management of multi-skilling practices. These authors argue that multi-skilling can help overcome common problems in the hospitality industry such as high labour turnover and the persistence of individual contracts. Multi-skilling, it is argued, places workers in a high-trust relationship with management which enhances the quality of their working lives when taken with the greater variety of work engendered by job rotation. In a second case study, Mars, Bryant and Mitchell show how the adoption of multi-skilling affected the Hotel Aeropolitan, a 400 bedroom establishment built at an airport by a large multi-national conglomerate newly involved in the hotel trade. The viability of the hotel was perceived as depending on the provision of high standards of service and the payment of higher than average wages in order to ensure attraction and retention of staff in a competitive local labour market. In order to overcome the cost implications of paying higher wages in a low productivity industry, the hotel management decided on a two-pronged policy of employing only local workers with no previous experience of the hotel industry and training them to perform multiple tasks. This policy was predicated on the belief that it would result in increased productivity and job satisfaction and higher wages could be afforded by the company. At the same time, traditional hierarchic structures in hotels would be broken down with payment relating to skill grades rather than official occupational grades, and labour retention increased by creating the possibility of internal promotion, i.e. ensuring the operation of an internal labour market. On implementation the policy was initially successful in terms of maintaining a comparatively low labour turnover rate. However, problems arose when the hotel, breaking with its policy, began to employ traditional hotel workers who were attracted to the hotel by the higher rates of pay but were subsequently unable to adapt to the multi-skilling practices employed. The major difficulty centred on the absence of individual contract making in the unit: the expectation of traditional workers that they would be able to manipulate the total payments system was not met and they were unable to cope with the lack of flexibility in the rewards system. Conflict arose between traditional and 'new' workers which led to an increase in labour turnover, ultimately corrected by the reassertion of the original policy.

Mars, Bryant and Mitchell's case studies are of interest not only for the early examples of functional flexibility but for their reporting of a now increasingly common strategy of employing workers with no experience of hotel and catering work, a practice common in many fast-food restaurants but also other types of operation. The worst effects of deskilling are arguably found in these highly capitalised operations in which skill and initiative and also control is vested in technology and process. One criticism is also worth airing here and that is the over-zealous concern of Mars, Bryant and Mitchell with breaking down traditional hierarchies in hotel and catering organisations and neutralising the effects of individual contracts and the informal payments system. Whilst these may be desirable aims in their own right, a significant element in the introduction of multi-skilling in Le Pays du Nord was the operation of a policy by the owner whereby staff could eat from the customer menu at half-price. Staff were also supplied with food at cost for their domestic requirements plus a free chicken each week or its equivalent (the equivalent is not specified!). The objective of this policy was to reduce the amount of knocking-off, the absence of opportunity for which is a key source of disgruntlement as has been shown, and is also, of course, for some workers at least a key element in remuneration. The problem here is that Mars and colleagues do not chart the effects, actual or potential, of this effective formalisation of 'knocking-off' on the beneficial labour relations that prevailed in the restaurant. It is thus uncertain as to the extent to which multi-skilling alone was responsible for the observed effects as opposed to other elements in operational practice – including for example the employment of 'untypical' catering workers as appeared to be the case with Le Pays du Nord no less than the Hotel Aeropolitan.

More recent reports on flexible working practices in hotels and catering are less evangelical than those of Mars, Bryant and Mitchell. Bagguley (1987) suggests that both numerical flexibility (firms changing levels of input in response to changes in demand levels by the use, for example, of temporary, short-term, part-time and contract and casual workers) and functional flexibility (the versatility of employees in the light of employers' strategies to move employees between different jobs according to changes in work loads) have had particularly important consequences for female part-time labour since the 1960s. In particular, he argues, male employees are more likely to be functionally flexible, i.e. engaged in a wider variety of tasks, than women who tend to be confined to operative roles. At the same time, the female workforce in the hotel industry is largely numerically flexible and numerically flexible workers are usually the least functionally flexible because the principal mode of numerically flexible working – part-time employment – limits the development of wide-ranging skills and experience and the scope for obtaining functionally flexible positions. If Bagguley is correct, then there has been a tendency for males to retain a monopoly of those jobs characterised by multiple functions and skills whereas women have been restricted to routinised, deskilled posts. This interpretation is at least superficially supported by the statistical data on female employment in the hotel and catering industry discussed in Chapter 2.

There is some general consensus that numerical flexibility is a common feature of low-skill operative grade work in hotels and catering. Kelliher (1989: 160) points out that many employers develop their own pool of temporary employees familiar with organisational practices who can be called upon as required. This is particularly true of the banqueting departments of hotels where the majority of staff are casuals, recruited on an *ad hoc* basis (Guerrier and Lockwood, 1989b). Having said this, the dangers of generalisation are ever present. Lockwood and Guerrier (1989) studied fifteen hotel groups and interviewed personnel executives on the subject of flexible working practices. They note that even within the same company, different hotels can be staffed in vastly different ways. Of particular interest is their finding that for those hotels with limited variations in activity levels over a week or year, numerical flexibility was simply not an issue. These hotels responded to their market position by employing mainly full-time staff, coping with seasonal and other troughs through natural wastage. Hotels facing wide variations in demand were more likely to employ large numbers of part-time and casual staff to provide necessary flexibility, sometimes attempting cost control through forecasting methods, more often than not relying on managerial judgement (see also Guerrier and Lockwood, 1989b). Further, the authors discovered that:

> Increasingly, these hotels are recognising their part-time and casual staff as key elements of the establishment and providing them with similar rewards to full-time staff. No longer are they seen as purely 'peripheral'. It is seen as desirable to attract local committed employees, even on a part-time basis, rather than depend on transient full-timers.
>
> (Lockwood and Guerrier, 1989: 14)

Lockwood and Guerrier go on to note that numerical flexibility is achieved, seemingly intentionally or otherwise, through reliance upon labour turnover to cope with short-term fluctuations in demand for labour.

On the basis of the foregoing, it would be clearly too hasty to generalise about the extent of numerical flexibility in the hotel and catering industry. The general trend seems to be a fairly extensive use of numerically flexible labour though in certain cases this may be less than is commonly supposed. One area in which numerical flexibility does seem to be an increasing feature of managerial strategy is in contract catering. Kelliher (1989: 164) studied contracting in the National Health Service and found that both in-house and external tenderers for catering contracts achieved a reduction in staffing levels through the use of numerical flexibility. Staff reductions were generally greater under external contractors. Reductions in working time were common in tendered operations as staff requirements were closely matched to demand, a process seemingly involving the conversion of some full-time jobs into part-time posts. One example cited by Kelliher (1989) is the case of the external contractor who employed 50 per cent of the workforce on a part-time basis compared to a previously full-time workforce. Of course, the process of contracting-out catering in the National Health Service has been a far from uniform one. Nevertheless, the traditional (relative) stability of the catering workforce in the NHS and other public service catering provides an environment for the controlled study of the introduction of flexible working practices not afforded by the commercial hospitality industry with its more unpredictable market circumstances and generally greater labour instability. What will be interesting to observe is the extent to which the commercialisation of public sector catering in Great Britain engenders a trend towards rendering the public sector as insecure and volatile as the commercial hospitality industry.

Turning to functional flexibility, the early studies by Mars, Bryant and Mitchell (1979) discussed earlier have found little sympathy in later research. Lockwood and Guerrier (1989) found little evidence of functional flexibility in their study of fifteen hotel groups. Short duration 'functional moves' such as working in different areas of the hotel during a single shift were not formally encouraged and where they did occur were almost always based on *ad hoc* arrangements between individual staff. Similarly, multi-skilling was evident in only one company. In another study, Guerrier and Lockwood (1989b) point out that a major impediment to functional flexibility in hotels is the persistence of departmentalisation. Not only do company head offices delegate considerable authority to individual unit mangers but also to departments, which are treated as cost or profit centres. This increases the emphasis on differentiation between departments which in any case exists in the cultural and attitudinal variations between staff of different departments. Further constraints on functional flexibility were manifest in the attitudes of senior management who, whilst favouring greater cross-departmental flexibility in principle, felt the need to put their own departments first in terms of meeting staff targets. Guerrier and Lockwood do note the common phenomenon of junior, trainee and other managers engaging in 'operative' activities, particularly in the food and beverage area, though in one hotel studied, there was little assistance loaned to the Banqueting Manager by other food and beverage managers involved in the restaurant. In housekeeping, Guerrier and Lockwood found that supervisory staff in the form of floor housekeepers were expected to be functionally flexible downwards, undertaking routine operative tasks in order to meet labour targets or cope with staff shortfalls. In their complementary study, Lockwood and Guerrier (1989) offer a case example of housekeeping. They begin by noting how difficult it is to recruit and retain chambermaids because of the pressure of the external labour market that makes women's cleaning skills easily transferable. Further, they claim that the work of a chambermaid is not attractive in status though, like Shamir (1975) (see Chapter 3), suggest that it contains certain positive features in terms of autonomy and involvement in work. The housekeeping department is, the authors claim, ripe for development in terms of functional flexibility strategies. In one hotel they report:

> Chambermaids have been given total responsibility for their own set of rooms and also for the checking of the room after servicing and its release to reception. The checking of rooms was previously done by floor housekeepers, who now maintain control of standards by random spot checking. The maids seem to have responded positively to this challenge, and, despite initial reservations, are now committed to the new system.
>
> (Lockwood and Guerrier, 1989: 15)

On the basis of work by Guerrier and Lockwood in hotels, it seems that functional flexibility is limited, at least in chain-owned establishments. As Kelliher (1989: 160) notes, it is as if functional flexibility is not commensurate with the range of demands made on anything other than the smallest hotels. More important than this however, as Guerrier and Lockwood emphasise, is the role played by organisational culture in buttressing the traditional rights of hotel managers to run their own units as they see fit. In the light of earlier discussions of the '*ad hocism*' entailed by traditional hotel management and the incipient conservatism and fatalism of hotel managers in their perspectives on the world outside of hotels, it is unsurprising to find that insofar as flexible working has made any impact on the hotel and catering industry at all, it is in the extension of already existing practices that treat labour as a 'hire and fire' commodity on the basis of secure knowledge about the availability of such labour in ready supply. Nor is the situation necessarily any different in the non-commercial sector. Kelliher's study of National Health Service contracting found that functional flexibility was not a common feature of managerial strategies. Where it did exist, it was the by-product of other processes. For example, where an in-house tender had been successful, functional flexibility and the rearrangement of work tasks had often been used to avoid staff redundancies.

An important and singular contribution to an understanding of the motivations of employers to adopt functionally flexible working practices is given by Hales (1987) who examined the adoption of 'Quality of Working Life' (QWL) measures in the UK hospitality industry. QWL measures are not necessarily synonymous with methods of creating functional flexibility but the two are closely related (cf. Lockwood and Guerrier, 1989). Certain methods of increasing functional flexibility may be regarded as falling under the 'QWL' heading. The crucial difference is in terms of motivation: the adoption of flexible working practices are quite clearly motivated by production and cost criteria. QWL measures in contrast may also be motivated by such concerns but are equally preoccupied with methods of improving, quite literally, the quality of working experience. This is a somewhat simplistic rendering of what is a complex topic arising out of the flexible specialisation response to the labour process debate but it is broadly sustainable (see Thompson, 1989; Rose, 1988 for a fuller account). Hales (1987) begins from the proposition that QWL measures are predicated on the belief that dissatisfaction with work arises from Taylorist and related principles of work organisation. QWL measures have been vaunted as a humanistic and instrumental solution to, respectively, workers' negative experiences of work and employers' constant concern with maintaining and improving productivity. In essence, the cry is 'happy workers are productive workers' and QWL measures are seen as a means of instilling interest in work and increasing employees' stake in the success of the organisation.

Hales argues that classical organisational principles at work involve horizontal and vertical specialisation at the level of both individual jobs and the organisation. At the level of individual jobs, vertical specialisation means that non-managerial work lacks autonomy whilst horizontal specialisation leads to detail work involving minimum skill and repetitive tasks. QWL measures advocate despecialisation. *Vertical despecialisation* involves diffusion of the conceptual elements of work which at the organisational level entails devolution of decision-making powers and greater participation by all parties in organisational management (e.g. via such means as works councils, consultative committees and worker directors). At the level of individual jobs, vertical despecialisation entails the addition of decision-making powers to employees' jobs principally by job enrichment programmes. *Horizontal despecialisation* at the organisational level entails the move towards multi-function work units by such means as autonomous work groups (groups empowered and enskilled to perform specific tasks), task forces and project teams (normally *ad hoc* groups with organisation-wide membership constituted to tackle a particular project) and quality circles (similar groups with a remit to identify potential improvements in the product or service offered by the organisation). At the level of individual jobs, horizontal despecialisation involves adding new tasks to postholders' existing responsibilities and this can be achieved by job enlargement (addition of particular tasks to a job) and job rotation (involving the retention of task-centred specialisation but the movement of workers between different jobs in order to alleviate monotony).

If the foregoing catalogue is compared to the strategies available for achieving workforce flexibility the overlap of interests between the two is easily discernible. Hales (1987) questionnaired and interviewed heads of personnel in a variety of commercial and non-commercial hospitality organisations. There was evidence that hospitality organisations favoured horizontal despecialisation measures at the level of the individual job (i.e. job enlargement and rotation, though job enrichment was also in evidence) whilst vertical despecialisation measures were favoured at the organisational level (notably works councils and/or consultative committees). The latter is perhaps an unsurprising finding in the light of hotel and catering organisations' valorisation of the managerial prerogative to inform and direct rather than consult. Indeed Hales found that the use of consultative committees and the like tended to serve as a safety valve for grievances and a means of deflecting employees' attention towards peripheral matters. These mechanisms were not generally regarded as forms of genuine participation but rather as downward instruments of communication, being favoured by management over trade unions precisely because they inhibited the development of trade union consciousness. In short, these bodies served to legitimate management power, a fact reflected in the use of restricted agendas and discouragement of discussion over terms and conditions of employment. Ironically, this did not stop Hales' respondents complaining about the narrowness of discussions, a paradox the author explains in terms of management preference for agenda items that would allow their views to prevail.

Hales found that job enlargement, enrichment and rotation strategies were far from the theoretical ideal insofar as in many cases they had evolved in an arbitrary and *ad hoc* fashion, rather than as an outcome of systematic planning to overcome monotony at work. Such measures were usually orientated towards increasing the responsibility of supervisory and management staff, often as a response, it was claimed, to the expressed willingness of staff to shoulder extra responsibilities. Job enrichment served as a means of rationalising organisational structure, usually by reducing middle and area management and redistributing their tasks to unit management. Job enlargement often involved little more than job extension; that is, increased use of generalist job categories where incumbents were required to move between different tasks during their shifts. Job rotation was a term often used to denote managerial career development via regular job changes and/or mobility for unit managers. Hales notes that there existed a generalised perception of non-managerial staff as neither capable nor desirous of greater responsibility in their work. However, job rotation was a common strategy adopted amongst manual as well as management workers, frequently entailing the use of general assistants as flexible labour to carry out duties on an *ad hoc* basis in order to reduce labour costs. Hales identified two hotel groups adopting the practice of employing mainly female labour to carry out breakfast waitress, chambermaid and bar duties over the course of a morning shift. Like Mars, Bryant and Mitchell (1979) before him, Hales found some companies expressing a preference for workers without previous hotel and catering experience, a preference deriving from the twin views of the absence of technical content from hotel and catering jobs and the idea that previous hotel and catering experience brought with it pre-conceptions of the nature of the work that may not be realised. Notwithstanding these findings, Hales also noted that whereas many organisations reported having adopted QWL measures in a range of occupations, this trend was far less marked in organisations concerned exclusively with hotel operations. He also discovered that where QWL measures were consciously adopted, as opposed to evolving in an *ad hoc* fashion, they were seen primarily as a means of increasing productivity rather than improving the quality of working life. Unsurprisingly, the adoption of QWL measures was reported by employers to have improved the morale of the workforce and, in the specific case of job rotation, led to a fall in labour turnover.

Hales' study paints a depressing picture of employers' motivations and handling of QWL measures in the hospitality industry. Where used, they appear to be little more than an excuse for economising on staff and extending managerial control. Indeed, as Hales himself recognises it is a central tenet of many critiques of job redesign that QWL measures increase the potential for managerial control along Taylorist lines, a point not lost, additionally, on Mars, Bryant and Mitchell (1979) who, however, appear to morally condone the fact that multi-skilling necessarily involves some deskilling in order to break down the traditionally rigid hierarchy of specialisms and skills on which individual contracts are based. It is, perhaps, unsurprising to find that hotels amongst all companies surveyed used QWL measures the least. Despite the fact that some form of 'multi-skilling' is the norm in those small firms that dominate the hotel and catering industry (Lowe, 1988), the *need* for functional flexibility or any desire to improve the quality of working life of employees by hotels with ready access to a relatively plentiful supply of labour is not a priority. Measures that improve the functional flexibility or quality of working life of the workforce can be costly, requiring training and attendant organisational changes. In conditions of demand uncertainty such as those facing many hotels, and where numerically flexible methods of labour management are both managerially and economically expedient, it is unsurprising that functional flexibility/quality of working life measures are not an issue for employers. The relatively 'high' levels of functional flexibility amongst managerial workers are superficially encouraging up to the point where it is recognised that functional flexibility or QWL measures perform a corresponding function at supervisory and managerial level to numerical flexibility strategies at operative levels, i.e. presents senior management with an opportunity to cut labour costs and organise administrative functions in a more rational way.

To round off this discussion of flexible working in hotels and catering, it is worth noting that the use of pay flexibility and distancing strategies in the industry has received less attention than either numerical or functional flexibility. Again, the hotel and catering industry has always had some form of pay flexibility established through such means as individual contracts, and the use by employers of tips to subsidise wages. Because hotel and catering general managers are given considerable scope in setting pay rates, they can, within limits, reward exceptional or shortage skills easily, as well as varying informal rewards. Lockwood and Guerrier (1989) found no general pattern in the role of distancing methods. In terms of the distribution of risk, there are areas that remain unelaborated, though, given the reliance of many hotel and catering organisations on prepacked and preprepared foodstuffs, it is surprising that this has not been considered seriously as an element in hospitality organisations' distancing strategies. Similarly, a historical perspective on flexibility in hospitality organisations may reveal the extent to which there has been a degree of intra-company and intra-industry distancing. The Department of Employment (1971) noted that much work had been removed from hotel units to centralised company operations, particularly in the field of reservations. Many current analyses of flexibility in the hospitality industry lack a historical dimension: the ready acceptance of, in particular, numerical flexibility as an enduring feature of hotel and catering organisation has perhaps obscured the extent to which the other processes described here have also figured as fundamental historical trends, rather than being simply contemporary aspects of work organisation made fashionable by academic scholarship.

CONCLUSIONS

The preceding discussion highlights two styles of commentary on the nature and extent of deskilling. The first embodies fairly straightforward 'matter of fact' assertions about the nature and extent of deskilling in the industry, and presents at least superficially convincing evidence to suggest that standardisation of hotel and catering products and services has reduced the need for costly skilled labour and has led, through greater capital intensivity, to deskilling and greater financial and technological control of work in hotel and catering operations. These commentaries are broadly supportive of the Braverman hypothesis in content but in tone lack any theoretical perspective or motivation. The second area of debate on flexible working is more open as to its conclusions. Some evidence at least suggests that multi-skilling and QWL practices have had some influence on the hotel and catering industry, entailing a degree of deskilling.

The absence of any firm conclusions about the extent of deskilling in hotels and catering reflects similar tensions to be found in the wider degradation debate. Superficially, there is a good case for arguing that deskilling has taken place in hotels and catering but to press this point is to raise questions about tendencies towards enskilling and the upgrading of jobs. It is probably fair to say that the weight of evidence supports the view that both deskilling and enskilling/reskilling have occurred in hotels and catering. The weight of evidence is not all that great, however, and the usual caveats apply about the need for more detailed study of workplace production processes and managerial control strategies. One area of investigation that may merit explanation is that of employer and managerial intention. Little is known in the hotel and catering context of deliberate managerial strategies to increase control through deskilling and the reorganisation of skill nor of the consequences of such strategies. If the evidence considered in this and previous chapters is anything to go by, then the essentially arbitrary nature of hotel and catering management suggests that distinct motivations to deskill are less likely than attempts to engender other changes in the production process. Riley (1981a) draws attention to the relationship between the market for hotel and catering services and the potential for deskilling (see also Gabriel, 1988). He suggests that deskilling can come about as a result of either changing consumer preferences and/or deliberate action by management to 'trade down' and permanently deskill occupations. The temptation to trade down is strong since many workers, notably core workers, are expensive. Further, total labour costs might be reduced by the more widespread elimination of individual contracts and associated covert forms of remuneration. For Riley, the consequence of trading down is the inhibition of skill accumulation and the lowering of standards. Trading down leads to skills falling into disuse, reduces the opportunities for workers to acquire skills (since markets become increasingly homogenous) and lowers the apex of skill attainment within the industry, certain 'higher' skills disappearing altogether. In such a situation, Riley argues, the culture of the hotel industry is undermined and parts of it at least disappear:

> No matter how far the culture is dispersed and creates demand, if it fails to induce people to learn its skills, it must die. . . .It follows from the above that to wither supply would be to choke off demand. . . .Thus

deskilling would, by definition, wither supply. The net result would be that fewer people would demand these standards, and fewer people would be able to supply them.

(Riley, 1981c: 102–103)

Riley's analysis goes some way to explaining the trend towards standardisation and moves away from traditional conceptions of skill, standards and service in hotels. There is evidence of an opposite trend, however, one that at least maintains, or at best increases, demand for the traditional culture of hotels predicated on the European model of personal service, *haute* gastronomy and unmitigated luxury. The disparate nature of the hotel industry makes generalisation impossible but some hotel users at least seem unwilling to accept the sterile environment of many of the chain-owned 'bed factories'. This tendency may not be equal to that of greater standardisation with its concomitant deskilling, but it is marked. The suspicion is that managerial strategies towards deskilling, like those evident in Hales' study of the adoption of quality of working life measures, are less a matter of unified intent than uncoordinated stumblings towards some hazy ideal of efficiency and administrative improvement.

6 Accommodating decline?

The future of hotel and catering work

According to Samuel Butler, 'Life is the art of drawing sufficient conclusions from insufficient premises'. On the basis of the evidence reviewed in this book, a sufficient conclusion would be that despite a general lack of wide-ranging empirical data, there is some measure of agreement that hotel and catering work is largely exploitative, degrading, poorly paid, unpleasant, insecure and taken as last resort or because it can be tolerated in the light of wider commitments and constraints. This is not to deny that there are many employed in a whole variety of work tasks who value their position and gain much satisfaction from their employment. Anyone who has even a moderate acquaintance with the industry is familiar with the many workers at all levels, 'the addicts', who work long hours in poor conditions for relatively little financial reward and for whom criticism of the industry is regarded as heretical. It remains to be demonstrated however as to whether these happy circumstances apply to anything more than a minority of the workforce.

INTERNATIONAL COMPARISONS

Insofar as it is possible to assess, the problems and experiences of the UK hospitality industry workforce are not unique, but are repeated on an international scale. In the mid-1960s and 1970s the International Labour Office (ILO) published a number of reports based on the proceedings of symposia held under the auspices of the International Labour Organisation (International Labour Organisation, 1965, 1974, 1980). A close reading of these rapidly reveals that little can be added to the judgement of Mars, Bryant and Mitchell:

> The I.L.O. reports describe the structural properties of the industry in a number of different countries. Although there are some very obvious cultural variations, particularly in terms of attitudes to the service role

the industry performs, many of the social and economic problems of the industry tend to have general applicability.

(Mars, Bryant and Mitchell, 1979: 153)

Mars and his colleagues have of course, identified that key difference between the UK and other countries which is supposed to mark the fact that other hotel and catering industries are in some way better than our own and their workers better off in some absolute terms. This is the attitude to service which can and does differ radically in *some* countries from the British aloofness and disdain for personal service industries. However, appearances have little to do with reality, particularly in the hotel and catering industry.

Nowhere is this clearer than in the case of the USA, the frequently lauded home of consumer-orientated consumerism. Ackerman (1981) makes five observations of interest about the USA hospitality industry:

First of all, employees are predominantly women and young people (women alone account for 56 per cent). Second workers have the shortest working week (an average of 26.4 hours). This means there are many part-time workers, simply paid by the hour. Third, wages are low: workers have the lowest average earnings per hour (excluding tips). Fourth, for many they are dead-end jobs, without any prospect for promotion or a career. And fifth, they are hardly protected by unionization.

(Ackerman, 1981: 448)

Ackerman's observations are confirmed in a study by Alpert (1986) of the American restaurant industry. His statistics are no less illuminating: 64 per cent of all restaurant workers are women; most workers are young, with half under the age of 25 and 32 per cent less than 19; most work less than twenty hours per week; most are relatively badly paid, restaurant workers' wages being only 52 per cent of employees in manufacturing. Alpert also claims in support of the British evidence that tipping is extensive and serves to subsidise the cost to the operator of service delivery (though only 37 per cent of restaurant workers are actually in service positions and therefore likely to receive tips); that deskilling in the industry is extensive as a result of increasing use of technology; and the level of unionisation is low at around 10 per cent. Hiemstra (1990) in a study of the personnel practices of a sample of American hotels and motels in response to an apparent labour shortage reports labour turnover rates of 89 per cent for hourly paid staff and 44 per cent for salaried staff per annum. When asked what personnel policies were being pursued in the light of the putative labour shortage, in a list of nine 'paying relatively high wages' came bottom with, just above, 'providing job security'. The most common hiring practice reported by

Hiemstra's respondents was local recruitment through newspaper adver-
tisements or personnel recommendation, thus emphasising the no less local
nature of labour markets in the American hospitality industry.

The evidence of Ackerman, Alpert and Hiemstra confirms the findings
of Henderson's 1965 study of the American lodging industry and, when
taken with the other North American literature discussed elsewhere in the
text, suggests that there are few fundamental differences in the nature and
experience of work on either side of the Atlantic. This appears to extend to
other countries. The picture of hotel and catering work in Australia differs
hardly at all. Worland and Wilson (1988) examined hotel and catering
labour in the state of Victoria and report above average levels of part-time
work and female participation in the labour force of the hospitality industry,
aspects of employment they suggest mirror national trends. Casualisation,
linked to trends in multiple-job holding, is also common. Tomoda (1983) in
a study of working conditions in Japanese hotels similarly found many of
the common industry characteristics described earlier. Wages were
generally low, women and part-timers were particularly affected in this
respect and, of course, many part-time workers were women. Explicit
discrimination appears to have been a feature of Japanese employment at
that time. Hardly any wage gap existed at all between men and women upon
graduation from high school but pay gaps increased markedly between the
second and fifth years of employment in the hotel and catering industry
largely, Tomoda suggests, as a result of some women receiving smaller
increments than their male counterparts. Men also enjoyed greater chances
of promotion within the industry.

A report in the industry magazine *Asia Travel Trade* (May, 1989)
focused on six countries with labour shortages and pointed up all too
familiar problems and practices. In Hong Kong, employers were seeking to
overcome the labour shortage in terms of offering more perks, poaching
staff from one another's hotels and in some cases paying large loyalty
bonuses – four months salary at Chinese New Year is the example cited.
Staff poaching was also common in the much smaller Malaysian hotel
industry where, however, the reports' authors note concern about the lack
of staff training. The Philippines appeared to be the least problem-ridden of
the countries examined and it is interesting to note that there is an established system of hotel management education in the Philippines! Labour
shortages and high labour turnover were both common problems in the
Singapore and Taiwanese hotel industry, compounded by reportedly poor
conditions of work and a view of the industry as offering low status jobs. In
Thailand, the authors of the report noted more fundamental problems in
terms of an acute skills shortage (including language skills) but found
recruitment to be buoyant as pay and conditions of work in the hotel

industry tended to be better than average for the country as a whole. This view is borne out in a study by Samalapa (1990) who suggests that Thais have a considered and positive approach to hospitality not necessarily characteristic of many other Asian societies. Personal and community bonds deriving from close religious observance render personal service a relatively valuable social commodity that is not regarded as degrading. At the same time, the Thai hotel industry is characterised by a substantial number of indigenous hotel companies and internationalisation is as yet in its infancy in terms of the presence of significant numbers of multi-national firms. The indigenous firms thus set employment standards in the industry and these tend to be predicated on the predominant social values of Thai society which are paternalistic but, at some levels at least, less inclined to economic exploitation.

This last observation is not without some significance. In many developing countries, those of the so-called 'Third World', the indigenous hospitality industry is often limited in scope to the needs of the resident population. The growth of the multi-national hotel industry is slowly changing the face of hospitality in many of these countries, at least in large cities and tourism destinations. Hotel companies operating in less developed countries may pursue a range of strategies in running their hotels: franchising the operation, utilising management contracts, and direct management by their own staff amongst them. Similarly, hotel construction can be achieved in a variety of ways: solely financed by the company, financed jointly by the company and the government of the country concerned and so on. Ultimately, however, the resulting product tends to be very much in the cultural traditions of Western hotels, unsurprising given that a substantial proportion of the tourist trade is drawn from the West. The spread of the international hotel industry to less developed countries may be seen as a form of cultural imperialism and though knowledge concerning the effects of development on employment is virtually non-existent, the effects of tourism on these and other non-industrialised countries have attracted the attention of some researchers.

For example, Belisle (1983) in a study of tourism and food production in the Caribbean notes how the requirements of the former distorts local food production. Many Caribbean islands import the majority of their foodstuffs. There are a number of reasons for this. Tourists prefer the type and taste of food they customarily consume at home, imported food is sometimes cheaper than local food and of a superior quality, and local farmers are unable to either change the type of food they produce or supply sufficient quantities of what they do grow. Importing food leads to loss of foreign exchange but, more significantly, there is a loss of opportunity to expand and diversify the indigenous food production and processing industries with concomitant loss of potential employment and income. This scenario is a familiar one to tourism analysts. In terms of employment local economies can be distorted by an over-emphasis on tourism and hotels as revenue generators. Employment patterns in support of tourism industries may develop in such a manner as to irrevocably alter and distort the economic and social fabric of whole communities and regions.

This process is not confined to less developed countries or established overseas resort destinations. In Britain, the recent growth of the 'heritage industry' and internal tourism, encouraged by government and others as a potential employment solution to long-term decline in traditional manufacturing and 'smokestack industries', has led many commentators to express concern at the growing dependence on so narrow an economic base. Arguments about the British hostility to service industries apart, the implications for employment seem clear: not only do the service industries appear incapable of absorbing sufficient numbers of workers from declining industries but service jobs are often part-time and of dubious 'quality' (Gabriel, 1988). But this does not have to be the case. The potential for wholesale distortion of economy and employment as a result of growth in service industries in general and tourism in particular is a potential that can be ameliorated by preventing unfettered development and taking action to provide an economic framework that accords service industries a central rather than peripheral role in economic policy. There is no intrinsic reason why service employment should be poorly paid: poor pay and conditions are a matter of employers' policies and these are mediated by wider social and political values and ideologies. Discussion of attitudes to service and service industries have recurred throughout this book (and are returned to several times below). Without seeming to trivialise what are obviously complex economic issues, it is nevertheless important to recognise that exploitation in employment is not a characteristic of particular types of industry but of the social and economic system in which industries operate – and all systems are susceptible, with varying prospects of success, to some form of management.

EMPLOYMENT TRENDS, PROFESSIONALISATION AND EDUCATION

Given the limited availability of detailed evidence, there is little merit to any extensive country-by-country account of the conditions of hotel and catering labour. What is clear is that despite cultural variations general trends can be perceived and these bear out much of what has been said about the degradation of work in the industry and the exploitation of employees in the UK context. Changes in the nature of hotel and catering employment in modern times have not, in the main, been for the better. The historical fact of low pay, low status and highly stigmatised jobs has been compounded by employer strategies to weaken further the power of employees by moving towards increased numerical flexibility in the use of labour; the increased employment of workers limited in bargaining power, most notably women; the creation of a multi-layered workforce incorporating a strata of low skill, deskilled and degraded jobs many of which are heavily sex-typed; and heightened divisions within the workforce engendered by the utilisation of greater numbers of peripheral casual and part-time workers at the expense of full-time core staff. The frequent efforts of employers to convince the outside world that the nature of hotel and catering work has improved or is improving look ever more shallow with each new piece of research confirming the true state of employment in the industry. So too do claims concerning the increased professionalisation of, in particular, hotel and catering managements. Views like these have always formed part of the rhetoric of hospitality industry employers, educators, representative organisations and professional associations. They now seem to be gaining wider circulation. For example, Crompton and Sanderson note that 'Within the hotel trade in particular it was constantly stressed that progress through management without an HCIMA [Hotel, Catering and Institutional Management Association, the UK's professional and educational association] qualification would be extremely difficult' (Crompton and Sanderson, 1990: 156). This is a pleasant fantasy that mistakes both the extent of unqualified managers in the industry (particularly in those areas where management functions have been devolved to largely unqualified 'supervisors' for the purpose of containing labour costs and increasing the value to the employer of certain categories of labour) and the nature of hotel and catering management education as a form of preentry socialisation to an occupation which itself is extremely degraded in terms of job content and remuneration except at the most senior levels.

Certainly, the hotel and catering industry has always been surrounded by the paraphernalia of education and certification (Lennon, 1990). To dignify this as evidence of professionalisation is, at its kindest, misguided for it makes certain unspecified assumptions about the content and quality of such education. Despite many pockets of excellence, detailed study of aspects of British hotel and catering management education raises serious questions about the quality and standards of provision (Department of Education and Science, 1987, 1988; Wood, 1988; Lennon, 1989, 1990). More important is the extent to which hotel and catering management education, at least in Britain, buttresses existing systems of inequality and exploitation in the industry by virtue of its very existence as a form of training separate and distinct from general business and management

studies. As Mars, Bryant and Mitchell (1979) imply, hospitality management education is something of an industry in its own right, promulgating
reactionary platitudes as potential managerial solutions to the 'problems'
faced by the hotel and catering sector. Education, the authors suggests,
'makes any problem appear soluble at an acceptable cost. . .[and]. . .has
allowed difficult decisions to be avoided by discouraging the kind of
searching analyses that may reveal unpalatable realities' (Mars, Bryant and
Mitchell, 1979: 129). Though they do not say it in so many words, Mars and
his colleagues appear to be suggesting, rightly, that management is, in the
words of the aphorism, part of the problem rather than part of the solution.

One thing is certain and that is that if the success of hotel and catering
management education was judged solely in terms of the contribution of
trained managers to the quality of working life in the industry then it would
be difficult indeed to find something even remotely charitable to say in
defence of both past and present performance. From the evidence reviewed
earlier (and some limited reading between the lines) it seems that the
situation in the education systems of other countries is not radically different. In Britain, there is a certain resistance in the hotel and catering industry
to the blandishments of educational institutions and great emphasis is
placed on practical skills and experience. Ironically however, there is a
lurking suspicion that one issue on which educationalists and industrialists
would be agreed upon would be the need for specialist separate hospitality
management education if there must be education at all. There are few
industries in the United Kingdom or elsewhere whose potential source of
managerial labour is trained quite so extensively at the taxpayers' expense
prior to them taking up their first job. The response of employers to this
considerable subsidy is to pay their management staff salaries which for the
most part are substantially below those of managers in other industries,
constituting further cost savings in the acquisition of skilled administrators.

At the time of writing there are over twenty degree courses in hotel and
catering studies available in UK higher education institutions compared to
just two courses in 1965. In addition there are innumerable Higher National
Diploma (sub-degree) courses and programmes leading to certification in a
variety of operative skills. The long-term post-war investment of government, not only in education but in training (via such organisations as the
Hotel and Catering Industry Training Board), has had ample time to show
concrete returns not only in terms of product quality but in the quality of
working life in the hospitality industry that might be engendered by 'professional' approaches to administration. No such returns are in evidence. The
hotel and catering industry has succeeded in talking about training and the
need for training whilst pursuing, at many levels, development and

employment policies designed to eliminate the need for motivated and accomplished employees.

BLAMING THE WORKERS

Management and management education is of course a soft target for the desk-bound critic and there are many, including academic commentators, who point with varying degrees of explicitness to the role of the workforce in perpetuating poor terms and conditions of employment. These arguments operate at a variety of levels. Hotel and catering workers are, supposedly by their own admission, 'different from other people' (Shamir, 1981). They 'enjoy' mobility and transient social relationships. As Crompton and Sanderson (1990) put it on a number of occasions, the industry is a 'turbulent' one. Turbulence is not a basis for sound industrial relations or collective action. The more these kinds of argument are analysed the more it becomes obvious that victim-blaming is still alive and well. The problems faced by many employees are not seen as the the the result of socio-economic inequalities and appalling management: workers themselves must bear at least some of the responsibility for their situation.

That hotel and catering workers tolerate their lot because, despite the privations of their employment, they derive some psychological gratification from being exploited or rather enjoy the instrumentalism forced upon them by a highly competitive work environment, is a view that is as fatuous as it is dangerous. From Orwell's autobiographical excursus through Whyte's study to much contemporary research, the idea that some or all hotel and catering workers obtain masochistic pleasure from performing degraded and unpleasant work tasks for minimal reward has provided an explanatory bolt-hole of extraordinary convenience. Sometimes, this aspect of hotel and catering work has reflected analysts' genuine puzzlement at the conditions under which industry employees are prepared to labour. On other occasions, researchers' dazzlement at the seedy and informal side of hotel and catering operations can be identified as the source of arguments predicated on victim-blaming. Too frequently, however, holding workers responsible for their own situation derives from an unwillingness to recognise the importance of labour market factors and more general trends in work that provide the wider context for conditions of employment in the hospitality and other industries.

Such an unwillingness has been, until relatively recently, at the heart of the orthodox view of research into hotel and catering labour. As suggested in Chapter 1, increasing research interest in hotel and catering employment has begun to widen perspectives and lead to a questioning of these orthodoxies. Despite this, there is an all too ready willingness when avoiding 'victim-blaming' explanations to accept that there is little that hotel and catering workers can or want to do to improve their situation. The sense of hopelessness experienced by many employees is in other words matched by a similar sense of hopelessness amongst researchers. Gabriel (1988) captures this well but signals a refreshing departure from much of the introverted navel-contemplation that characterises many of the existing debates in industrial sociology when he says:

> I would also dispute the view that the workers have lost their ability or will to resist, fight and contest the power of capital. While the workers whose views were described here come from some of the most vulnerable and exploited sections of the working class – foreign, part-time, female, teenage, unskilled – and while their position is aggravated by economic collapse, their discontents mirror the hidden injuries of class of many generations of workers who have reluctantly sold their labour power to capital. Their lot is boring work, poor working conditions, arrogant management, and above all, lack of control over those forces which dominate their lives. Like generations of workers before them, they experience deep ambivalence, depending on capital for their livelihood, feeling impotent in the face of capital and yet fighting back in significant ways.
>
> (Gabriel, 1988: 167–168)

The point is, of course, that the extent of workers' resistance is limited as a result of the general lack of importance attached to employment welfare and particularly that of workers in service industries. General social disdain for service employment is complemented in common-sense perceptions by a curious attitudinal paradox that on the one hand sees service work as 'not quite the thing' and on the other as offering opportunities for 'helping' others and thus performing valuable tasks. Most of the general public only ever appreciate hotels and catering in terms of the work of waiting staff and other front of house employees and this can lead to the 'lion and hyena' situation whereby the vulture, having observed the lion rip the hyena to shreds, alighted next to the unfortunate victim and, upon being asked with a dying groan why he had not come to the hyena's aid replied 'You were laughing so much I thought you were enjoying yourself'. The general social perceptions of hotel and catering and other service work, with all the contradictions they entail, have far more concrete implications. Apart from minor concessions to wages protection, government takes little interest in the lot of service workers and other low-paid employees (a point elaborated upon briefly in the next section). Trades unions have demonstrated what by any standard is only marginal interest in the hotel and catering industry and more significantly have failed to back both their rhetoric and frequently stated desire to maintain membership levels in the provision of resources necessary for organising the industry. It is interesting to reflect upon the plight of hotel and catering workers in terms of the root character and purpose of their labour – the provision of food, drink and shelter, and to consider just how widely the majority of people take these things for granted. Hotel and catering workers have always been taken for granted and their situation, far from being a product of their own inertia, constitutes more the outcome of wider social attitudes to service and hospitality that are ruthlessly exploited by those who provide it.

FUTURES PERFECT AND IMPERFECT

What then is the future of hotel and catering work? One view based on current trends might be that the UK is developing along similar lines to the situation that seemingly exists at present in America if writers such as Alpert (1986) are to be believed. The industry is becoming a sector in which people work for a brief time, it is a staging point on the career path that leads to somewhere better. This scenario is supported in the American context by the observation that the hotel and catering industry offers a ready and plentiful supply of part-time jobs particularly valuable to young people in education who require sources of finance to support their studies (Alpert, 1986). Similarly, in the UK Crompton and Sanderson (1990) have questioned the rigidity of the sex-typing of low-grade service jobs in hotels and catering and pointed to a similar possibility:

> lower level work in the hotel trade has not been firmly sex-typed. In this highly competitive industry it is necessary that labour should be cheap, rather than it should be one sex or another. Thus, despite evidence of what may appear to be quite extensive segregation by gender, the realities are more complex. An 'inverse statistical discrimination' operates. Female labour is used because it is both cheap and available at the right time of day and season. If another source of cheap labour becomes available it will be used as well. The economic recession, in combination with central government policies, has made young people such a source. Unemployment rates are particularly high amongst the younger age groups, and the system of benefits has been structured so as to make it more likely that they will accept poorly-paid work. More young people are staying on into the sixth form, and/or going into further education. The declining value of student grants and pressures on parental incomes has further increased the necessity for part-time work of some kind.
>
> (Crompton and Sanderson, 1990: 148)

Crompton and Sanderson undoubtedly paint the prospect of an industry that has little qualms about employing the cheapest labour. The substitutability of labour (or should it be disposability?) is a matter of little concern to employers where part-time and casual employees enjoy few legal rights of protection and can be excluded by law or company policy from certain remunerative benefits such as holiday pay and work-related bonuses. Certainly, in the case of young workers under the age of 21, where the encouragement to low pay is enshrined in statute law, Crompton and Sanderson's arguments acquire special salience. It would be dangerous, however, to fall into the trap of regarding such a scenario as either wholly real or unavoidable. The hotel and catering industry is not heterogeneous and it is clear that local labour markets are an important factor in determining both the supply and price of labour as well as hotel management's attitudes to staffing. As the earlier study by Lockwood and Guerrier (1989) demonstrated, there are certain areas in which hoteliers build up a core of more or less permanent staff. Just as it is clear that in some areas practices such as these are alien to hotel managements then there are locales and sectors in which labour stability is an important factor in employer strategy. Nor does this apply only to full-time staff. There are many instances of even casual, seasonal and part-time staff working for only one firm or unit as the need demands (cf. Lowe, 1988). Youth labour is likely to remain an important element of the supply for hotel and catering labour in many countries and it seems that in some cases at least, 'the young' will predominate in the workforce overall. Some employers, notably McDonald's in the USA (with whom 7 per cent of the working population gain their first job – Transnationals Information Centre, 1987), have made a point of employing older workers, including the early retired, but this trend does not seem to have gathered momentum elsewhere. Clearly the shifting composition of the hotel and catering workforce will remain an interesting focus for research, though it is important to remember that the action (or indifference) of employers and prevailing influences in the labour market are not the only variables of importance in considering the changing nature of hospitality work.

This is particularly true in industries such as hotel and catering traditionally 'protected' by legislative structures centred on pay regulation. Here governments can make a difference. During the 1980s in Great Britain a central plank of employment policy has been, as indicated earlier in the text, to lower the cost to employers of youth labour through a variety of devices including exclusion of under-21s from the scope of Wages Councils in protected industries. There is nothing necessarily inevitable or concrete about such policies however and a government of different political colour may well reverse these legislative measures or at least make important adjustments to them. In one form or another, the Trades Union Congress (TUC) is committed to pressurising government for the introduction of a statutory minimum wage (SMW). Under a government of the Labour Party such a development is not unlikely, though nor is it necessarily practicable. The United Kingdom's membership of the European Community is also a likely important influence on industry and employment in general and low-pay industries like hotels and catering in particular. The attempts by the European Community to introduce a 'Social Charter' regularising *inter alia*, employment rights in member states was resisted by the British Government to the extent that Britain was the only country not to sign the Charter in December 1989. European-wide influences on both employment legislation and employment itself seem likely to increase in importance, especially with the advent of the Single European Market in 1992. Certainly, the failure of the hotel and catering industry in Britain and elsewhere to 'put its own house in order' (a charitable description) means that it is only action by governments that will make any real change to the nature of hospitality sector employment. Even here, however, past experience shows that the scope for government is limited if policy is merely directed towards employee protection. Wages Council protection is of little use if it is not policed rigorously. For this reason, even returning under-21s to Wages Councils protection would probably make little difference without substantial improvements to monitoring the system. The kind of governmental intervention that would be required to ensure that hotel, catering and all other employers provided decent terms and conditions would require a radicalism not seen in British politics for many years, if at all. Even then, it is not certain that many industry employees, given their diverse motivations, would either welcome or benefit from such changes. Employers and proprietors could no doubt be relied upon to respond with their usual hostility. It is a measure of the extent to which service industries in Britain are viewed as unworthy of serious attention that tourism, hotels and catering – one of the nation's biggest money-earners – are not represented significantly in the higher reaches of government, either in policy or administrative terms. The United Kingdom has no Ministry of Tourism, it has no coherent set of policies on tourism development and the internal administration of tourism is handled by a range of bodies that are not co-ordinated in any significant way. There is little or no unifying focus for tourism-related industries nor any widespread sense of their value and limitations to economy and society more generally. This *laissez-faire* approach seems likely to continue for the foreseeable future, with all that entails in terms of the continuing misery of employment for those who service the leisure and business needs of others.

LAST ORDERS?

Predicting the future is a sometimes interesting but rarely meaningful exercise. Chivers (1973) suggested that the deskilling of cooks and chefs would lead to a greater unionisation of that occupation. A similar portent was divined by Mars and Mitchell (1976) in respect of the growing involvement of breweries in the ownership of hotel and catering organisations. Breweries, they argued, had sophisticated management and personnel administration techniques and were unlikely to tolerate the workplace practices common in the hotel and catering industry. These were optimistic prognoses and they have (so far) been proved quite wrong. Indeed, any understanding of both the history of the hospitality industry and the laws of probability suggest that optimism about the future of hotel and catering work is bound to be misplaced. Each new study of employment in the industry tends to 'rediscover' the wretched situation of many hotel and catering workers. The provision of hotel and catering services at anything other than the most basic level has always entailed an element of the feudal, of the poor servicing the rich. Conflict in the workplace is not a new phenomenon in hotels and catering but one, as Gabriel (1988) suggests, with its roots very firmly planted in the soil of capitalist exploitation. In these respects, hotels and catering differ little from other industries and it is the similarities that the industry has with others that deserve to be stressed, not the putative differences on which many employers, educationalists and academic researchers repeatedly dwell.

To take refuge in platitudinous generalisations is, of course, to abandon the responsibility for accepting that improvements are possible within any social and industrial system. Mars, Bryant and Mitchell (1979) argue for reducing the importance of individual contract-making and breaking down the informal rewards system by encouraging multi-skilling and the employment of workers with little or no experience of hotel and catering employment and therefore limited expectations of industry traditions and conventions in respect of additions to basic pay. To a certain extent, many large hotel and catering organisations have pursued just these policies. However, there is every suggestion that, insofar as they ever existed at all extensively, individual contract-making persists as do informal reward elements in remuneration. Mars, Bryant and Mitchell's goals are directed towards an essential undermining of the culture of hotels. Thus in arguing for multi-skilling, they accept that one price for this will be some deskilling. They are not so clear about the necessary corollaries to elimination of individual contract-making and informal rewards, i.e. higher basic wages. Their still eminently realisable objectives could be achieved by management action but this would require the uniformity of purpose and level of foresight necessary to the sparking of a conversion of the kind unseen since that of Saint Paul. More importantly, without the concomitant provision of decent basic pay and conditions, many workers would be disadvantaged. Partnership between industry and government, with action by the latter to introduce an element of compulsion into the process of reform would be one alternative. Indeed, whilst laudable, it is difficult to see how the sorts of objective Mars, Bryant and Mitchell have in mind could be realised without government intervening to either initiate or contain reforming action.

This is clearly the view of campaigning groups. In Britain, the Low Pay Unit network of regional pressure groups has for some considerable time performed singly what should be a role shared with trade unions, that of campaigning to protect low-paid workers in hotels, catering and other industries. Potter (1988) concentrates on the extent to which employment conditions in hotels and catering might be improved as a result of developing highly co-ordinated local strategies of monitoring, control and action involving the tourism departments of local authorities, trades unions and other interested parties. There is a rather sad air in Potter's work reflected in her exclusion of employers from a potential list of 'action points'. Considering employers' track record on innovation and change it is probably realistic to assume that it is only legal and quasi-legal controls and external pressures that are likely to produce significant improvements. However, given the local nature of hotel and catering product and labour markets, it would be unwise to assume either that hotel and catering employers can be negated in any strategy for change or that *all* employers would themselves be opposed to involvement in a scheme that could be designed to bring manifest benefits. Certainly, one benefit of local strategies to combat conditions of work in hotels and catering is that they can take account of local circumstances and need not rely on the idealistic hope of initiatives by central government. The main stumbling block is of course the willingness of local authorities to participate in such schemes which, it is safe to hazard, would be ideologically unacceptable to some forms of political control.

Discussion of the kinds of policies that are needed to effect meaningful change to the terms and conditions of hotel and catering workers inevitably returns attention to the scope for making generalisations about what is an industry of considerable diversity. And yet generalisation is possible. The evidence reviewed in this book is suggestive of a deep-rooted and widespread malaise in the hotel and catering industry. It is a malaise also to be found in many other low-paid industries. The issues are somewhat blurred in the academic literature by the persistence of arguments concerning the willingness of hotel and catering workers to accept their lot 'with a nod and a smile'. These arguments must contain an element of truth but they should not be regarded as typical. For the most part, their expression is itself the result of researchers examining relatively untypical examples of hotel and catering operations. Perhaps the biggest obstacle to change in hotels and catering however is the widespread prejudice that goes hand-in-hand with concepts of service. To reiterate the point, service is simply not regarded as important in contexts where it is associated with things like food, drink and accommodation, things that most people take for granted. By association, those who work to meet these needs in the public sphere of hospitality receive little acknowledgement of their efforts and only limited acknowledgement of their service. It is a wretched situation made more wretched by the knowledge that change is possible but unlikely.

References

Ackerman, W. (1981) 'Cultural values and social choice of technology', *International Social Science Journal* 33, 3: 447–465.

Advisory, Conciliation and Arbitration Service (ACAS) (1988) *Labour Flexibility in Britain*, London: ACAS.

Airey, D.W. and Chopping, B.C. (1980) 'The labour market', in R. Kotas (ed.) *Managerial Economics for Hotel Operations*, Guildford: University of Surrey Press.

Alpert, W.J. (1986) *The Minimum Wage in the Restaurant Industry*, New York: Praeger.

Arnaldo, M.J. (1981) 'Hotel general managers: a profile', *Cornell Hotel and Restaurant Administration Quarterly*, November: 53–56.

Asia Travel Trade (1989) 'Manpower', *Asia Travel Trade*, May: 12–21.

Atkinson, J. (1984) 'Manpower strategies for flexible organisations', *Personnel Management*: August: 28–31.

Attewell, P. (1987) 'The deskilling controversy', *Sociology of Work and Occupations* 14, 3: 323–346.

Bagguley, P. (1987) *Flexibility, restructuring and gender: changing employment in Britain's hotels*, University of Lancaster: Lancaster Regionalism Group.

—— (1990) 'Gender and labour flexibility in hotel and catering', *The Service Industries Journal* 10, 4: 737–747.

Bain, G.S. (1970) *The Growth of White Collar Unionism*, Oxford: Clarendon Press.

Barron, R.D. and Norris, G.M. (1976) 'Sexual divisions and the dual labour market', in D. Barker and S.L. Allen (eds) *Dependence and Exploitation in Work and Marriage*, London: Longman.

Baum, T. (1989) 'Managing hotels in Ireland: research and development for change', *International Journal of Hospitality Management* 8, 2: 131–144.

Becker, G. (1964) *Human Capital*, New York: Columbia University Press.

Beechey, V. (1982) 'The sexual division of labour and the labour process: a critical assessment of Braverman', in S. Wood (ed.) *The Degradation of Work? Skill, Deskilling and the Labour Process*, London: Hutchinson.

—— (1987) *Unequal Work*, London: Verso.

Belisle, F. (1983) 'Tourism and food production in the Caribbean', *Annals of Tourism Research* 10, 4: 497–513.

Boella, M.J. (1986) 'A review of personnel management in the private sector of the British hospitality industry', *International Journal of Hospitality Management* 5, 1: 29–36.

Bowey, A. (1976) *The Sociology of Organisations*, London: Hodder & Stoughton.

Braverman, H. (1974) *Labor and Monopoly Capital*, New York: Monthly Review Press.

Brighton Council Economic Development Committee (1988) *Great expectations: the aspirations of Brighton's unemployed and recruitment difficulties in Brighton's hotels*, Brighton: Brighton Borough Council and Brighton Polytechnic.

Brown, M. and Winyard, S. (1975) *Low pay in hotels and catering*, London: Low Pay Unit.

Burns, T. and Stalker, G.M. (1961) *The Management of Innovation*, London: Tavistock.

Butler, S.R. and Skipper, J. (1981) 'Working for tips', *The Sociological Quarterly* 22, Winter: 15–27.

Butler, S.R. and Snizek, W.E. (1976) 'The waitress–diner relationship', *Sociology of Work and Occupations* 3, 2: 209–222.

Byrne, D. (ed.) (1986) *Waiting for Change*, London: Low Pay Unit.

Chivers, T.S. (1971) 'Chefs and cooks', unpublished Ph.D. thesis, University of London.

—— (1973) 'The proletarianisation of a service worker', *Sociological Review* 21: 633–656.

Chopping, B.C. (1977) 'Unionisation in London hotels and restaurants', unpublished B.Phil thesis, University of Oxford.

Collins, H.M. (1984) 'Concepts and methods of participatory fieldwork', in C. Bell and H. Roberts (eds) *Social Researching*, London: Routledge & Kegan Paul.

Commission for Racial Equality (1991) *Working in Hotels*, London: Commission for Racial Equality.

Commission on Industrial Relations (1971) *The Hotel and Catering Industry Part I: Hotels and Restaurants*, London: HMSO.

Corcoran, J. and Johnson, P. (1974) 'Image of four occupations', *Hotel, Catering and Institutional Management Association Journal*, June: 13–19.

County of Avon Careers Service (1988) *Tomorrow's Avon: Hotel and Catering*, Bristol: County of Avon Careers Service.

Cousins, J. and Foskett, D. (1989) 'Curriculum development for food production operations teaching for the hospitality industry: a system framework', paper given at the Operations Management Association Conference, Dunblane, May.

Crompton, R. (1989) 'Review of Y. Gabriel (1988) *Working Lives in Catering*', in *Work, Employment and Society* 3, 1: 129–130.

Crompton, R. and Sanderson, K. (1990) *Gendered Jobs and Social Change*, London: Unwin Hyman.

Croney, P. (1988) 'An investigation into the management of labour in the hotel industry', unpublished MA thesis, University of Warwick.

Dann, D. and Hornsey, T. (1986) 'Towards a theory of interdepartmental conflict in hotels', *International Journal of Hospitality Management* 5, 1: 23–28.

Delamont, S. (1983) 'Lobster, chicken, cake and tears: deciphering wedding meals', in A. Murcott (ed.) *The Sociology of Food and Eating*, Aldershot: Gower.

Dennis, N., Henriques, F. and Slaughter, C. (1956) *Coal is Our Life*, London: Tavistock (reissued in 1969).

Department of Education and Science (1987) *A survey of degree courses in hotel and catering studies in public sector higher education in England*, London: Department of Education and Science.

—— (1988) *Report by Her Majesty's Inspectors of a survey of one-year graduate entry courses leading to management qualifications in hotel and catering studies*, London: Department of Education and Science.

Department of Employment (1971) *Manpower study no. 10: Hotels*, London: HMSO.

—— (1976) *Manpower study no. 11: Catering*, London: HMSO.

Doeringer, P.B. and Piore, M.J. (1971) *Internal Labor Markets and Manpower Analysis*, Lexington, Mass: D.C. Heath.

Donald, E.B. (1982) *Debrett's Etiquette and Modern Manners*, London: Pan Books.

Dronfield, L. and Soto, P. (1980) *Hardship Hotel*, London: Counter Information Services.

Dunkerley, D. (1975) *Occupations and Society*, London: Routledge & Kegan Paul.

Education and Training Advisory Council (ETAC) (1983) *Hotel and catering skills – now and in the future, Part II: jobs and skills*, Wembley: HCITB.

Edwards, R. (1979) *Contested Terrain: The Transformation of the Workplace in the Twentieth Century*, London: Heinemann.

Ellis, P. (1981) *The Image of Hotel and Catering Work*, Wembley: Hotel and Catering Industry Training Board.

Forte, C. (1986) *Forte: the Autobiography of Charles Forte*, London: Sidgwick & Jackson.

Friedman, A. (1977) *Industry and Labour: Class Struggle at Work and Monopoly Capitalism*, London: Macmillan.

Gabriel, Y. (1988) *Working Lives in Catering*, London: Routledge & Kegan Paul.

Guerrier, Y. (1986) 'Hotel manager: an unsuitable job for a woman?', *The Service Industries Journal* 6, 2: 227–240.

—— (1987) 'Hotel managers' careers and their impact on hotels in Britain', *International Journal of Hospitality Management* 6, 3: 121–130.

Guerrier, Y. and Lockwood, A. (1989a) 'Developing hotel managers – a reappraisal', *International Journal of Hospitality Management* 8, 2: 82–89.

—— (1989b) 'Managing flexible working', *The Service Industries Journal* 6, 3: 406–419.

Hales, C. (1987) 'Quality of working life: job redesign and participation in a service industry: a rose by any other name?', *The Service Industries Journal* 7, 3: 253–273.

Henderson, J.P. (1965) *Labour Market Institutions and Wages in the Lodging Industry*, Michigan: Michigan State University, MSU Business Studies.

Hicks, L. (1990) 'Excluded women: how can this happen in the hotel world?', *The Service Industries Journal* 10, 2: 349–363.

Hiemstra, S.J. (1990) 'Employment policies and practices in the lodging industry', *International Journal of Hospitality Management* 9, 3: 207–221.

Hill, S. (1981) *Competition and Control at Work*, London: Heinemann.

Horowitz, M.A. (1960) *The New York Hotel Industry*, Cambridge, Mass: Harvard University Press.

Hotel and Catering Economic Development Committee (HCEDC) (1967) *Your manpower: a practical guide to the manpower statistics of the hotel and catering industry*, London: HMSO.

—— (1968a) *Why tipping?*, London: HMSO.

—— (1968b) *Service in hotels*, London: HMSO.

—— (1969) *Staff turnover*, London: HMSO.

—— (1975) *Manpower policy in the hotel and restaurant industry – research findings*, London: HMSO.

Hotel and Catering Industry Training Board (HCITB) (1970) *Development and training for potential managers*, Wembley: HCITB.

—— (1983) *Manpower changes in the hotel and catering industry*, Wembley: HCITB.

—— (1984a) *Women's path to management in the hotel and catering industry*, Wembley: HCITB.

—— (1984b) *Manpower flows in the hotel and catering industry*, Wembley: HCITB.

—— (1985) *Hotel and catering manpower in Britain*, Wembley, HCITB.

Hotel and Catering Training Board (HCTB) (1987) *Women in the hotel and catering industry*, Wembley: HCTB.

—— (1989) *Lifting the barriers: summary report*, Wembley: HCTB.

Howe, L.K. (1977) *Pink Collar Workers*, New York: Avon.

Humphreys, R. (1985) 'The survival of "scientific management"', *International Journal of Hospitality Management* 4, 3: 124–127.

Hyman, R. (1975) *Industrial Relations: A Marxist Introduction*, London: Macmillan.

International Labour Organisation (1965) *Tripartite technical meeting on hotels, restaurants and similar establishments, Report I: review of the social and economic problems of employees in hotels, restaurants and similar establishments*, Geneva: International Labour Office.

—— (1974) *Second tripartite technical meeting for hotels, restaurants and similar establishments: conditions of work and life of migrant and seasonal workers employed in hotels, restaurants and similar establishments*, Geneva: International Labour Office.

—— (1980) *Employment in the hotel and catering industry*, Geneva: International Labour Office.

Jameson, S.M. and Johnson, K. (1985) 'The hotel shop steward – an emerging role in British industrial relations', *International Journal of Hospitality Management* 4, 3: 131–132.

—— (1989) 'Hotel shop stewards – a critical factor in the development of industrial relations in hotels?', *International Journal of Hospitality Management* 8, 2: 167–177.

Johnson, K. (1978) 'Personnel matters: an overview or an oversight?', *Hotel, Catering and Institutional Management Association Journal*, January: 21–23.

—— (1980) 'Staff turnover in hotels', *Hospitality*, February, 28–36.

—— (1981) 'Towards an understanding of labour turnover?', *Service Industries Review* 1, 1: 4–17.

—— (1982) 'Fringe benefits: the views of individual hotel workers', *Hospitality*, June: 2–6.

—— (1983a) 'Payment in hotels: the role of fringe benefits', *The Service Industries Journal* 3, 2: 191–213.

—— (1983b) 'Trade unions and total rewards', *International Journal of Hospitality Management* 2, 1: 31–35.

—— (1985) 'Labour turnover in hotels – revisited', *The Service Industries Journal* 5, 2: 135–152.

—— (1986) 'Labour turnover in hotels – an update', *The Service Industries Journal* 6, 3: 362–380.

Johnson, K. and Mignot, K. (1982) 'Marketing trade unionism to service industries: an historical analysis of the hotel industry', *Service Industries Review* 2, 3: 5–23.

Johnson, K. and Whatton, T. (1984) 'A future for wages councils in the hospitality industry in the UK', *International Journal of Hospitality Management* 3, 2: 71–79.

Jones, B. (1982) 'Destruction or redistribution of engineering skills? The case of numerical control', in S. Wood (ed.) *The Degradation of Work? Skill, Deskilling and the Labour Process*, London: Hutchinson.

Jordan, D. (1978) *Low pay on a plate*, London: Low Pay Unit.

Kelliher, C. (1989) 'Flexibility in employment: developments in the hospitality industry', *International Journal of Hospitality Management* 8, 2: 157–166.

Kelliher, C. and Johnson, K. (1987) 'Personnel management in hotels: some empirical observations', *International Journal of Hospitality Management* 6, 2: 103–108.

Kelliher, C. and McKenna, S. (1987) 'Contract caterers and public sector catering', *Employee Relations* 10, 2: 8–13.

Knight, I. (1971) *Patterns of labour mobility in the hotel and catering industry*, Wembley: HCITB.

Kumar, K. (1978) *Prophecy and Progress*, Harmondsworth: Allen Lane.

Larmour, R. and McKenna, M. (1983) 'Room at the top', *Hospitality*, July: 8.

Larwood, L. and Wood, M. (1977) *Women in Management*, Lexington, Mass: D.C. Heath.

Lee, D.J. (1981) 'Skill, craft and class: a theoretical critique and a critical case', *Sociology* 15, 1: 56–78.

Lennon, J.J. (1989) 'Industrial "needs" and education provision: the case of hotel and catering management', *International Journal of Hospitality Management* 8, 3: 227–235.

—— (1990) 'Social science in hotel and catering degree education', Unpublished M.Phil. thesis, University of Strathclyde.

Lennon, J.J. and Wood, R.C. (1989) 'The sociological analysis of hospitality labour and the neglect of accommodation workers', *International Journal of Hospitality Management* 8, 3: 227–235.

Levitt, T. (1972) 'Production-line approach to service', reprinted in W.E. Sasser, R.P. Olsen and D.D. Wyckoff (eds) (1978) *The Management of Service Operations*, Boston: Allyn & Bacon.

Ley, D.A. (1980) 'The effective General Manager: leader or entrepreneur?', *Cornell Hotel and Restaurant Administration Quarterly*: November: 66–67.

Littler, C.R. (1982) *The Development of the Labour Process in Capitalist Societies*, London: Heinemann.

Lockwood, A. and Guerrier, Y. (1989) 'Flexible working in the hospitality industry: current strategies and future potential', *Contemporary Hospitality Management* 1, 1: 11–16.

Lowe, A. (1988) 'Small hotel survival – an inductive approach', *International Journal of Hospitality Management* 7, 3: 197–224.

Lucas, R. (1989) 'Minimum wages – straightjacket or framework for the hospitality industry into the nineties?', *International Journal of Hospitality Management* 8, 3: 197–214.

—— (1990) 'The Wages Act 1986: some reflections with particular reference to the Licensed Residential Establishments and Licensed Restaurant Wages Council', *The Service Industries Journal* 10, 2: 320–335.

Macfarlane, A. (1982a) 'Trade union growth, the employer and the hotel and restaurant industry: a case study', *Industrial Relations Journal* 13: 29–43.

—— (1982b) 'Trade unionism and the employer in hotels and restaurants', *International Journal of Hospitality Management* 1, 1: 35–43.

McKenna, M. and Larmour, R. (1984) 'Women in hotel and catering management in the UK', *International Journal of Hospitality Management* 3, 3: 107–112.

McKenna, S. (1990) 'The business ethic in public sector catering', *The Service Industries Journal* 10, 2: 377–398.

Mars, G. (1973) 'Hotel pilferage: a case study in occupational theft', in M. Warner (ed.) *The Sociology of the Workplace*, London: Allen & Unwin.

Mars, G. and Mitchell, P. (1976) *Room for Reform*, Milton Keynes: Open University Press.

—— (1977) 'Catering for the low paid: invisible earnings', *Low Pay Unit Bulletin* 15, June: 1–3.

Mars, G. and Nicod, M. (1981) 'Hidden rewards at work: the implications from a study of British hotels', in S. Henry (ed.) *Can I have It In Cash? A Study of Informal Institutions and Unorthodox Ways of Doing Things*, London: Astragal Books.

—— (1984) *The World of Waiters*, London: Allen & Unwin.

Mars, G., Bryant, D. and Mitchell, P. (1979) *Manpower Problems in the Hotel and Catering Industry*, Farnborough: Gower.

Mazurkiewicz, R. (1983) 'Gender and social consumption', *The Service Industries Journal* 3, 1: 49–62.

Mennell, S. (1985) *All Manners of Food: Eating and Taste in England and France from the Middle Ages to the Present*, Oxford: Basil Blackwell.

Mintzberg, H. (1973) *The Nature of Managerial Work*, New York: Harper & Row.

Mullins, L. (1981) 'Is the hotel and catering industry unique?', *Hospitality*, September: 30–33.

Murcott, A. (1982) 'On the social significance of the "cooked dinner" in South Wales', *Social Science Information* 21, 4/5: 677–696.

Nailon, P. (1968) 'A study of management activities in units of an hotel group', unpublished M.Phil. thesis, University of Surrey.

—— (1978) 'Tipping – a behavioural review', *Hotel, Catering and Institutional Management Association Review* 2, 4: 231–243.

National Economic Development Council (1986) *Changing working patterns* (report by the Institute of Manpower Studies), London: National Economic Development Office.

Orwell, G. (1933) *Down and Out in Paris and London*, Harmondsworth: Penguin (1986 reprint).

Palmer, G. (1968) 'Inter-union dispute in the Torquay hotel industry', *British Journal of Industrial Relations* 6: 250.

Paterson, E (1981) 'Food work: maids in a hospital kitchen', in P. Atkinson and C. Heath (eds) *Medical Work*, Farnborough: Gower.

Pine, R. (1987) *Management of Technological Change in the Catering Industry*, Aldershot: Avebury.

Potter, T. (1988) *A candy floss economy? Tourism and employment in the West Midlands*, Birmingham: West Midlands Low Pay Unit.

Prus, R.C. and Vasilakopoulos, S. (1979) 'Desk clerks and hookers – hustling in a "shady" hotel', *Urban Life* 8, 1: 52–71.

Quest, M. (1978) 'Unequal portions', *Hotel, Catering and Institutional Management Association Journal*, August: 13–14.

Riley, M. (1980) 'The role of mobility in the development of skills for the hotel and catering industry', *Hospitality*, March: 52–53.

—— (1981a) 'Recruitment, labour turnover and occupational rigidity: an essential relationship', *Hospitality*, March: 22–25.

—— (1981b) 'Labour turnover and recruitment costs', *Hospitality*, September: 27–29.

—— (1981c) 'Declining hotel standards and the skill trap', *Tourism Management* 2, 2: 99–104.

—— (1984) 'Hotels and group identity', *Tourism Management* 5, 2: 102–109.

—— (1985) 'Some social and historical perspectives on unionization in the UK hotel industry', *International Journal of Hospitality Management* 4, 3: 99–104.

Riley, M. and Turam, K. (1988) 'The career paths of hotel managers: a developmental approach', paper given at the International Association of Hotel Management Schools Symposium, Leeds, November.

Robinson, O. and Wallace, J. (1983) 'Employment trends in the hotel and catering industry in Great Britain', *The Service Industries Journal* 3, 3: 260–278.

—— (1984) 'Earnings in the hotel and catering industry in Great Britain', *The Service Industries Journal* 4, 2: 143–160.

Roebuck, J. and Frese, W. (1976) *The Rendezvous: A Case Study of an After Hours Club*, New York: Free Press.

Rose, M. (1975) *Industrial Behaviour: Theoretical Development Since Taylor*, Harmondsworth: Penguin.

—— (1988) *Industrial Behaviour*, Harmondsworth: Penguin (2nd edn).

Salaman, G. (1974) *Community and Occupation*, Cambridge: Cambridge University Press.

—— (1986) *Working*, London: Tavistock.

Samalapa, C. (1990) 'Problems associated with utilising indigenous labour in international hotels in Third World countries with special reference to Thailand', unpublished M.Sc. thesis, University of Strathclyde (The Scottish Hotel School).

Saunders, K.C. (1980) 'Head Hall Porters', *Employee Relations* 2, 2: 12–16.

—— (1981a) *Social Stigma of Occupations*, Farnborough: Gower.

—— (1981b) 'The influence of the menu structure on social relations in the kitchen', *Hospitality*, June: 14–18.

—— (1985) *Who is your kitchen porter?*, London: Middlesex Polytechnic.

Saunders, K.C. and Pullen R.A. (1987) *An occupational study of room-maids in hotels*, London: Middlesex Polytechnic.

Shamir, B. (1975) 'A study of working environment and attitudes to work of employees in a number of British hotels', unpublished Ph.D. thesis, University of London.

—— (1976) 'Resistance to change', *Hotel, Catering and Institutional Management Association Journal*, March: 7–9.

—— (1978) 'Between bureaucracy and hospitality – some organisational characteristics of hotels', *Journal of Management Studies* 15: 285–307.

—— (1981) 'The workplace as a community: the case of British hotels', *Industrial Relations Journal* 12, 6: 45–56.

Simms, J., Hales, C. and Riley, M. (1988) 'Examination of the concept of internal labour markets in UK hotels', *Tourism Management* 9, 1: 3–12.

Snow, G. (1981) 'Industrial relations in hotels', unpublished M.Sc. thesis, University of Bath.

Spradley, J.P. and Mann, B.J. (1975) *The Cocktail Waitress: Women's Work in a Man's World*, New York: John Wiley & Son.

Stacey, C. (1987) 'Top spot for women', *Hospitality*, November: 12–13.

Taylor, R., Airey, D. and Kotas, R. (1983) 'Rates of pay in the British hotel and catering industry', *International Journal of Hospitality Management* 2, 3: 157–159.

Thomas, C. and Erlam, A. (1978) *Unequal portions: a survey of pay in the hotel and catering industry*, London: Low Pay Unit.

Thompson, P. (1983) *The Nature of Work: An Introduction to Debates on the Labour Process*, London: Macmillan.

—— (1989) *The Nature of Work: An Introduction to Debates on the Labour Process*, London: Macmillan (2nd Edn).

Thompson, P. and McHugh, D. (1990) *Work Organizations: A Critical Introduction*, London: Macmillan.

Tomoda, S. (1983) 'Working conditions in the hotel, restaurant and catering sector: a case study of Japan', *International Labour Review* 122, 2: 239–252.

Touraine, A. (1962) 'An historical theory in the evolution of industrial skills', in C.R. Walker (ed.) *Modern Technology and Civilisation*, New York: McGraw-Hill.

Transnationals Information Centre (1987) *Working for Big Mac*, London: Transnationals Information Centre.

Tunstall, J. (1969) *The Fishermen*, London: Routledge & Kegan Paul.

Twigg, J. (1983) 'Vegetarianism and the meanings of meat', in A. Murcott (ed.) *The Sociology of Food and Eating*, Aldershot: Gower.

Venison, P. (1983) *Managing Hotels*, London: Heinemann.

Watson, T.J. (1980) *Sociology, Work and Industry*, London: Routledge & Kegan Paul.

—— (1988) *Sociology, Work and Industry*, London: Routledge & Kegan Paul (2nd edn).

Whyte, W.F. (1948) *Human Relations in the Restaurant Industry*, New York: McGraw-Hill.

—— (1949) 'The social structure of the restaurant', *American Journal of Sociology*, 54: 302–310.

Whyte, W.F., Hamilton, E.L. and Whiley, M.C. (1964) *Action Research in Management*, New York: Irwin Books.

Witz, A. and Wilson, F. (1982) 'Women workers in service industries', *Service Industries Review* 2, 2: 40–55.

Wood, R.C. (1988) 'Against social science?' *International Journal of Hospitality Management* 7, 3: 239–250.

—— (1990a) 'The image of the hotel in popular literature: a preliminary statement', *International Journal of Hospitality Management* 9, 1: 5–8.

—— (1990b) 'Sociology, gender, food consumption and the hospitality industry', *British Food Journal* 92, 6: 3–5.

Wood, S. (ed.) (1982) *The Degradation of Work? Skill, Deskilling and the Labour Process*, London: Hutchinson.

Wood, S. and Pedlar, M. (1978) 'On losing their virginity: the story of a strike at the Grosvenor Hotel, Sheffield', *Industrial Relations Journal* 9, 2: 15–37.

Woodward, J. (1958) *Management and Technology*, London: HMSO.

—— (1965) *Industrial Organization: Theory and Practice*, Oxford: Oxford University Press.

Worland, D. and Wilson, K. (1988) 'Employment and labour costs in the hotel industry: evidence from Victoria, Australia', *International Journal of Hospitality Management* 7, 4: 363–377.

Worsfold, P. (1989) 'Leadership and managerial effectiveness in the hospitality industry', *International Journal of Hospitality Management* 8, 2: 145–155.

Name index

Subject index